D0874566

Animators of Fil
and Television

1867089
FO-C.
BA

Animators of Film and Television

*Nineteen Artists, Writers,
Producers and Others*

NOELL K. WOLFGRAM EVANS

McFarland & Company, Inc., Publishers
Jefferson, North Carolina, and London

Library of Congress Cataloguing-in-Publication Data

Wolfgram Evans, Noell K., 1973–
     Animators of film and television : nineteen artists, writers,
producers and others / Noell K. Wolfgram Evans.
          p.   cm.
     Includes bibliographical references and index.

     ISBN 978-0-7864-4832-6
     softcover : 50# alkaline paper ∞

     1. Animators — United States.   2. Animated films — United
States.   3. Animated television programs — United States.
I. Title.
NC1766.U5W65   2011
741.5'8092273 — dc22   2011010254

British Library cataloguing data are available

© 2011 Noell K. Wolfgram Evans. All rights reserved

*No part of this book may be reproduced or transmitted in any form
or by any means, electronic or mechanical, including photocopying
or recording, or by any information storage and retrieval system,
without permission in writing from the publisher.*

Cover art and design by David Landis (Shake It Loose Graphics)

Manufactured in the United States of America

*McFarland & Company, Inc., Publishers
   Box 611, Jefferson, North Carolina 28640
   www.mcfarlandpub.com*

Many thanks go to my parents, who let us watch TV and encouraged us to explore. Thanks to my sister for sharing the remote (once we got one) and to my brothers for helping me to rediscover old favorites.

The greatest amount of appreciation and thanks, on a level not yet invented, belongs to the five people who continually offer me untold levels of support, encouragement and ideas. It is to Cara, William, Ella, Luke, and Anna that this book is most appreciatively dedicated.

Table of Contents

Preface

Saturday Morning Fever

I am a child of Saturday Morning Television. *Real* Saturday Morning Television. Eight to Noon. All morning. Pajamas and pounds of cereal. Like any set of children, my sister and I had a complicated system worked out to navigate between the offerings of NBC, ABC, and CBS (our only options at the time). Like master stockcar drivers, we weaved our way through the programs, avoiding the roadblocks that were randomly thrown up (yes, even to my indiscriminate eyes I knew shows like *Mr. T* and *Hulk Hogan's Rock and Wrestling* could rot my brain) to get to what we saw as gold. We also underwent a master negotiation process that allowed her to watch *Shirt Tales* so I could stay with whatever version of *Super Friends* was on.

As much as I loved Saturday, though, Sunday was always a little more televisiony important to me. It was Sunday mornings at 8 A.M. that Channel Eight ran classic cartoons (Bugs Bunny, Popeye, Daffy Duck, Droopy and the like). It was only half an hour, and our timing was rushed and hectic, but you knew that you were watching something special. I particularly remember falling under the spell of the shorts where you would be led through some seemingly benign place — a library, a general store, the zoo — and you would see what would happen when the lights went out. These stood out to me like few cartoons had. (I would later discover that many of my favorites in this sub-genre were the work of directors Tex Avery and Frank Tashlin, two men who helped shape our collective comedic vernacular.)

In 1943 critic Manny Farber, writing for *The New Republic* about the animation output of Warner Brothers, declared, "The surprising facts about them are that the good ones are masterpieces and the bad ones aren't a total loss."[1] It's a sentiment I wasn't aware of until much later, but I am sure my younger self would have agreed wholeheartedly.

Once we *finally* got cable, our cartoon diet expanded to include regular doses of Tom and Jerry, the Flintstones, and Bullwinkle. And then we got a

1

VHS player, which was, in so many ways, a time travel device. Countless trips to the library unveiled Silly Symphonies, Betty Boop, Johnny Quest, and nearly every feature-length animated film that was released. My mother would shout at us to stop wasting our time in front of the television, but it wasn't a waste. We were being entertained and educated; we were communing with a time long past and developing an appreciation for a true art form, for drawing, and design, and music. And sitting with my sister, and later our brothers, we were forming a collective vernacular. And we were laughing. Our brains were downloading things we couldn't even process, and yet we couldn't get enough. In a very modern way, we were in a sense taking part in a tradition that spanned all of the years of human history.

The Influence of Animation

Now a *single* drawing, especially the cartoon, has always been capable of expressing a great many ideas. A drawing of a man, for instance, can glorify him or ridicule him. Further, it can emphasize aspects of his physical form and subdue or eliminate others. It can combine ideas, such as a human face on a locomotive, an animal in a tuxedo, a skeleton with a cloak and scythe, etc. It can represent a specific object (a portrait, a landscape, a still life). Or it can represent a symbol of *all* men, *all* trees; the drawing of Uncle Sam representing America; the eye representing sight; the skull representing death: the single image can represent the *general* idea. The part can be interpreted as a symbol for the *whole*.[2]

Like any art form, animation is a subjective medium. Unlike other art forms, though, it's also an anonymous one. Of all of our popular entertainment outlets — animation, live action films, books, music, episodic television programming, painting, photography — animation may be the only one where the creators are relatively unknown. It is true that there are some universally known names — Walt Disney, Walter Lantz, William Hanna and Joseph Barbera — but do we really understand what the people behind those names did? More importantly, what of the people whose names the general public can't readily rattle off? The day-to-day workers whose work altered our popular consciousness — those who taught a generation how a bill becomes a law and that three truly is a magic number; who showed us from a young age how to laugh at authority; who still make us laugh — 60 years after they told their joke; who brought independence to mainstream eyes; who rose to the top and then used their power to fight for their friends; whose designs still influence the way we look at the world; whose "subversiveness" is now taken for a cultural icon.

What's Inside

This is not meant to be an all-encompassing biography of each artist, nor is it intended to act as a full history of each artist or the industry. What you will find here are glimpses of an artist in a particular time and place, and what you will see is how the decisions he or she made and the artistic paths he or she took changed the medium and in turn had a residual effect on the popular culture of the day, an effect we continue to feel. You will find that the singular moment of change for each artist is different — for some the moment can be found within the confines of a single film, while for others that moment stretches across years and careers. This is due as much to the nature of the business as to the unpredictableness of the creative mind.

There are 18 artists and one artist "conglomerate" featured within. The term *artist* is being used, and will be used throughout, in the broadest way possible. While there are some artists as the word has historically been used, there are also writers, directors, technicians, and even members of the armed services. Each artist is listed under a group label. These labels are not meant to pigeonhole anyone, but rather they are in place to categorize like-minded individuals.

Part of what makes these artists so special is that their influence isn't confined to animation — their fingerprints can be found across popular culture. Their working vocabulary has become the standard that guides artists across media today. Working across time and countries, they have each skillfully handled the collective thread that somehow weaves its way through the rolling projector and binds us together. And that is what this book will attempt to explore. Within these pages we will look at the artists who found a way to utilize the medium to create work that transcends the form and affects culture across all levels.

It will (hopefully) be interesting to discover that while each person had, and showcased, a singularly unique talent, this talent shined brightest in concert with others. Either in direct working relationships or as passing acquaintances whose significance is not truly discovered until the time has long gone by. It's the truth of the old adage "Talent begets Talent" — Hubley worked for Tashlin, before leaving for his own place, where he hired Scott and Babbitt. Scott and Maltese worked at Warner Brothers, and then Scott and Benedict worked for Jay Ward where Scott was a key influence on Groening, while Benedict heavily influenced Kricfalusi. Selick professes a deep debt to Harryhausen, who steps outside of the whole affair in wonderment. As we shall see, that list continues to twist and grow as more and more people are exposed to the work of each of these talented individuals.

Following each artist's story is a listing of their career awards. Of course no artist creates strictly for the awards, but a little recognition, especially those awards coming directly from peers, is always nice. For our purposes, it is revealing to see how artists who now are considered the best at what they did were scantily recognized at the time where they were most active.

A selective filmography is included for each artist. In some cases these are their best-known works, while in others they are little-known gems that hold moments when the parameters of animation shifted. In all cases they are films that should be respected, watched, studied, and enjoyed.

Of course any piece, book or otherwise, that is focused on animation contains within it some vestige of Walt Disney; such is his importance within the industry. While not a direct subject featured here, he still is threaded through many of the individual narratives, sometimes as a player, sometimes as a catalyst, and in at least one occasion, as the perceived villain. (For clarification I will follow the convention of using *Disney* when discussing the Walt Disney Studios and *Walt* when discussing the man.) While Walt did not invent the animated form, he and his studio have held the most influence over the medium. Perhaps his biggest contribution was giving us Disney-branded entertainment, but in doing so, he opened a veritable Pandora's Box. Much of what we have today, as we will see, can be traced back, as a result or reaction, to what he brought forth.

> *"Animation can explain whatever the mind of man can conceive."*
> — Walt Disney[3]

The Idealists

1. Art Babbitt:
Working with Idealism

FRANK STARK: You can't be idealistic all your life, Jim.
JIM STARK: Except to yourself.
      —*Rebel Without a Cause* (1955). Screenplay by
      Stewart Stern. Adaptation by Irving Shulman.

The story of Art Babbitt (10/8/07–3/4/92) is the story that we wish others would tell about us. Talented. Fair. Generous. Willing to put everything on the line to do the right thing.

Babbitt was one of the top animators at Disney, the top animation studio in the world. One of the most talented and respected animators at the studio, he worked on the Wicked Queen in *Snow White and the Seven Dwarfs* (1937), *The Three Little Pigs* (1933), *Pinocchio* (1940), *Dumbo* (1941), *Fantasia* (1940). He was also a prime catalyst behind the creation of Goofy. In his position at the studio, he could have had anything he wanted, except for one thing. Equality.

At the Disney studio, at every studio, really, there was a definite class system. Those at the top did very well; those at the bottom ... well, most had to take on outside assignments just to get by. There was a chasmic disparity in responsibility and pay not just among departments but within as well. Amongst animators top artists could be earning $200 a week while others might be making $25. Some spoke up about this disconnect, but it wasn't until Babbitt took a stand that anything was done. And in that moment of defiance toward the studio that made him, Art Babbitt altered the history not only of the Disney Studios but also of the animation business as a whole.

While Babbitt's career is closely tied to Disney, that is not where he got his start in animation. When his plans to study medicine in New York fell through due to financial constraints, Babbitt fell back on his artist skills and became a commercial artist. One day a client asked him to create what he called a "medical film" — an animated "commercial" on some particular health topic that would run in the local theater. It was his first experience on the other side of animation. Soon thereafter sound was introduced, and Babbitt knew that if he wanted to continue in the medium he would have to go somewhere a tad more "professional," which is how he found himself at Paul Terry's studio. Babbitt stayed with Terry until he had a chance encounter with Walt Disney. Or, more truthfully, one of his shorts.

Go West

In 1932 Babbitt sat enraptured in the darkness of a local movie house as skeletons danced in time across the screen. He was watching a re-release of Disney's *The Skeleton Dance* (1929) and thinking to himself that if there was a studio making movies like that, he had to work there.

Shortly afterward he was on a train to California. He arrived there with one intention, to work for Walt Disney. He only had one hurdle, he had no appointment or connections in the studio. Undaunted, he set about "writing" a letter of introduction on a piece of paper 20 feet by 15 feet, which he sent to Walt's secretary. He was invited in for an interview the next day and was hired soon after.

His first scenes appeared in 1932's *Santa's Workshop*. The work he created belies his screen experience most likely because he was a very strong learner and went out of his way to study, practice, and improve his natural abilities.

To this end, in the fall of 1932 Babbitt began holding life drawing classes at his home in the Hollywood Hills. As with any other life drawing class, this one occasionally involved the study of the human body. The *nude* human body.

Walt found out about this and summoned Babbitt to his office. Walt was not against the idea of studying or education per se, but he was concerned about anyone outside of the studio (i.e., the press) finding out that there was a group of Disney animators holed up in a house drawing pictures of naked women. He rightly felt that it would be hard for the studio to recover from that. Babbitt countered that he understood the concern but that the classes would be instrumental in the development of the artists and, by extension, the studio. It was the only argument that Walt needed to hear. He agreed to bring the classes in-house and hire a professional instructor. Babbitt stayed with the classes for about four more weeks as a "monitor" until Don Graham from the Chouinard Art Institute came onboard. This would evolve into the Disney Art School. (The success of these classes would influence Walt's decision in 1961 to coordinate the creation of CalArts.)

Babbitt quickly and impactfully made his mark at the studio. His animation was strong and confident; his characters were filled with logical personality and were technically very fluid. He animated with a strong sense of perspective, which helped his drawings achieve a sense of cartoon realism that was new to the industry but exactly what Walt had been searching for. By 1936 he hit his stride with *Moving Day* and *The Country Cousin*. This led to him being asked to animate the Wicked Queen in *Snow White and the Seven Dwarfs* (1937). It was a piece of watershed animation, filled with malice and dread, but entirely relatable. For all of the power in those drawings, one could argue that it was still not his best work of this period.

"Our craft is still in its infancy — to call it an art is a wishful exaggeration. We are barely learning to stumble on stage ... and a whole world of action, acting, design, caricature, humour and storytelling awaits us. Our field is wide open; it has barely been touched."[1]

Art and the Goof

If there is one character who is distinctly Babbitt, it would have to be "The Goof." Under various guises and personality versions Goofy made a number of appearances in the early 1930s. It wasn't until 1935 in *Mickey's Service Station* that he became the Goofy we know today. As animated by Babbitt, Goofy finally steps out of the shadows as a supporting player and becomes a fully fledged studio star. Babbitt's Goofy is less focused on the "cartooniness" of the character and more on the personality. This Goofy has a sort of helplessness about him, like a victim trapped in a series of mechanics far greater than he would ever understand. And yet he maintains a good-naturedness about him that either showcases his simplicity or belies a greater understanding of his position.

Babbitt would later lecture on Goofy and the best way to animate him both from a technical perspective and to take maximum advantage of his personality:

> Think of the Goofy as a composite of an everlasting optimist, a gullible Good Samaritan, a half-wit, a shiftless, good natured hick, he is loose jointed and gangly, but not rubbery. He can move fast if he has to, but would rather avoid any over-exertion, so he takes what seems the easiest way. He is a philosopher of the barber shop variety. No matter what happens, he accepts it finally at being for the best or at least amusing. He is willing to help anyone and offers his assistance even when it is not needed and just creates confusion. He very seldom, if ever, reaches his objective or completes what he has started. His brain being rather vapory, it is difficult for him to concentrate on any one subject. Any little distraction can throw him off his train of thought and it is extremely difficult for the Goof to keep to his purpose.[2]

And later, with the best first line physical description of perhaps any character ever:

Never think of the Goof as a sausage with rubber hose attachments. Though he is very flexible and floppy, his body still has a solidity and weight. The looseness in his arms and legs should be achieved through a succession of breaks in the joints rather than what seems like the waving of so much rope. He is not muscular and yet has the strength and stamina of a very wiry person. His clothes are misfits, his trousers are baggy at the knees and the pants legs strive vainly to touch his shoe tops but never do. His pants droop at the seat and stretch tightly across some distance below the crotch. His sweater fits him snugly except for the neck and his vest is much too small. His hat is of a soft material and animates a little bit."[3]

He continued his studio ascension with his work on Geppetto in *Pinocchio* (1940), the Chinese Dance in *Fantasia* (1940), and Mr. Stork in *Dumbo* (1941). Each of these characters, and actually every Babbitt character, works in shades and nuances of character that were quite unusual to find in animation at this time. This is because Babbitt put some thought and backstory into everything he did. As animator Tom Sito explained, "He studied the acting theories of internalization of Stanislavsky and Boleslavsky, as any actor of his time would."[4]

The World Around Him

While Babbitt's stature grew among the studio, so did his vision, and he started to see and really understand the large working differences within Disney. When an internal union was started, he was elected and accepted the position of president.

Walt was attempting to head off any outside influence on his studio by establishing a union and calling it the Federation of Screen Cartoonists. It started in 1938 and initially attracted great attention and interest from the employees. At their first meeting, more than 600 employees registered and elected Babbitt as president. Babbitt took the responsibility very seriously and worked hard to help quell grievances and bring some equality to the workplace. Unfortunately that was a harder task than perhaps it should have been.

At this same time there was a push amongst unions to organize the workforce of Hollywood. This was all the impetus Babbitt needed to take action. In 1941 he went to talk to Walt Disney about the current working conditions. Not only were his opinions not heard, but also Walt took this as an opportunity to "re-evaluate" his staff. The next day, Babbitt was escorted from the lot after having been summarily let go for, essentially, attempting to unionize. The very next day over 300 studio employees walked out.

Babbitt could have walked off into the sunset, moved to any other studio in Hollywood, or accepted his lumps and sold himself back to Disney, but none of these options were in his character. For Babbitt, the only option was to stand and fight, for himself just as much as for everyone in the studio.

It would have been easy, and less trouble, for him to brush off these issues as "not my problem," but Babbitt understood that, at their core, these concerns were bigger than any one artist. The strike quickly divided the studio: many top artists walked out, but an equal number remained — particularly animators in supervisor roles.

There were a number of people, such as Dave Hilberman, who played an instrumental role in the preparation and execution of the strike, but it was Babbitt's participation that was key. People saw in him a man who had nearly everything, and yet he was willing to put that all on the line for the people on the opposite side of him.

For his part Babbitt saw his participation as a near-moral obligation. In many ways he understood that he had the life he had because of the hard work of so many others and felt as if they should receive equal treatment for their contributions.

Casualties

The strike raged on for nearly four months before Walt finally relented to the union's demands. Many strikers returned to the studio, but other key creative talents moved, or had already moved on, including Frank Tashlin, John Hubley, Maurice Noble, Bill Meléndez, Bill Tytla, Walt Kelly, Virgil Partch, Zack Schwartz, David Hilberman, and others. The ones who stayed found themselves in a physically familiar but mentally very different place, as the studio went from an artistic quasicollective to a job.

There were also large artistic ramifications that extended outside of the realm of animation. The exodus from the strike sent a number of forward-thinking artists out, and many banded together. Their graphic predilections were set against a strike-induced desire to move far away from the Disney style of art. The result was a push toward modernism, perhaps best seen in the output from UPA. "The Disney strike had HUGE industry effects on style, too," Tashlin later stated. "After the strike, people felt they could try anything [graphically] and they did."[5]

And then there was Babbitt. One of the results of the strike settlement was that Disney was court-ordered to re-hire Babbitt into his old position. They did it, but they didn't make it easy. Babbitt, flush off of the strike victory, decided to test the waters himself and sued Disney for back pay and bonuses. A trial ensued that played out less like a presentation of the facts and more like the final machinations of a couple who have broken up but just haven't realized it.

Shortly after the strike, Babbitt headed into the Marine Corps. Discharged in 1945 he headed right back to Disney, where he stayed, continually battling, until 1947, when both sides essentially ran out of gas.

Moving On

His next permanent position was to join a number of Disney refugees at United Productions of America (UPA) in 1949. Their modernist approach to animation must have seemed like a foreign language to the more classically minded Babbitt. Yet he completed some innovative and engaging work, including *Ragtime Bear* (1949), *The Four Poster* (1952) and most particularly *Rooty Toot Toot* (1952). The film, directed by John Hubley, is a masterwork of stylized design that works with the story not just as design. For his part, Babbitt animated the character of Frankie, and he had footage of ballerina Olga Lunick shot to use as a guide.

When John Hubley was forced (fired) from UPA, he started his own studio called Storyboard, which had a focus on animation for television commercials. Babbitt was one of the lead animators at the studio. In 1955, Hubley moved his studio from California to New York. Babbitt stayed behind and, together with two other former Storyboard artists — Stan Walsh and Arnold Gillespie — formed Quartet Films. (The fourth member of the group was production manager Les Goldman.)

From there Babbitt went where every animator goes at one point — Hanna/Barbera. He worked strictly doing television commercials, though, avoiding the Saturday-morning trap. But his next major contribution to the industry came as he entered the second phase of his career — teacher.

London-based animator Richard Williams headed a studio that had won over 200 awards from nearly every imaginable organization. Williams, though, thought they could be doing better. To that end he invited some of the world's best animators to visit his artists and offer a "Master Class" in animation. In August 1984, Babbitt made the journey and spoke for over a month's time about his career and what he learned. Babbitt spoke for three hours a day on the "rules" he followed (and in some cases wrote) around animation in the classical sense. This was a brave and calculated risk for Williams, who gave away hundreds of hours of training to his animators; it was a move that more than paid off, though, with films such as *Who Framed Roger Rabbit* (1988).

Babbitt was no stranger to the studio, either; he had been animating there since 1977 and remained there until his retirement in 1983.

This was not the first time that Williams had made an arrangement like this, either. Twice before, in the early 1970s, Williams had held similar classes with Babbitt holding court. There was also a secondary motive driving Williams for this series: he wanted to capture, while he could, the advice, techniques, and mechanics of these master animators not just for his studio but for all time. Animator Tom Roth, who worked for Williams at the time, remembers the Babbitt teaching sessions quite well:

> Wednesday afternoon from 5 to 6 was chosen by Dick to be our weekly lecture from Art because that's when the Disney classes were held. Dick was fanatical about doing everything the Disney way, even if it made no sense. The class consisted of a lecture on a particular subject, say, for example a type of walk or the progressive bending of joints at which we took notes, including Dick who had heard it all before. Then we'd be given an assignment to do on our own time. Next week he'd look at the assignments on our video pencil tester and make comments. His comments were frank objective criticism but never really harsh. Overall, I'd say those who took his teaching seriously benefitted from him greatly. Much of what I know today came from him.[6]

Art Babbitt was perhaps one of the most talented men to ever work in the animation business. Perhaps even greater than the contributions he made with his pencil, though, were the advances he pushed through in regards to studio working conditions. His leadership in the Disney strike prompted a watershed moment in employee relations in Hollywood. While we will never know exactly what would have occurred at Disney had the strike somehow been averted and the talented artists remained in place, we can be sure that we would not have experienced anything as free-form and artistically forward-thinking as the UPA Revolution.

Toward the end of his career, when no one would have faulted him for resting on a beach, Babbitt sat in a crowded London studio and shared all that he knew about the animation industry. Some 40 years later, he was again full of fire as he tried to inspire yet another revolution, although perhaps this time of a strictly artistic variety.

> *"I look forward to the day when real artists who are more than craftsmen, who have developed their art, will come into this business, will pay it the attention it deserves as a potentially serious art medium.... Disney and other studio heads have actually held the industry back by years by their 'out-of-the-world' fantasies, by their refusal to deal with real life and by their enchantment with 'calendar art.' I want to see those days go by the board. I want to see real artists assume leadership in this game."* — Art Babbitt, 1941[7]

HONORS

Winsor McCay Award, International Animated Film Association, 1974
Golden Award, Motion Picture Screen Cartoonists Awards, 1985
The Walt Disney Company, Disney Legend, 2007

SAMPLE FILM SELECTION

Moving Day (1935)
Snow White and the Seven Dwarfs (1937)
Fantasia (1940)
Rooty Toot Toot (1951)
Everybody Rides the Carousel (1975)

2. John Hubley: The Modernist

"I am an artist. I have a right to say what I want. And I have a right to say what I don't want."
— John Hubley to the House Un-American Activities Commission.[1]

There are certain seismic shifts that have occurred over the years within animation — the introduction of sound, the addition of color, the incursion of the television, the innovation of computers. Somewhere on this list one could also add "the theories of John Hubley." Hubley (5/21/14–2/21/77), a designer whose primary work period was during the middle of the twentieth century, led the charge to bring to animation a new aesthetic. This shift from the realism of Disney to the modern stylings of mid-century America marked more than just a change in artistic temperament; it created a philosophical shift in the discussion and acceptance of animation.

The story of John Hubley is also an important one because it transcends animation, integrating its self deep in the human psyche. Art, belief, friendship, betrayal, conviction. It's a story that continues to captivate because at its essence, it is the tale of a man working to break out of the system, gain artistic freedom and perhaps start a revolution along the way. A revolution to make a thing as great as it possibly can be.

John Hubley was born in 1914 in Wisconsin. One can only assume that he spent the long Wisconsin winters with pen and paper in his hand, as it wasn't long before he found himself working as a background artist on *Snow White and the Seven Dwarfs* (1937). As Disney ramped production up on Snow White, he hired in a large group of new animators and artists. These were essentially the first people to be hired *into* the company, the previous (current) employees, for the most part, had started with Walt or had been involved with the studio in its early inception in some way. These original employees felt a loyalty to Walt and a complete faith in the direction he was leading animation. This blind subservience to the Disney way of animation was not something so easily shared by the newer employees. Many of these new artists had been college-trained and had studied the fine arts, unlike their studio-bred counterparts, who learned their trade as they created it. These newer recruits felt that there were more ways into which animation could (and should) expand and grow.

These differings of opinion all came to a head in the spring of 1941, when over 300 Disney employees went on strike. Ostensibly the strike came about due to Disney's intermittent payment practices, but it is hard not to believe that some of the workers did not see this as an opportunity to rebel, to make a statement, against the Disney system. John Hubley fell into this latter group. While not one of the visible leaders of the strike, his beliefs permeated the line.

The strike and its final settlement had major repercussions at the Disney Studio and throughout Hollywood as well; one of the consequences was the scattering of many members of the Disney staff. For Disney, one of the worst repercussions of the strike had to be the loss of so many talented people (although at the time Walt may have been happy to be rid of them on a personal level). Among those who left just before, during, or after the strike were Bill Meléndez, Maurice Noble, Art Babbitt, Bill Tytla, Walt Kelly, Virgil Partch, and Preston Blair.

A New Start

Hubley was also in this group moving to Screen Gems at Columbia Pictures. He joined several of his former co-workers, including most pivotally Frank Tashlin. Director/writer Tashlin had come over to Screen Gems with the idea that he would be heading up a "unit." Not long after his arrival, though, he found himself as essentially the lone man standing after a mass layoff. Suddenly, and really by default, he was not heading his own unit but leading the entire studio. Tashlin had two very important traits that were key to those working under him — he was interested in exploring where animation could go, and he trusted his artists. It was like a dream come true for this migrating group, who had just come out of Disney and were seeking respite from the tightly controlled, almost dictatorial ways of *that* studio. Many of these artists held a prevailing belief that the further Walt strove for realism in his films, the more he violated the basic aesthetics of animation. A cartoon was, after all, drawings on a flat piece of paper. By adding dimensions and depth, Disney was moving the medium away from its natural origins. Under Tashlin the artists were encouraged to explore their ideas and experiment with the techniques that previously they had regulated to the privacy of their drawing books. While Tashlin fostered this environment, there were still certain constraints imparted from a higher level that had to be managed. So while the artists were experimenting, they had to make their experiments work within the established Columbia cartoon characters library. It would be a few years, and take a new location, for Hubley to begin to put all of the theories and artistic elements together and make the kind of film that he wanted to.

Not long after Hubley's arrival, Dave Fleischer was brought in to take over for Tashlin. (It was a move that management made based on more of a pro–Fleischer attitude than an anti–Tashlin sentiment.) While the artists feared that this would mean a return to the old ways, they were pleased to find out that Fleischer had plans to simply "phone it in," and his indifference allowed the artists at the studio to continue their "experiments." When Fleischer was brought in, one of his first acts was to give John Hubley a promotion from layout artist to director. While involving himself more and more in the production of a picture, Hubley came to realize that the further you pushed a design forward, the stronger the emphasis grew on the writing. It was a thought that would drive Hubley's work for the rest of his life.

With the talent and cooperation assembled, there is no telling how high the Screen Gems studio could have climbed. As World War II entered America, though, it was a question that would go unanswered. As World War II started, many areas of the government (particularly the Armed Forces) set up film units in Hollywood to produce instructional and informational shorts to be shown to their "employees." In 1942 John Hubley joined the Army and was assigned to the Army Air Force First Motion Picture Unit (FMPU). It was a diverse group run by Rudy Ising (of MGM) and included such artists as Frank Thomas (of Disney). The diversity of recruits into the FMPU worked well for the animators, as it forced them to become completely involved in the filmmaking process. For the first time, animators had to assume a variety of tasks; one day you might be doing fill-ins, and the next you were working layouts, and on the third day you were washing cels. This work helped the artist to get a complete, hands-on understanding of how an animated film *really* worked. It also gave the animators a chance to really get together and exchange ideas and theories and opinions about where the medium was headed.

In March 1942, Hubley contributed some of his ideas to an issue of *The Animator*, an industry publication.

> A progressive, intelligent approach to animation, and realization that it is an expressive medium, is imperative if we want to keep animated cartoons from stagnating. Development and growth of animation is dependent upon varied, significant subject manner presented in an organized form, evolved from elements inherent in the medium. Among the least understood of these elements

are the graphic ones. In spite of the fact that animation is almost entirely concerned with drawings, drawings which must function in both time and space.[2]

The Wake-up Call

In 1943 Hubley saw the Warner Brothers cartoon *The Dover Boys* (directed by Chuck Jones). It was the story of three men, a woman and a villain as set in the Gay Nineties. Its linear drawings and stylized images, so different from anything else done at the time, helped prove to him that his thoughts on animation were correct. Hubley would often speak fondly of the way Jones used new animation techniques on a story of comedy on a human level, as opposed to the typical cartoon of comedy for comedy's sake.

The army was a great training ground, if you will, because they were concerned completely with getting their message across, however possible. This left a lot of open ground for people to work in. This is not to imply that all of the pictures that came out of these situations were experimental masterpieces. Indeed the majority of the work done was very "standard." At the FMPU many of the pictures they produced did have new elements to them, but these were all basically works in progress, experiments and attempts to find the right notes and combinations.

Hubley spoke at a UCLA Writers Conference in 1943 and shared some of the findings of the work at the FMPU: "Writers have been forced to deal with positive ideas, and there have been significant new developments in techniques as a result. But the material has been essentially technical ... the inherent human appeal of the medium and its application to all forms of cartoon production has just begun to be realized."[3]

While in the FMPU Hubley directed a short called *Flat Hatting* (1944). The premise of the piece was to show pilots the danger of flying straight down and then leveling out the plane (or Flat Hatting). Where the film stands out, though, is through its early renditions of what would come to be known as "50s Design" and in its use of "limited animation" principles.

This was not just a test for Hubley's animation theories; it was also an opportunity to test the idea of using animation as a mass scale educational outlet. The result was that after the showing of this film to service men and women, the number of flat-hatting incidents dramatically decreased. While Hubley was widely known in the animation community and had been an active member for a number of years, it could be said that this is the film that made him.

Hubley was not the only artist seeking the future and truth in the animated film; others had similar thoughts and were working on them. They wrote papers, taught classes and founded studios. One such studio was founded by Zack Schwartz (previously of Screen Gems), Dave Hilberman (a former Disney employee whom Walt derided as being a Communist and whom he held responsible for the 1941 strike) and Steve Bostustow (a former animator and employee at Hughes Aircraft). Schwartz and Hilberman had founded a small studio on the idea that they would finally be able to create the types of things that they wanted to. Soon though, thanks to the large amounts of government work floating around, they found that their studio had grown from two men painting in a small room to an actual operation. The company did well, but its best was yet to come, and 1944 proved to be an important step in that direction. To begin with, on May 1 the company changed its name to United Film Production. More importantly though, this was the year that brought John Hubley into the fold.

In 1944 Hubley had been approached by the United Auto Workers to produce a cartoon that would encourage the re-election of Franklin Roosevelt. He worked out the storyboards and designs and then took the project to United Film to be completed. The team at United Film was more than pleased to take this task on. They were of course happy for the work as, if they produced a good film, it could lead to a long and profitable partnership with the powerful auto union. There was also the underlying political aspect that appealed to them. The majority of the artists at United had a very liberal view of the world, and they felt a strong connection to FDR's victory. For all of the work that was done by many skilled freelance artists (the picture was actually directed by Chuck Jones), this was still, in its essence, Hubley's film. In his design of the film, he tried out many of the ideas of stylization he had been working through in his mind, many of them proving successful.

Hell-Bent for Election was a major success, and the studio, rightfully, felt very proud of itself— so proud in fact that they decided to change their name again, this time to showcase the full encompassing canvas of their work. So it was that on December 31, 1945, United Productions of America (UPA) was officially born. Unfortunately for the studio World War II was over, and with that the government work, which had once been their bread and butter, started to slow up. Bostustow, Hilberman and Schwartz all began looking for other opportunities into which they could take the company. As they talked, it soon became apparent that Hilberman and Schwartz had one vision of the company, while Bostustow had a completely different view. In 1946 Bostustow bought out Hilberman and Schwartz and proceeded to move forward, gobbling up as many remaining government contracts as he could find. Before he did anything, though, he named Hubley supervising director.

In 1947, an event occurred that foreshadowed the eventual demise of the studio. It was around this time that "Communism Fever" dug its roots deep into America. The FBI began their quest to find those Americans with Communist leanings, and one of the first places they looked was in Hollywood. UPA was a prime investigative target, thanks to the large number of government films that they made. As has already been stated, UPA was constructed by freethinkers, experimentalists. Many of the employees had left-leaning political views, and several (including John Hubley) had been members of organizations with loose affiliations to Communism. The FBI compiled quite a detailed report, which was presented by J. Edgar Hoover to members of the defense community. Whatever Hoover said, it worked, as the government and industrial contracts quickly disappeared. By 1948 Bostustow, in order to save the company, was forced to shift its direction. It was a decision that would cement UPA's place in film history.

UPA Takes Off

UPA decided to sign a contract to produce theatrical films for Columbia (who had recently shut down their Screen Gems division). UPA would be given a budget of $27,500 plus 25 percent ownership in everything they created. Monetarily it was a decent deal; the downside to the contract was that UPA had to work with Columbia's two cartoon "stars": The Fox and The Crow.

The first two films released under the contract were, while stylistically interesting in places, still the same thing that other studios had been putting out. In late 1949 UPA finally pulled something different together. *The Ragtime Bear* would have been just another run-of-the-mill story had it not been for the supporting character of Mr. Magoo. Although many artists, including Jim Backus (as the voice of Magoo), had a part in Magoo's creation, his essence came straight from Hubley. The shortsighted, bald, obstinate old man was immensely popular in part because he was funny and in part because there was something about him that was fresh and new.

This cartoon is doubly significant because it displays one of the first real uses of UPA's famed limited animation style. Whereas Disney used one cel for each frame of film, UPA used one cel for every two to three frames of film (partly a style decision, partly a decision of cost). It is often stated that the artists at UPA were forced into their trademark "limited" style of animation because they had no money to work with; this is not exactly the case. The average budget given to them by Columbia was $27,500 per picture. This is equal to (and in some cases more than) what other cartoon units were receiving at this time. The problem, as Hubley pointed out in later years, was that each artist was a perfectionist, and in working each image to be exactly as they wanted it, they would quickly eat through their budget, so compromises had to be made. That they were able to work through their monetary problems to produce consistently appealing cartoons shows the enormous talent of the animators.

These talents were on full display in 1951 when theory and practice came together in the groundbreaking *Gerald McBoing Boing*, directed by Bobe Cannon. In a perfect collaboration, UPA married a Dr. Seuss story to their graphic ideals, and the results are incredible. *Gerald McBoing Boing* was a layered story about a boy who could not speak. Whenever he opened his mouth, instead of words, sounds came out. His parents and friends shunned him, and he was left to find his own way in the world. Gerald is essentially the story of a "handicapped" boy who is unloved. (This reflects what Hubley said nearly ten years earlier, that the farther out the graphics go, the stronger the writing must become. The graphics for this picture were daringly minimal; for example, there were no distinctions between floors and walls. Cannon's team boiled the story down to its essence and that is all that was shown on screen.) So although Hubley himself did not direct *Gerald*, his style and ideas can be felt all over the picture.

The 1951 Academy Award that Bobe Cannon won for directing *Gerald* struck Hubley deeply. There had always been a rivalry between the men, and this only deepened it. Determined to prove that he could perform his ideas better than anyone, Hubley essentially "split" UPA into two sides, with Cannon leading one and Hubley leading the other. While Cannon took animation in a limited form to the extremes to make a statement, Hubley pushed artistically. In 1952 UPA released *Rooty Toot Toot*, which was the picture Hubley had been working toward his entire artistic career. Along with Paul Julian, John Hubley had finally partnered design with animation. This retelling of the Frankie and Johnny story used flat images, colors, lines and settings to evoke and provoke the mood and feel of the picture. Although he lost that year's Academy Award, Hubley's revolution had begun.

> *"So many wonderful animated films and filmmakers have influenced me. If I have to pick just one film I think it would be UPA's* Rooty Toot Toot *by John Hubley. Besides being smart, funny and inventive, that film made me aware of how close animation is to the dance. That animation is choreography and we don't have to be limited by realistic actions. Thank you, John Hubley, for your innovations."*— Bob Kurtz, animator[4]

Advertising and art directors everywhere began consistently pushing their teams to copy the UPA style. Warner Brothers produced two films in 1954: *Goo Goo Goliath* and *From A to Z-z-z-z*. UPA's greatest compliment may have come in 1953 when Disney released *Toot-Whistle-Plunk-Boom*. It was the supreme validation of what UPA had been "preaching," that the ideas of form and content in an animated film could merge together in a manner that may not provide the ultimate realism, but rather may enhance the story and, in hand, the ultimate experience.

Blacklisted

The 1950s were not a proud time in Hollywood (or American) history, in particular 1951–1952, when there was a witch-hunt not seen since the days of Salem. Only this time there were not witches being searched for, there were Communists. At the center of this countrywide display of anti–Communist force was the House Un-American Activities Committee (HUAC), before which prominent citizens were called and asked to reveal any connections they, their friends, neighbors or relatives had to the Communist Party. Some people talked; they "named names." Those who were named or those who would not talk were blacklisted, essentially cast out of society. With its freethinking members and frequent themes of social reformation, Hollywood was an especially live target for HUAC. Hit hard by the Committee was UPA. Many in the organization were asked to sign papers, rescinding their previous actions, and some were asked to testify before the committee. John Hubley made no apologies for things he may have done; to him the past was the past. Unfortunately the government saw things differently, and as Hubley refused to cooperate, pressure was placed on UPA to take action. On May 31, 1952, John Hubley was fired from UPA. (There have often been stories that Hubley resigned for the "good of the studio," but John's wife, Faith, insists that he was fired early in the process because of his political associations.)

When John Hubley left UPA, he took with him the creative spark that had taken the studio to such glorious heights. Yes, UPA still had Gerald and Magoo, but they no longer had their "edge." In a matter of years UPA would be turning out the same formulaic cartoons that they had been formed to rail against. With its principal creators forced out, there was a type of poetic justice to the studio's demise.

A Commercial Influence

Hubley decided to start his own Los Angeles studio and, in order to avoid any new conflicts, gave it the intentionally generic name of Storyboard Films. The studio survived at first and then flourished by creating animated commercials for television. Since commercials are a creditless medium, Hubley encountered less friction than he might have if he had tried to get back into theatrical animation. Hubley's commercials not only produced results but also tracked well. Closer examination reveals that while the commercials are scripted well and have a unique graphic style, it's what's under those that people seemed to attach to. As a museum press release put it, "Fluid and enigmatic as well as joyously entertaining, Hubley Studio animation always has an air of spontaneity and improvisation."[5]

It would have been very easy for Hubley to continue creating animation that hearkened back to his work at UPA. While it would have most assuredly been profitable, for Hubley it would have been creatively damning, and so what he chose to do was hearken back to the *spirit* of his work at UPA and use his studio to continue to explore the animated form.

Amid Amidi believes that as much as the work Hubley did at UPA influenced American animation, what he created at Storyboard "directly influenced European animators and helped usher in the flourishing foreign animation design scene of the early 1960s."[6]

The bulk of the work the studio did, particularly in its early years, was television commercials. Hubley employed jazz musicians, mixed media materials (including doing things like adding wrapping paper to provide texture to a cel), and even utilizing the satirist Stan Freberg as the narrator (which today sounds innocent enough, but at the time satire in advertising was considered definitely off-limits). These pieces were coupled with striking design decisions such as anthropomorphic products, "blobulous" shapes representing everyday objects, and human figures both realistic and stylized. The resulting shots are expertly put together, with every item in its perfect place and paced with an amazing amount of control. When you see one of the commercials from this period one of the things that hits you midway through is the organic feeling, as if you're just watching things unfold and not necessarily viewing a preplanned story. Such is the genius of John Hubley. "(The commercials) transcend their mercantile origins and succeed remarkably as animated films," wrote one critic.[7]

In 1956 the studio moved to New York City, where Hubley and his wife, Faith, continued to create television commercials while slowly shifting their focus to more personal, artistic projects. They actually made the pledge to create one "personal" film a year as part of their wedding vows. These films would reach great critical and artistic acclaim and three of them — *Moonbird* (1959), *Everybody Rides the Carousel* (1975), and *A Herb Alpert & The Tijuana Brass Double Feature* (1966) — would go on to win Academy Awards.

In 1966 they also completed the short *Urbanissimo*. This six-minute short was commissioned by the housing authority to give an overview of the issues of urban housing. In a standard Hubley move, he set the film to a soundtrack of jazz with original music by Maynard Ferguson, Ray Brown, Pete Jolly, and Benny Carter. (All told, they would partner with Carter on eight shorts overall.)

Throughout his career Hubley turned to jazz as the soundtrack to his films. As Faith explained: "There's a remarkable connection between animation and jazz. There's something about jazz's bending of time within a rigid format that also applies to animation. Film time is different from regular time, and animation time is even further removed from film time. It stretches and bends, the same as it does in music and particularly in jazz. That's why they work so well together. It's a marriage made in heaven." It was a connection that Hubley had made early on. He had a great reverence for the music style as a fan and a fellow artist, and jazz musicians loved to work with him because he wasn't looking for a song to simply mark time or act as an underscore. For Hubley, the music was the key to the animation, not the other way around.

> I feel that the composer has to have freedom and I think that the music has to go first. Then the artist isn't burdened with having to do everything to the split second. So the first thing we did was throw the click-track in the garbage and let the composers work the way they used to when they created the great scores in film history. We would do a storyboard first — or sketches for the storyboard — and then talk to the composer. If something felt musically that it should be a little longer, or something great was happening, we had the flexibility to open it up and take advantage of it.[8]

Educating the Next Generation

The studio also put a particular focus on education, providing animated sequences for *Sesame Street* and *The Electric Company*. For these PBS series Hubley and a studio writer (generally Chris Cerf) would receive a syllabus for the show season and from that plan out their sequences. Across seasons, Hubley and his team took part in the creation of at least 60 of these animated efforts including the popular Letterman series on *The Electric Company* and, for *Sesame Street*, sequences such as *F, Football*, where a football player discusses his favorite sport, and *Letter S*, where the letter S meets up with a face that turns out to belong to a snake.

Education was always a particular focus for Hubley. One of the things he loved was to discuss art theory and expression ideas. In 1963 he was given an opportunity to do just that in a large-scale setting, when Robert Gardner, the director of Harvard's Film Study Center, hired John and Faith to teach a semester at Harvard.

Throughout his career, Hubley was smart enough to look for inspiration in unlikely places. While at Storyboard he frequently spoke with, among others, Bob Guidi, a noted illustrator who created album covers. Prior to that, at UPA, Hubley would bring in live-action screenwriters like Bill Roberts to provide a fresh set of eyes and a different perspective to the issue (and it was not always a script) at hand.

These meetings allowed Hubley to step outside of his comfort zone and challenge himself and his creative team. They were also indicative of his great desire to pull from all aspects of the world as inspiration.

Hubley was a serious student and apostle for the animated form as art. He often spoke about animation, held classes to talk about and discover techniques, and was actively involved in the International Association of Film Animation (ASIFA), even serving as president.

The impact that John Hubley had across the animation industry cannot be overstated. No less of a legend in his own right, Bill Scott explains Hubley's importance in this way: "He was one of the first to bring both social and moral passion into animation and to expand the frontiers beyond what it had been."[9]

HONORS

Winsor McCay Award, International Animated Film Association, 1975
Cannes Film Festival, Jury Prize, *A Doonesbury Special,* 1978
Academy Award, Best Short Subject, Cartoons, *Moonbird,* 1959
Academy Award, Best Short Subject, Cartoons, *The Hole,* 1962
Academy Award, Best Short Subject, Cartoons, *A Herb Alpert & The Tijuana Brass Double Feature,* 1966

SAMPLE FILM SELECTION

Flat Hatting (1944)
Ragtime Bear (1949)
Rooty Toot Toot (1951)
"I Want My Maypo!" Maypo Commercial (1956)
Moonbird (1959)
The Hat (1964)
Everybody Rides the Carousel (1975)
The Electric Company—Letterman Stories (1971–1977)

THE MAVERICKS

3. John Kricfalusi: The Throwback

"I liked Warner Brothers cartoons because they were rude, and nasty. Just like REAL people."

— John Kricfaulsi[1]

John Kricfalusi (b. 9/9/55) is the kid in your seventh-grade class who drew *all* the time. While everyone else was paying attention to a photosynthesis lecture, he was drawing a character of a leaf and detailing out the backstory of a group of heroic archea. Now, unlike that kid in your seventh-grade class, Kricfalusi managed to turn this "idle pastime" into a groundbreaking career. In the 1980s and 1990s he became a leading voice for creator-driven animation of the kind that hadn't been seen outside of film festivals since the Hollywood studios came to prominence.

What Kricfalusi did was swing the pendulum back from the mass-produced Saturday-morning star-based animation series to programs that were singular, unique, and reflective of one creative, driving force. In doing so he opened the door for series as diverse as *The Power Puff Girls* and *SpongeBob Squarepants* to, it can be argued, *The Simpsons*.

There are many parallels that can be drawn between Kricfalusi and the Golden Age (primarily the 1940s) creatives he so deeply admires. They held an animation perspective that was truer to the intent of the medium than others in later years would subscribe to. Those "early" animators spent time analyzing their work, but not overthinking it, and created from the gut, and where they had to learn how to move their medium from theatres to television, Kricfalusi had to handle a television-to-Internet transition. He was, in fact, the first animator of stature to look at the Internet as a viable content-delivery medium, using his animation studio, Spumco, to explore the options, and in 1997 the result was unveiled. On October 15 of that year Spumco launched *The Goddamn George Liquor Program*. Created in Flash, the show became the first cartoon series to be created exclusively for the Internet.

Back to School

Others followed, as did some sporadic television work, but as the twenty-first century moved forward, Kricfalusi had a new plan. He closed the daily operations of *Spumco* and became a latter-day version of Art Babbitt, with the establishment of a "Cartoon College." This online, invitation-only university (of sorts) would send talented artists through a series of animation classes where they would learn throwback animating techniques. The intent of the college is twofold — to provide true artistic guidance and training and to allow Kricfalusi an opportunity to establish a network of freelance artists with whom he could work.

> *The kind of cartoons I make require these skills, and I can't afford to teach them during a production. Cartoon budgets go down every year and so I need people who already understand what I'm looking for and are functional. I always want to do layouts in my cartoons — it's what separates my cartoons visually from so many others, but layout is mostly not done anywhere anymore. Nowadays, they just design the characters from a couple different angles, take them into Flash and then move the still pieces around like paper doll puppets. I can't make my kind of custom stories and acting using that system. I need talented and SKILLED people to help. It's worth it to me to help out before a production begins, but it will be up to you to practice and apply and critique yourselves according to what you learn. I will give some critiques and everyone here can learn from each other's studies.* — John Kricfalusi about starting his "Cartoon College"[2]

Kricfalusi can be tied back to Art Babbitt by more than just a desire to impart animation techniques, though; both are idealistic artists in an industry that claims to want art but treasures commerce and control. Unfortunately, both are also similar in that they found this out the hard way.

Growing up, Kricfalusi was a child of Hanna-Barbera. He has cited time and again the effect that the Ed Benedict designs for the early Hanna-Barbera series such as *Huckleberry Hound* and *The Flintstones* had on him. So there was no small amount of excitement when he got to a working age and found himself walking those same Hanna-Barbera halls that he had fantasized so much about as a child. Granted this Hanna-Barbera lacked much of the innovation, verve, and artistic sensibilities that he had always imagined, but still he most likely believed that the only way to enact change was from the inside.

So there was the inevitable letdown when he was assigned to work on series like *Flash Gordon* (1980); *Pac-Man* (1982); and *Heathcliff & the Cadillac Cats* (1984). John was "lucky" enough to have worked on all of those, and he tried, but his personal style was not in line with what Hanna-Barbera had become. Finally, perhaps thankfully, he was let go after complaints that he was drawing the Snorks too flat. A forgivable offense for most people.

The Bakshi Years

It was a bittersweet opportunity because, for him, the medium that was about personal expression and interpretation had become watered down through needless corporate collaboration. In 1987, he finally found the series that would restore his faith in the way animation should be done. *The New Adventures of Mighty Mouse* was a Ralph Bakshi production for Saturday morning. To this day that's still a funny sentence. It's still not clear who gave Bakshi, the noted auteur behind *Fritz the Cat* (1972), *Wizards* (1977), and *Cool World* (1992), the keys to Saturday morning, but it's a good thing they did. From 1987 through 1988 Bakshi and his animators created something entirely new for broadcast television at that time, a stylized, personality driven, gag-filled, animation series. From the attitude of its characters to the look of the streets, this was unlike any other series; it bore the very distinctive thumbprint of Bakshi.

The idea of a piece of animation reflecting so strongly one individual's aesthetic is not a new one. In the early years, animated shorts were each distinctly original and imbued with the sensibilities (in design, manner, characterization, poses) of its guiding creator, but as mediums shifted and a corporate model became the de facto production process, much of this originality was lost. That's what makes this series so special. Bakshi made one brilliant decision when starting the series, which sealed the fate of the series and created a star. He hired John Kricfalusi. The young, Canadian-born animator was looking for the chance to create an experiment of sorts. Although the business had drastically changed, could he create an environment that replicated, in spirit, what they had on the Warners lot in 1943?

Kricfalusi raided all of the local animation houses and found as many like-minded individuals as he could. His next step was to find a way to keep the majority of the key animation creative moments at the studio, as opposed to overseas, where those things usually went. By devising a creative strategy that included using portions of the original Terrytoons Mighty Mouse shorts, he was able to save a significant amount on production. Even more than physical details, though, he was able to shift their fundamental working style backwards to a more directorial-led "unit." This was key to his overarching plan because it gave one person, in the end, ultimate control over the finished creation. This was not just for an ease of process but for a unification of ideas, temperament, and overarching characterization.

As with everything new and slightly different, certain groups pressured the network to drop the show, and after some intense lobbying, they did just that. When *Mighty Mouse* was not renewed, Kricfalusi got the opportunity to fulfill a fan's ultimate dream and work with some of his favorite characters.

This was the continuation of a trend for Kricfalusi, who has a spectacular reverence for the series and characters of the past. In fact, in many ways his career provides a mirror counterpart to the history of animation — he worked on his "Golden Age" series (*Mighty Mouse*), moved into early television (*Beany and Cecil*), created a success in modern television (*Ren and Stimpy*), took animation to a new medium (the Internet), and then took a moment to make sure the latest generation of animators had the right skills, knowledge and appreciation of the past.

So, following his departure from CBS, he was given the opportunity to work with two of the most popular characters ever shown — Beany and Cecil, the characters originated by perhaps his number one animation hero, Bob Clampett. "Clampett's influence on John K's cartoons is undeniable. His work is crazy, often crude, exaggerated to the max, and, well ... just plain cartoony."[3]

It was a bright spot in an otherwise monotonous Saturday-morning animation wave. The trouble with working in animation in the 1980s, John said, was "the whole system (was) just geared to ensure that nobody's individual contributions ever made it to the screen."[4]

It was this mentality that he was hoping to find a "cure" for in Mighty Mouse, as he used the opportunities he had there as a test run for his big smash, the series that would put him on the animation map in places that had never before been commercially explored and at the same time throw him into the center of a pop-culture craze. A series that would also redirect the flow of programming development dollars from standard paint-by-numbers work to more original programming. That series was of course *Ren and Stimpy,* perhaps the oddest mainstream animated series ever to become a hit.

Kricfalusi's films may be so original because his range of influences is far broader than many others. Instead of turning to art or animation, his mind casts a wider net. Harvey Kurtzman, Segio Aragones, Hank Ketcham, Vivien Leigh, and the Three Stooges are among his miscellaneous study targets.

Along with co-creator Jim Smith, Kricfalusi dreamed up a series that played as a 1940s Warner Brothers cartoon short with 1990s sensibilities, organically designed, and filled with great "cartooniness."[5]

Ren and Stimpy debuted on August 11, 1991, and people went crazy for the adventures of the asthmatic Chihuahua and his cat friend. While the show was immensely popular, it also quickly courted controversy, and by 1992 Kricfalusi was on the block. He was given an ultimatum — adapt the show to more mainstream (meaning network) standards, or be fired. He stuck to his program and was unceremoniously released from the series that he had created. It was a maddening defeat, particularly because the series remained on the air. This was Ren and Stimpy in name only, though. The show limped along until

1996, but the glow was off. The public could tell that they were not watching the "real" Ren and Stimpy in action but someone trying to figure out how to put the pieces together.

Like many an animator before him, Kricfalusi turned to commercials to keep the lights on in the studio. Fortunately for him he also had something none of his heroes did — the Internet. Even in its early iteration, Kricfalusi saw the Internet as more than just a viable delivery medium. He had learned from the mistakes of so many of his animator heroes years ago who sneered at the emerging marvel of television as an evil stepchild. For him, the space Kricfalusi saw in the Internet was a virtual home for his studio.

While Spumco was already a working studio ("The Cartoon Studio for Cartoonists"), the Internet would give it a position as a latter-day version of Hanna-Barbera's marketing acumen along with Jay Ward's physical Dudley Do-right Emporium. On top of providing original short animated series, it also fulfilled fans' desire for merchandise, including figurines and a quasi–home-animator kit complete with studio executive mask. Sure it was all tongue in cheek and slightly campy, but in reality those were two of the traits that made a Spumco cartoon so popular.

Kricfalusi continues to animate to his particular mash-up of ages and genres. In 1999 he had the chance to work with one of his animation heroes when he teamed with Ed Benedict on the short *Boo Boo Runs Wild*. The piece was commissioned by *Cartoon Network* and was an interesting experiment with Fred Flintstone.

What happened to Kricfalusi is a cautionary tale for both artists and studios. A creator-driven series can be inventive and exciting; it can also be a scary proposition to the upper level of studio executives, who spend more time reviewing the bottom line and not the innovation chart. Thankfully for Kricfalusi he was able to pick up and move on, but one has to wonder that in that time, how much did we, the viewing public, miss?

HONORS

Annie, Outstanding Individual Achievement in the Field of Animation, 1992
Winsor McCay Award, International Animated Film Association, 2008

SAMPLE FILM SELECTION

The New Adventure of Mighty Mouse (1988)
The Ren & Stimpy Show (season one)
Boo Boo Runs Wild (1999)
The Goddamn George Liquour Show (1999) (Internet programming)

4. Terry Gilliam:
The Accidental Animator

Throughout the history of the animated film many artists have left their mark through unique storytelling, artistic advances, artistic style or technological advances. Of this group of animation innovators, there are but a select few whose work and style are instantly recognizable by both the student of animation and the casual fan. Terry Gilliam (b. 11/22/40) is one such artist. Now a respected and successful live-action director (*Brazil* [1985], *The Brothers Grimm* [2005], *12 Monkeys* [1995]), Gilliam was once creating revolutionary (and hilarious) animations for the comedy group Monty Python.

His short works are seemingly free-association collections of ideas that build on, but more often subvert, both the animated image and the medium's form; his work is as rich in detail as it is crude in composition; the work is hilarious, influential, unique and perfect for what it needs to be. The animation in a Gilliam short is very organic; things don't follow a predetermined path as much as they *happen*. The short animated sequences are filled with more satiric subversion and surprise than most filmmakers can cram into a full-length feature. All in all, it's not a bad feat for a boy from Minnesota who was just trying to find his way.

What Makes You, You?

Terrence Vance Gilliam was deposited on Earth in Minneapolis, Minnesota, in 1940. He had a rather uneventful childhood that was marked by a move to California ("the California of Tim Burton's *Edward Scissorhands*"[1]). If there was anything during his early years that could be looked back on as an inspiration, it would be his love affair with the audio aspects of the world. The Gilliam family was without a television for a long period of time (of course this was during a time when few people had them), and so for entertainment they relied on the radio. "I think radio gave me all my visual skills"

Gilliam has said. "(It) is an extraordinary thing — because you have to invent, it's not there. The sound effects are there, the voices are there, and you've got to invent the costumes, the faces, the sets. It's the most incredible exercise for visual imagination."[2] (In an interesting twist, years later Gilliam's first professional animation would be created to a soundtrack comprised solely of a radio disc jockey's on-air riffs[3]).

After high school Gilliam enrolled at Occidental College in California. Although he wanted to study art, he understood there was probably more career to be had in the sciences, so he took up physics. He could never really get art out of his system, though (or physics into his head), and so he transferred into the Fine Arts Department. His time in the studios was short-lived, though, because after repeated frustrations, including a run-in with a professor over his drawing style, he transferred his focus again, this time to Political Science. This change stuck, and he maintained a Political Science major up through graduation. This ability to shift with the situation would be a great benefit to Gilliam as he moved into the working world.

At Occidental, Gilliam joined the staff of *Fang*, the college's literary magazine. Influenced strongly by *Pogo*, *Mad Magazine* and *Help!* (a national humor magazine), he moved the magazine away from its literary roots and transformed it into a humor magazine, with a heavy bend toward the visual arts.

Overall, Gilliam's influences were wide-ranging and varied. They include Brueghel, Bosch, Redon, Walt Disney, Shel Silverstein, Salvador Dali, Goya, Boucher and Harvey Kurtzman.[4] The citing of so many classical painters of course stems from the inspiration received by using them as source material in his animations. It's also arguable that earlier on, as he was still forming himself, they helped to shape his sense of space, detail and composition. As for the others on the list, Shel Silverstein seems an obvious influence with his humor both dark *and* sunny and oftentimes completely unexpected. As for Kurtzman, he could be the seminal influence in Gilliam's life; it's a relationship that will be discussed in further detail in a moment. That takes us to Disney. Walt Disney and Terry Gilliam aren't names you might normally link together; for Gilliam, though, Disney and his studio's output appear at key moments in his life and career. Gilliam has said that "as an American growing up in Minnesota, Walt Disney *was* animation." When pressed for what it was about the works of the Disney Studios that captivated him, he's cited the visual power and detail. "The Disney universe is complete, complex. Compared to Disney, Chuck Jones was a joke. Disney is far superior. The real art is superior."[5]

Many artists cite Disney as an influence only to turn away from the Disney aesthetic as they grow their talents. As Gilliam's career has progressed, though, he seemed to embrace the elements of Disney even tighter. In many respects it was an issue of career necessity. The Disney films helped to condition the public to how animation worked, how a story flowed, etc. Gilliam created pieces that played off of this now-conditioned understanding of the medium. In a Gilliam piece, the Princess may now find her Prince Charming, but a foot will probably fall out of the sky and smash him. Gilliam's work shocks and entertains us because it *is* so completely unexpected, and that comes from an audience's expectation from Disney animation (style and storytelling). Gilliam wasn't out just to subvert Disney, though; there was a real inspiration that he felt from this work, and his fondness for that comes out in some of his shorts, although in true Gilliam fashion, it's in a dark way.

TERRY GILLIAM'S PICKS FOR THE TOP TEN ANIMATED FILMS[6]

Pinocchio (1940)
Red Hot Riding Hood (1943)
The Mascot (1934)
Out of the Inkwell (1938)
Death Breath (1964)
Les Jeux des Agnes (1964)

Dimensions of Dialogue (1982)
Street of Crocodiles (1986)
Knick Knack (1989)
South Park: Bigger, Longer and Uncut (1999)

And Then There Was Harvey

By the time Gilliam reached college, Harvey Kurtzman had become a legend in the comics industry. He had worked for several publishers before really making a name for himself writing for EC Comics, where he created stories known for their detail and factual truth. This attention resulted in highly stylized, detailed and dramatically flaired stories. It's important to recognize that style, and the substance in it, here because Gilliam carried much of this same ethic and belief into his own work. While Kurtzman uses detail to help ground the story, Gilliam uses it to sell the surprise. Gilliam's obsession to detail helps to create an aura of realism that makes the surrealism and absurdity that lay just under the surface of each animated world even more impactful. (A great example can be seen in the segment set on a very Victorian street. A woman is pushing a baby carriage, and as people bend in to see the baby, the carriage closes on them, and they are eaten. It's a perfect juxtaposition of the unreality of a "real" world.)

Another piece of Kurtzman that rubbed off on Gilliam was his satirical streak. Kurtzman had a great outlook on the world, and many of his stories carried instances of this, sometimes macabre, sometimes satiric, sometimes unexpected, but always perfectly timed and funny. This all came to a head in

1952 when EC publisher William Gaines asked Kurtzman to oversee the publication of a humor comic. And in that seemingly innocent request, *Mad* was born. *Mad* was a shot across the bow of an Eisenhower-era establishment set in its structured, suburban ways. Witty, irreverent, satirical, hilarious —*Mad* lampooned everything in sight. Kurtzman's attention to detail was perfectly fit for the comic, as he was so attune to society that he knew right where the cracks in the foundation, and the subsequent jokes, were. Its biting brashness was comedy that hadn't really been seen before, and the public ate it up. For a number of reasons, in 1955 Kurtzman departed EC. *Mad* continued to flourish, though, and remained heavily under Harvey's influence, so strong was his presence and philosophy. For his part, Harvey took his brand of humor to three other magazines. Although none approached the popularity of *Mad*, they all carried out the distinctive humor of Harvey Kurtzman.

In his appreciation for Harvey, Gilliam says, "Harvey was the great idol of my generation. *Mad* comics inspired everything we ever did. Then when he started *Help!* magazine, I was in college at the time and started the college humor magazine and copied a lot of things that Harvey was doing in *Help!*."[7]

Help! was the most popular of all of Kurtzman's post–*Mad* ventures. This was most likely because it attracted a number of the day's top comedians like Woody Allen, Sid Caesar, Ernie Kovacs, Jerry Lewis, Mort Sahl, Jean Shepherd and Dick Van Dyke. It also featured the early work of underground and independent artists including Skip Williamson, Dennis Ellefson, Don Edwing, Stew Schwartzberg, Gilbert Shelton, Jay Lynch, Jim Jones, Hank Hinton, Robert Crumb and Joel Beck. *Help!* presented its comedy in new and innovative ways. One of these was a photography segment known as *fumettis* (an Italian description for images purposely arranged in a comic-book style), which featured photos both found and new (or a combination) presenting outlandishly complex scenarios and fitted with comic captions.

In the midst of all of this, one day there came a knock at the door of Kurtzman's apartment. On the other side stood Terry Gilliam, bright-eyed, apple-cheeked and fresh out of school. "Here I am," he announced to everyone and no one at the same time. Such was the first meeting of Gilliam and his idol, and it couldn't have relieved Kurtzman more.

Help!

Gilliam, in an effort to be accepted by one of his idols, would routinely send copies of *Fang* to Kurtzman in New York City. After receiving several issues, Kurtzman sent Gilliam a note of appreciation and respect. It was the acceptance that Gilliam had been waiting for, and it boosted him energetically and creatively. The two sporadically traded letters back and forth until Gilliam's graduation, when he wrote to inform Kurtzman of his intention to come to New York and work. Kurtzman respectfully tried to dissuade Gilliam from making the trip, telling him that the city was big and bustling and not all that it was made out to be. The words were read by blind eyes. In 1962, Gilliam boarded a bus to New York to start a career and (perhaps more important to him) meet Harvey Kurtzman.

Meanwhile, in a destiny-filled twist of fate that seems to happen only in stories like this, the assistant editor of *Help!* was quitting at just the same time that Gilliam showed up on the magazine's doorstep. With his previous correspondences, great resume, and precision timing, Gilliam was offered the job.

One particular area Gilliam oversaw was the popular fumettis. He worked with the concepts, helped stage the photography and hired the talent to appear in each story. One day he was presented with an idea for a fumetti — a story about a man who lusted after a doll. Not only did he love the idea, but he also thought that he knew the perfect comedian, one who had the perfect mix of gravity and goofy. Just a few weeks earlier he had seen the Broadway production of the *Cambridge Circus*, a revue from England. Among the performers in the show was one John Cleese. During a down period for the show, Cleese agreed to star in the fumetti, and in that a seed was planted for much greater things.

It was at this time that Gilliam started experimenting with animation. His work was just that, experimental and probably more artistic expression than anything else. He and friends used to go to film studios and gather up any blank film stock they could find in the trash. They would take it home and draw on the frames. It was an exercise that gave him a feel for the sheer process of animation, helped him to understand detail even further and provided a base understanding of how the medium works.[8]

Gilliam worked at *Help!* until financial issues shut the magazine down. He then moved back to California, where he worked in advertising for a while before he jumped at an opportunity in 1967 to move with his girlfriend (a reporter) to Europe. It was in Europe that Gilliam got the need to start animating full time. Although it wasn't really *his* need.

Making Pictures Move

In the late 1960s and early 1970s Terry Gilliam found himself living in various European locales doing freelance work and enjoying the culture. He worked for numerous print outlets like *Pilote* in Paris but aspired to get into television and film. So when he finally landed in England, he looked up the one English performer he knew, John Cleese, and asked if Cleese could point him in the right direction. Cleese introduced him to Humphrey Barclay, a television producer who was working at the time on a new children's program called *Do Not Adjust Your Set* (1967–1969). When Gilliam finally worked his way into a meeting with Barclay, he figured the only way to break in would be as a writer, and so he took with him some written sketches. Barclay enjoyed the sketches so much that not only did he buy them for the program, but he also hired Gilliam to be a member of the writing staff, a staff that included Eric Idle, Terry Jones and Michael Palin.

Do Not Adjust Your Set turned out to be a critical and cultural hit. In 1968 Barclay tried to continue the magic of this show in creating his next series: *We Have Ways of Making You Laugh* (1968).

We Have Ways of Making You Laugh was a combination comedy/sketch/talk show. As an added attraction, Barclay, who, it turns out, was an amateur cartoonist and had recently discovered Gilliam's penchant with the pen, hired him to sit in during the talk show segment and draw real-time caricatures of the guests.

A guest on one episode was a popular British DJ who was known for his rapid-fire, rhyming patter. As they began preparations for the show, one of the technicians came forward with an audio recording. For several weeks he had been recording the DJ's radio show; he then edited out everything except the DJ's speeches, splicing them together, one after the next, to create a surreal monologue. Gilliam sensed there was something in this strange bit of audio, and he went to Barclay with a desire to do something with it. It was decided that Gilliam would produce an animation with the tape as the soundtrack. There was, though, very little money and nearly no time to do this. Because of these restraints Gilliam was forced to work with found materials, mainly previously produced imagery. He took images from magazines and old photographs, cut them up, and animated them in a stop-motion (what he calls the Magpie Approach) fashion. The result was a surreal stream-of-consciousness animation that was the start of the "Gilliam style."[9]

This style was born half out of necessity and half out of inspiration. With time and budget pressing against him, he focused in on his background and found something he could cannibalize. While he was living in New York he had the opportunity to see *Death Breath* (1964, Stan van der Beek). It was a simple, stop-motion short starring (pictures of) Richard Nixon trying to talk but having trouble because his foot kept literally getting stuck in his mouth. The simplistic surrealness of it made a significant impact on Gilliam, who took the seed of this idea and cultivated it into his own unique interpretation of animation.

The DJ animation that Gilliam produced went over so well that he was asked to create more animated segments for the second season of *Do Not Adjust Your Set*. Gilliam used these animations to find his form — he fine-tuned his style, explored pacing and expanded his focus on the details. One example of his work during this time is a short of Christmas card scenes where a church spire takes off like a rocket and the Magi go off after an increasingly jumpy star. What sound like seemingly simple bits of animation are actually finely developed, layered experiments in audience expectation. It was pure Gilliam showing his understanding of the audiences' (in this case primarily children's) expectations and using his creative fearlessness to not simply riff off of those expectations but to take things down an opposite and completely unexpected path. That's where the joy in his work comes from, the initial humor as well as the wonder at being shown the unexpected, the unseen.

While the black-and-white animations created for *Do Not Adjust Your Set* may have been unpolished they most definitely were impactful: "Yesterday, the show included a new feature, some really clever animated cartoons done by Terry Gilliam. These cartoons were as good as you would get at any hour on television. The equal of cinema cartoons" (a review of *Do Not Adjust Your Set* by Stanley Reynolds for *The Times*, April 8, 1969[10]). (Sadly the BBC had a habit of recycling program tapes, recording new shows over the old ones, and so the majority of this early work is lost.)

Always one to push ahead, in 1968 Gilliam pushed his animation skills to the limit when he created the eight-minute short film *Storytime*. It's an ambitious effort and a great exercise in structure. He continued expanding when Marty Feldman asked him to create some animated bits for his new BBC-2 program *Marty*.

Python

In 1969, three British comedians, Eric Idle, Terry Jones and Michael Palin, who had worked with one another on various BBC programs, contacted John Cleese and his sometimes-writing partner Graham Chapman about doing something as a group. While they weren't really sure *what* they wanted to work on, they knew that it had to be something other than the standard sketch show. After much searching they decided that in fact they *would* do a sketch show, but it would be set around the comedy and not the format. Rather than have a show filled with sketches that had a traditional open, middle and end, they decided to allow the pieces to go where they (both the group and the comedy) wanted. This meant that sometimes sketches would never really end, but instead just roll into each other, while other times they might not "end" at all, at least in the traditional sense; instead they would just stop when the premise had played itself out. While the sketches would have a similar overarching theme, they would vary wildly in terms of design and tone. It was at this point that Terry Gilliam's name came up.

The acknowledged problem with a show like this is getting all of the separate bits to somehow be a part of a cohesive program. So Gilliam was called in and asked to create short animated segments that could help keep the momentum of the show driving forward while also bringing some of the disparate live-action pieces together. It was the addition of this crucial piece that really brought about the birth of Monty Python. The troupe first brought their brand of satiric, anarchic, surprise-filled, forward-thinking comedy to the masses via *Monty Python's Flying Circus* on October 5, 1969.

While he occasionally acted and wrote sketches, Gilliam's main function was creating these animated segments, which helped the viewer get from a sketch set in a cheese shop that sold no cheese to one featuring a group of hairdressers scaling Mount Everest with the express purpose of opening a salon.

One of the hallmarks of these animations was his use of well-known paintings and iconic imagery, all acquired through the media library of the BBC. (One of these images, that of a massive foot descending from the sky, squashing whatever happens to be below it, has become one of the defining images of the group. That foot, perhaps the defining visual image of Python, was taken from *Venus, Cupid, Folly and Time* by Agnolo Bronzino.[11]) As at every other point in his career, the choice of these images was part inspiration, part necessity.

Python was not yet *Python*, and Gilliam again found himself hampered by the constraints of budgets and time, but he used his deadlines to focus his vision. He would attend the first set of writing meetings each week to get a full sense of what the subject and feel of the show's sketches would be. As the sketches started to take basic shape, he would give some broad outlines to the group as to what he proposed to do with his segments. More often than not he was given free rein to take his pieces in whatever direction he saw fit, as long as they started and ended as in and out points for the preceding and following sketches. With these show outlines, he would go lock himself in his room and animate (with his assistant, Katy Hepburn, who was Terry Jones's sister-in-law), re-emerging on the day of filming with completed animations in hand. Gilliam's limits on time and budget forced him to cut things tightly. He wouldn't animate intricate mouth movements but move a character's jaw up and down, approximating the words being spoken. Objects moved herky-jerky through a scene, and in some sequences you could practically see the hands manipulating the objects. It sounds amateurish and cheap, but put together with Gilliam's humor and style, the pieces worked to create a very effective whole. Animation historian Jerry Beck puts it this way: "The cheapness of it all adds to the charm."[12]

Gilliam had an uncanny ability to find the perfect images to supplement the humor and situation of a scene. In more traditional animation there's a certain unlimitedness because you can draw whatever you need to fill a sequence. When using cut-out animation, though, you're at the mercy of your materials. Given the time crunch he was often under, it would have been easy for Gilliam to take an image and *make* it work in each particular scene, but his tutelage under Kurtzman taught him the importance of detail, and so he and his assistant would spend the time to find the exact right image. The images were often ones that had an emotional or mental recall for the audience. This was part of the reason they were chosen: their familiarity immediately transported the audience to a place or a mood, which he could then manipulate.

When asked his thoughts on why so many famous paintings appear in his animations, Gilliam had this to say: "I only started off with paintings of famous artists because everybody knew them and understood them; and then I turned them into something stupid."[13] It's an understated way of categorizing his ability to take something known and understood and get inside of it and show it from the looking-glass side and making it funny and shocking at the same time.

The attention to detail in choosing his imagery is impressive, and it paid off, as it's part of what makes each short work as well as it does, giving the segment its grounded quality, providing it a richness (richness that was lacking in the production values overall) and helping sell the joke and make the action seem that much more absurd.

The segments that he created for Python are probably more aptly described as "stream of sub-conscious" works. For example in the animation in which an old woman leans into the baby carriage, secretly, deep down we all hope that the baby does something to her. We've all witnessed this scene before on street corners or at the mall; we know that these poor babies have to undergo a torrent of cheek pinching, and we always feel for them, secretly wishing that they got justice somehow. Gilliam explodes this secret desire and allows the (unseen) baby to pull the woman into the baby buggy and presumably eat her. It's a shock to be sure but a shock followed by a laugh tinged with happy justice along with the pleasure of seeing things we wouldn't always admit to thinking take form.

Gilliam's animations are manic and organic, moving along with a twisted purpose. The actions of the animation may appear outrageous, but the objects performing these actions do them in a logical and completely realized (for them) way. This only renders them even more absurd. When you're viewing Donald Duck, you prepare yourself for a certain reaction because of the unreality of the situation. When you view a photo of a criminal standing in a darkened alleyway, you're not sure how to prepare yourself because there is a reality in the photographic image, a reality that's heightened when the criminal jumps in front of an innocent man and demands that he raise his arms. After a moment, the man raises his left arm, than his right one, then another left and another right and another left and so on and so on. And as the arms keep raising, your emotions go from unease to humor as the reality turns to absurdity.

Gilliam's animations have a very relatable quality to them, which is also part of their appeal. When you look at something like *Cinderella* (1950, Walt Disney Studios), you marvel at the beauty of the images and stand in wonder of the artistry of the work. Most people look at animation like that and appreciate it and stand in reverence of it (and enjoy it), but they know that they will never be able to achieve something like that because that is not where their talents lie. On the other hand you'll be hard pressed to find someone who at some point in their life hasn't picked up an inanimate object, like a picture, and acted as if it were talking to you or made it a "live" part of some "funny" skit. Gilliam has taken this basic party practice and pushed it down the line in artistic and unexpected ways.

His contributions to the success of Monty Python cannot be stated enough. No less an authority on the group than Michael Palin has said, "Terry provided the element which made Python different than anything else."[14] And Python was completely unlike anything that had been seen before. Glenn Whipp of the *Los Angeles Daily News* surmises Python's humor as "(making) anarchy smart, funny and palatable."[15]

While Gilliam says that he was never consciously a part of the 1960s underground movement, subconsciously he must have felt its grasp because traces of that scene can be found flowing through his work, not so much in style as in tone and message. No one was safe from his reach, especially historical figures past and present who often came up against a sublimely silly antagonist. Others who met their just ends were figures who might not have been immediately recognized as leaders but who had an upper-class/ruling-class manner to them (well dressed men, overly proper women, judges, etc.). Even figures from famous works of art, such as Venus in Botticelli's *Birth of Venus*, were fair targets for Gilliam. (The Botticelli work would become a frequent touchpoint for him, particularly in his live-action work.) Gilliam wasn't overly malicious, just deflationist. He seemed to be saying that we were all equal and that was really how the world should treat us.

Another mark of Gilliam's animations is their focus on the macabre.

There is a very Victorian feel to his work. His shorts have a dark undertone (with frequent appearances by skulls and monsters), which provides the viewer a sense of uneasiness and heightens the disorientation that the animation may invoke. The actions of these (macabre) films still elicit a smile, but it's a smile tinged with nervousness.

An example can be found in one episode where a live action actor visits the "Home for the Severe Over-Actor." When he opens one door, the scene transitions into an animated piece featuring four figures dressed as Shakespearean actors reciting "To be or not to be." As they chant this over and over, they proceed to open their heads, remove their skulls and give the speech to them. Then they remove their heads, place the skulls on their shoulders and speak from skull to head. It's scary in the way that *The Addams Family* is, and these macabre touches are often part of his best work.

Other Work

With the success of *Monty's Python's Flying Circus*, Gilliam saw many opportunities to expand his creative visions.

In 1970 he created the opening animated title sequence for the forgettable Vincent Price film *Cry of the Banshee*. The sequence is typical Gilliam — humorous and dark — and features, among other things, Price's head splitting open and a torrent of demons spilling out. It's inarguably the best part of the film.

In 1971 Gilliam was asked by American television legend Larry Gelbert (writer on *Your Show of Shows*, *M*A*S*H*, *Tootsie* and *A Funny Thing Happened on the Way to the Forum* among others) to come to work on a television special starring British comedian Marty Feldman. Gilliam agreed to create 25 minutes of animation for *The Marty Feldman Comedy Machine*, a decision that was marked by numerous battles with American sensors. Gilliam was attempting to change his general material; he just discovered that some people were not prepared for it.

In 1972 he created the title sequence for a CBS television special on Shakespeare called *William*. That same year he also tapped into his advertising experience when he created a campaign for the British Gas Board.

Through this all, Gilliam has been honored with numerous awards and nominations, mainly for his work in live-action film as a director, producer and writer. In 1970, though, he did win a BAFTA (British Academy of Film and Television Arts) for his animation work in the 1969 season of *Monty Python*.

He has also turned from drawing to writing. In 1978 he authored the book *Animations of Mortality*, which featured artwork, sketches and text all looking into the mind of an animator. In 1996 the book was turned into an interactive CD-ROM complete with several new Gilliam-produced and -inspired animations and images.

No More

"Terry Gilliam is a mastermind of creative exploration."
— John Ramo, president and CEO of Enteractive, Inc.[16]

On December 5, 1974, the final episode of *Monty Python's Flying Circus* aired. There had been 45 regularly broadcast programs as well as two shows that were created specifically for German television. When they left the air, it wasn't a cancellation but a conscious decision by the group to end the series while still hitting their high marks for creativity, originality and comedy. The group also had other aspirations, one of which that was met later that year when their first original feature film premiered — *Monty Python and the Holy Grail* is a completely skewed take on the Arthurian legend; it is brash, bold and hilarious. (They had appeared in 1971's *And Now for Something Completely Different*, but that was a film compendium of show clips.) *Holy Grail* is inarguably a comedy classic. It is filled with sublimely ridiculous moments, all augmented by animations supplied by Gilliam. As the plot was really just a loose framework to hang extended sketches on, Gilliam was again called upon to create animations that could advance the story. From musical interludes (in the film's one production number) to some inspired sequences featuring God (sequences that somehow manage to be both reverential and absurd) to scenes of characters running in one direction or another, Gilliam managed to maintain the cheap quirkiness of his television work and still make it feel cinematic.

For fans of Gilliam the animator, this was a bittersweet moment. While it was great to see his work on the big screen, it also marked the end of a career path. Gilliam had always harbored a desire to direct a live-action feature film, and with *Holy Grail* he was given the opportunity to live out this dream (as co-director with Terry Jones). Although they were inexperienced and the experience was arduous, they were hooked. While Monty Python continued their run in live-action films (*Life of Brian* [1979] and *The Meaning of Life* [1983]) and Gilliam continued to provide animations for them, his attention turned more and more toward live action.

In this way he is like Frank Tashlin, a prominent early–twentieth-century figure in animation who made a conscious decision to walk away from the medium in favor of working in live-action films. Terry Gilliam is the only animator in memory who had such influence and success animating even though he most likely never really wanted to get into the field in the first place.

> CRANKYCRITIC: "Will we see any more animation out of you?"
> TERRY GILLIAM: "Nope. That was another guy. Same name, different guy."[17]

Having never been a member of the animation community, Gilliam was really unaware of the "rules" he was supposed to play by and untouched by the pressure that is often felt by a member of a trade community. This "outsider" status allowed Gilliam to create in an unjaded and rather uninfluenced atmosphere. He never had to prove himself to animators that he met climbing the ladder; all he had to do was entertain. His unfiltered style allowed him to purely pour his past, experiences, humor, politics, personality and feelings into his work. This made his work very personal; it gave his animations a very instinctive quality, which translates when you are watching them into a feeling that in production they were more felt than planned.

This is one of the lasting marks of Gilliam's influence, the way that story structure held less importance than the idea, an idea that often was expressed in a stream-of-conscious manner. Gilliam's work is very organic. His shorts are an essay in exploration; watching them you feel as if you are watching the creative process unfold before you. It's as if all of the crazy ideas and thoughts one has were poured from their head and allowed to run free on paper. It was all a form of controlled chaos, but it was perfect and exactly right.

Gilliam is a true auteur and a certain member of the DIY school of animation. He is one of the few animators who wrote, directed, shot, edited and often created the audio for his works. Each of his animations, while shaped by the sentiments and humor of the group, was purely and uniquely created in his voice. He wasn't born into the medium. He converted. This is important because you only ever convert to things that you are really, really called to.

Gilliam's influence in animation can be seen in those that have proclaimed their allegiance to and tried to follow his style and spirit. It's an interestingly wide-ranging group that includes Phil Vischer (*VeggieTales*), Philip Fairbanks, Nick Park (Aardman Studios), Andrew Stanton (*WALL-E*), Joe Murray (*Rocko's Modern Life*), and Matt Stone and Trey Parker (*South Park*). His work also freed many animators from following traditional routes. Gilliam had primed an audience for something new, and now others could continue feeding them interesting, funny and fresh animated shorts.

After *Meaning of Life*, the members of Monty Python drifted off to pursue their other interests. For Gilliam, this meant moving completely into the world of live-action filmmaking. The group occasionally got together, like in

1994 when they all collaborated on the CD-ROM *Monty Python's Complete Waste of Time*, but they have produced no other major works to date.

In the history of film and television, there have been few people who have been able to work effectively in two distinct mediums and be influential in both. Terry Gilliam is the rare individual who has made a distinct contribution in two diverse areas (animation and live-action films). While we may lament Gilliam's decision to stop animating, we also must be thankful for the work he produced. His ability to take the images of normal, everyday things and make them act in the most surprising and outrageous ways has not only entertained us, but also shown us what the medium of animation is truly capable of doing. Gilliam's passion, artistic sense, brilliantly wicked humor and attention to his audience led him to create some of the most innovative and funny animations of the latter half of the twentieth century.

HONORS (FOR ANIMATION ONLY)

Monty Python's Flying Circus, Special Award (for Graphics), British Academy of Film and Television Arts (BAFTA), 1970

Monty Python's Flying Circus, Michael Balcon Award for Outstanding British Contribution to Cinema, British Academy of Film and Television Arts (BAFTA), 1987

Monty Python's Flying Circus, Special Award (for Graphics), British Academy of Film and Television Arts (BAFTA), 2009

SAMPLE FILM SELECTION

Storytime (1968)
We Have Ways of Making You Laugh (1968)
Monty Python's Flying Circus (1969–1974)

WRITINGS

The Do-It-Yourself Film Animation Book, by Bob Godfrey and Anna Jackson, with contributions from Terry Gilliam, 1974
Animations of Mortality, by Terry Gilliam, 1978

The Technicians

5. Max and Dave Fleischer

> "If it can be done in real life, it's not animation."
> — Max Fleischer[1]

Technology as Art

There was a period (and in some circles this is probably still true) when the Walt Disney Studio was viewed as *the* pinnacle of animation. For many there was Disney and then there was everyone else, and to be fair, during certain periods, it's hard to break this argument. The gap between the output of Walt's artists and every other studio was so great at times it was almost unfair. (This argument can be continued, or remade, into the twenty-first century discussion thanks to Disney's acquisition of Pixar in 2006.) And yet, while this may have been the *public* perception, other studios didn't, or more accurately couldn't, buy wholeheartedly into this same school of thought because in doing so they would, in a roundabout way, invalidate the existence and need for their own work.

This pervasive thinking propelled artists elsewhere to work harder both out of a desire to elevate their own artistic output and as a way to show that there was "another way" in place of the Disney school. While individual artists shined from studio to studio in the 1930s, there was only one total studio that seemed to find one of those "other ways" and, for a brief period of time, use that to give Disney a run for the title. The Fleischer Studio, run by brothers Max (7/18/1883–9/11/72) and Dave (7/14/1894–6/25/79), provides an interesting counterpoint to Disney, not just in terms of artistic output but in the business and personality parallels as well.

The comparison and contrast between the Fleischer and Disney Studios is an interesting one to look through and discuss because there were so many similarities between the two. By understanding the path that Walt and Roy Disney took, one can have a better context when looking over the path that Max and Dave Fleischer took and the missteps they made along the way.

Both studios were run by brothers (although the Fleischers, unlike Disney, had three other brothers mingling through other occupations within the studio); both studios had a level of reliance on technology, which they used to achieve their initial success; and both saw the importance of music in their work. In terms of the artists at each location, both studios had similar working conditions, which accounts for why both were hit by labor strikes, which ultimately changed the direction of each studio. While they shared these, and other traits, the direction that each pair led their studio in and the results from those moves were markedly different.

From a very base level, the relationship between each set of brothers was completely different in terms of business positions. Walt and Roy Disney are inextricably linked, and need to be based on the personalities of the two men and the dynamics within their relationship. Walt was the clear figurehead — spiritually, creatively, business-wise, and in a manner technologically, within the studio. Roy's primary responsibility was to assist his brother and see that *his* dreams came true.

While Max and Dave Fleischer are linked, that may be unfair to their legacies, for although they worked together, their greatest contributions to the art of animation were more individually devised. Perhaps it was a New York streak running through them, but the Fleischers did not share the clean division of responsibilities that Walt and Roy had between them. Both Dave and Max operated strongly and independently within their chosen spheres of expertise. What they accomplished was more a result of personal determination than reaching for an overarching goal.

Max and Dave operated their animation studio out of New York City, 3,000 miles away from the Disney lot. This placement was more than a geographical difference; it was an artistic one as well, as it allowed the Fleischers to incorporate a distinct New York-ness into their shorts, a streetwise sensibility that was more than the remembered and reconstituted brashness that would develop within in the output from the West Coast–based Warner Brothers studio (although a particularly understood New York attitude was certainly prevalent in those shorts), more a daily, place-based worldliness.

The New York base gave the Fleischer films an "urbane sophistication" that was a marked departure from the middle-of-the-road, saccharine quality of most studio produced shorts. It also gave their films immediacy; for example, while Disney was rooted firmly in an idealized past, and the films from the Warner Brothers, which sat stylistically (depending upon the director) somewhere between Disney and the Fleischers, also offered more of a look back, the Fleischer Studio output sat in the immediate present.

This is all to say that the Fleischers presented a very real alternative to much of the animation that was being produced at the time, and yet in the way this work was done, their films didn't age as well as others because so much of it lives to be understood within a context of the time it was created. Their legacy, then, is not an accumulated output of work but more one of attitudinal influence, technical achievement, and an understanding of the strengths of the medium (as can be seen in their "house style").

Dreams Come to Life

"The black and white animated universe of Max and Dave Fleischer was bizarre, otherworldly and dreamlike. It was characterized by spectacular metamorphic effects where rubbery characters could easily transform into other creatures and where inanimate objects could randomly gain lives of their own."[2]

Fleischer shorts, particularly those of the early 1930s, while immediately recognizable as such, are still hard to describe because so many of them play like a dream. Their best efforts are enveloped in a surreal atmosphere where things just sort of seem to happen. While there are stories, in a traditional sense, they are not always linearly told, and in fact many play as if there is a start and a finish and maybe one or two certain stops to make along the way, but the path between those points is left up to the wind. This, though, is also what makes the shorts work so well and why they have stood across the years. The films are not indecipherable but entertaining and exuding joy; there are times when you can feel the animator's energy ripping across the page.

These films are remarkable for how distinctly they embodied the flapper attitude, spirit, language, and music of the day. Take their incorporation of jazz. The Fleischers saw inherent value and artistic merit in this music form, treated as a passing novelty by others. To the New York boys brought up in the streets of the city, it made perfect sense to them to transfer this tough, brassy, and even sexy world to the screen through pen and ink.

All of these components only meant that the Fleischers' films could suffer from a type of schizophrenia. Packed into each Fleischer short is a mix of surrealism, expressionism, and free-ranging thought that mirrored the attitude that sat over the nation during the time and was particularly prevalent along the upper portion of the eastern seaboard.

To produce and showcase these innovations and ideas, in 1919 the Fleischers established the Out of the Inkwell Studio. Here, at the dawn of the jazz age, the studio output wasn't trying to recapture a time past or find a safe, middle-of-the-road storytelling spot; rather their films "expressed the impudence of the age. Authority existed to be mocked; rules were made to be defied or concealed" (Stephen Kanfer[3]).

The Technicians

From the very beginning, Max and Dave Fleischer had forged an uneasy working relationship. Dave had designs on greater opportunities not so much within the studio but within the motion picture business overall, and Max did not have the personality or passionate drive to push himself into a "figure-head" position at the studio. This created a type of leadership vacuum, particularly of the personality leadership that Walt practiced so well. While the Fleischers' relationship and their studio could subsist on the positions as they were, it was a tenuous stand and one that could not be held over time. For as long as they could, though, they made it work. One of the areas that they could continually turn to in agreement and collaboration was the technical side of the business. While their interest in, and practice of, technology was great, it may have in fact superseded their ambitions in being known as animators. It's important to understand the Fleischers' technical prowess because it lays the foundation for all the work that followed. In direct contrast to what was happening at Disney, the Fleischers took a technical advancement or idea and then tried to craft a story around it. It was a reverse of the old architectural adage — function following form.

Max Fleischer's first "media" job was a telling one — he was art editor for *Popular Science* magazine. This job, seemingly just a job at the time, foretells the mindset he would use to guide his studio. In fact, he even entered the animation business not with any particularly lofty artistic designs but on a technical bent in the form of the rotoscope.

The rotoscope process was used to create hyper-realistic animation with the result looking as if a traditional live-action film and an animated short had a child. To achieve this effect, an actor, in costume, would be filmed performing the actions for a scene against a bare backdrop. This film was then rear-projected one frame at a time onto the back of a specially constructed animation table that allowed the animator to trace the actor frame by frame onto the animation paper. These drawings were then photographed and would become an animated sequence.

The first appearance of a rotoscoped scene coincided with the first appearance of Koko the Clown in the inaugural *Out of the Inkwell* (1919) cartoon. *Out of the Inkwell* is one of those key shorts in film history because it did introduce one of the first "stars" of the medium, the chameleonic clown Koko. The short is also important because of its link to this new technology, which helped (for better or for worse) push the art and style of the animated short.

(It's interesting to note that there is some question as to whether or not the brothers ever intended to turn to entertainment-focused animation with this device. In their U.S. patent application there is a drawing of the rotoscope in action, and within that it appears to have live-action implications, or at least the drawing hints at a use in creating education-focused animation, which did hold a particular interest for Max.)

The best and most famous use of the rotoscope may have been in the *Superman* series (which ran from 1941 through 1943 and included 17 install-ments in total). The choice to use rotoscoping in that series was a good one because, given its subject matter, the technique helped to ground the series and make it feel more "true." By placing these fantastic situations and actions in what was a realistic, although hyper-realized, setting, there was a certain amount of drama that could be cultivated. On the other side, by adhering to such realistic moments, the animators were handcuffed in terms of their artistic decisions, which in turn lent an artificiality to each installment.

What this means is that while the Superman stories are told through cartoons, they are not cartoony and therefore lack some of the benefits that come along with the medium. For all of the hype and potential within these films, the Fleischers missed a great opportunity to create a long-lasting series that would really define and develop one of the truly great American charac-ters.

Popeye — In Three Dimensions!

The rotoscope was the first of numerous technical innovations that the studio would bring to the industry. In 1936 Max applied for yet another U.S. patent for a machine that would copy the animator's pencil drawings directly onto cels. This process would see sporadic use until 1961 when Disney used a similar Xerox-based process to great acclaim on the feature *101 Dalmatians* (1961).

While that process brought a flatness to films, the Fleischers developed a separate system to take things in the opposite direction and add depth and dimensionality to their work. The brothers saw benefits in adding visual depth to their films, not as a gimmick, but to enhance the dramatic presence of the story.

They were not the only ones either. During this period several studios used the multiplane camera, which was an effective tool for establishing a location, but it lacked the mobility needed to create a 3D effect during a strong action sequence. What they ended up creating was another roto — the Rotograph. The Rotograph is essentially a miniature set onto which animation cels can be placed. The set is mobile and built at a forced perspective so that it can accommodate action across a wide expanse with a net effect being that the character of the scene inhabits, in a seemingly natural way, a fully realized physical space. The first practical use of this tool occurred with a Betty Boop short, *Poor Cinderella* (1934).

In order to sell the illusion that the characters were actually walking through this hard set, Max insisted that the sets be built with objects in the foreground, which does more than simply build space; it also replicates the parallax effect that the eye undergoes by pulling the eye to that section of the screen and manipulating the perception of focus. This adds a heightened sense of realism, for at times characters are obscured by objects they pass by, just as we might observe them in the street. The severest use of this perspective occurs in *Popeye the Sailor Meets Sinbad the Sailor* (1936) when Bluto, as Sinbad, travels across the island and at one point disappears behind a mountain base for a five-second stretch. It's not a terribly long period of time on paper, but a near eternity on screen and an impressive artistic (and perhaps somewhat egotistical technical) choice. It was a shot unheard of at the time, a long stretch of animation where the only thing onscreen is a rock. And yet it works because it is within the character of the story, happens so naturally in camera, and, when it comes right down to it, succeeds and is accepted partly because of its audacity.

The Popeye film was a seminal one in the history of the studio, notable for the great use of this technology; it was also Popeye's first color cartoon, the first Fleischer cartoon to receive an Academy Award nomination and, at two reels, the longest cartoon (at that point in time) ever created (as *Snow White and the Seven Dwarfs* [1937] was still a year away).

The Fleischers were certainly not the first animators to mix the real world with the animated one, but they did it like no other. Their interest in mixing the two had actually been in play at the studio since the early adventures with Koko the Clown. Those films famously introduced the animated Koko into the "real" world in each installment by having him emerge, or be unleashed, from the animator's inkwell. This merging of the real and imagined was often done through double exposing the film and precision-executed editing. As the film series wore on and the public, and the artists themselves, grew to expect a grander and grander opening, other techniques had to be employed. One of the more ingenious was to use still photographs as stand-ins for the live-action film footage. This happened in more elaborate sequences where Koko had to interact in detail with a "physical" set piece such as a building or a statue. To make this as simple as possible, a frame from the film would be taken and "frozen" to be used as a background to animate to. The result gives the illusion that continuous motion has occurred.

The Players

Each animation studio had their stable of stars, but those found at the Fleischers' were unique. What made those stars so special was that they were distinctly of their time. Just as live-action stars were products of their era, the Fleischers' three main draws, more than any other studio's stars, embodied the time they were living in. First there was Koko the silent, plucky clown; next in the spotlight came Betty Boop and all her flagrant sexuality; and then of course there was Popeye, the honest, hardworking, ingenious sailor who, for a time, rivaled Mickey Mouse as the most popular animated star in the world.

What's interesting is how judiciously the brothers used their stars. Other studios would introduce a new character, and then, if they caught on, that character would be pimped out and propped up, twisted, promoted, sold, and stretched for as long as possible. And then for a little longer. The Fleischers were more concerned with impact over shelf life, and they had the sense to retire a character when the time was right. Before doing so, though, they would use the initial character to introduce the next potential star, a sort of passing of the torch for the characters and a sign of acceptance and approval to the audience.

Koko

Koko's first appearance was in *Out of the Inkwell* (1919). Born out of a certain mix of necessity and ingenuity, Koko achieved his prominence not as much through personality as through, more fittingly, technical advancements. Koko was a "manufactured" character in that he was, initially at least, the rotoscoped likeness of Dave Fleischer. The initial popularity of Koko came from the lifelike precision with which he moved, but eventually he developed an impish personality, which he used to endear the public. While Koko was popular, as sound enveloped the industry room had to be made for others who were better suited to the changing medium.

Betty

Dizzy Dishes (1930) introduced the world to Betty Boop (at least an early incarnation, for when she was "born," she was an odd dog-human hybrid). Betty is a fascinating character in the history of animation, for she was the medium's first true sex symbol. More than just eye candy, though, Betty had a vivacious pluck and, like any true star, understood her persona and worked it to the best of her ability. Betty excelled at mixing naïveté with a sexual awareness that had never been seen before in animated films. This is perfectly shown in *Boop-oop-a-Doop* (1932), where Betty sings "Don't take my Boop-oop-a-doop away." You can't get any more plainly suggestive than that. Unfortunately Betty's ascendency to the upper echelon of motion picture stars was stopped by the moral right and their heavy-fisted Production Code.

The Man of Steel

As mentioned earlier, the studio also counted Superman among its stable of stars. While not a homegrown creation (credit for that goes to Joe Shuster and Jerry Siegel at DC Comics), the innovative work that was done with the superhero in the series definitely left its mark on the character's persona.

Popeye

As big as Betty and Koko were, even they couldn't hold a candle to Popeye. In fact no one could, as shortly after his introduction on the silver screen he rivaled Mickey Mouse in polls for the most popular animated character.

Popeye was created by E.C. Segar for the *Thimble Theatre* newspaper comic strip, and the Fleischers turned to him in a moment of desperation. With Betty's act stifled by the newly formed Production Code, the brothers needed a new star. Their choice of Popeye was an inspired one. Something about this hard-working, spinach-loving sailor struck a chord with the viewing public, and while his shorts were held to a certain formula, the public never tired of them.

Sound Innovations

One of the key production differences between a Fleischer film and others is one of the things that made the Popeye series so popular: all of the audio tracks were post-recorded. The standard set up was that voice tracks would be pre-recorded, and then the animators would draw to what the actors said; the Fleischers, though, flipped that convention, which left some slide room for improvisation by the voice actors who took the opening provided to them and ran straight through it. A particular culprit was the voice of Popeye, Jack Mercer. Mercer was notorious for his on-mike (in-character) mutterings and asides. Not only do they add to the spontaneity of the shorts, but they really also helped define who the character of Popeye was.

It was this type of effect that gave the Popeye series, which seemed to continually rework the same plot structure, the loose feeling that was visually evident in their earlier shorts. Even before that, even before anyone really, the brothers were testing the limits of how sound and animation could be combined.

A holdover from vaudeville, the sing-along remained a popular attraction of early motion-picture exhibition. As part of a theater's "bill," the house organist would play a popular song, and the audience would sing along. If they didn't know the words, it was okay, because they were projected on the screen through the use of slides. The Fleischers thought it would be ideal if the lyrics were placed on film, a straightforward concept that they took a step further by adding some "guidance" for the singing audience. That guidance came in the form of an on-screen ball that, in time to the music, jumped across the words as they crossed the screen. And so came the rallying cry across the country — "Follow the Bouncing Ball." This series, known as the *Song Car-Tune*, was an immediate success. The initial series of shorts in the series were rather visually plain, just some words on screen and a moving ball really. After a short span of time, though, the Fleischers began to experiment with the overall concept of what would be done. They started to add characters (particularly Koko and the dog Bimbo) into the mix. These were not narrative choices, though; they were artistic ones. Koko served to add an additional level of entertainment to the songs by acting out some of the scenes the lyrics suggested. (In doing so, a position could be made that this was also the start of what we know today as the music video.) The characters didn't just remain staid during each short; they rolled and morphed with the music. If the lyrics called for a car traveling the road on a happy Spring day, Bimbo would have morphed into that car and traveled down a swaying road as an anthropomorphic sun smiled down from overhead. These transitions allowed the characters to serve the song and in doing so showcased what would become one of their most well-known filmic traits.

While Max was the public face of the studio, Dave was its driving creative force, fulfilling the role that Max couldn't, or wouldn't, as overarching creative director. He was involved in some capacity in nearly every film they worked on, and among them all there was one consistent directive — find the gag. He believed that there should never be a moment on screen when there wasn't something funny happening. During set pieces this was easy, but he even demanded the funny in incidental scenes, and so when a character walked through, say, a house, the only option was to bring the household objects to life. Were this to happen once, it's a throwaway gag; if it happens in the same short multiple times, it's being done to service the story, but if it's happening over and over, it becomes the house style. And that was the story at the Fleischers, and it became one of the things that is so remembered by anyone who has ever seen even just one of their films.

On top of all of this, though, perhaps what made the *Song Car-Tune* stand out was its eventual inclusion of the *tune*. In 1928 Disney released *Steamboat Willie*, the first Mickey Mouse cartoon with sound and a short, assumed by many, to be the first cartoon with a synchronized soundtrack. Actually that honor belongs, and it should be unsurprising given their affinity for technology, to the Fleischer Studio, as in 1926 they released the *Song Car-Tune—My Old Kentucky Home*. The result was less than perfect, but the studio continued to work and refine the processes involved.

The Fleischers had partnered with DeForest Phonofilm and Red Seal Pictures Corporation for the production of these shorts, but unfortunately in 1926 bankruptcy struck both of those firms, and the *Song Car-Tune* series was shut down. The Fleischers would return to the series after a few years, but at that point, sound on film was prevalent, and the novelty was lost. Still the milestone had been achieved, but the inability of the studio to capitalize on this points to a larger concern within the studio. Time and again the studio would mark a technological breakthrough or make an artistic move forward only to have the innovation become stagnant, forgotten, or mis-handled. This was a marked contrast to Disney, which, as an institution, would grab hold of any innovation or seminal success and ride it, hype it, grow it, and build on it on the way to the next success.

The End

In 1937 the Fleischers became the first American animation studio to work through a labor strike. The animators had walked off the job for a myriad of reasons including the popular strike topics of pay and workday hours. When the strike was settled (not long after it started and in favor of the workers), the studio became a changed place. A feeling of distrust settled across the building. Max was particularly taken aback. He was a changed man, befuddled as to this turn, a betrayal, from his "family" of employees. All of this change and the residual sentiment was part of the impetus for the Fleischers making yet another ground-breaking decision, this time to literally break ground in the creation of a new studio in a somewhat unlikely location — Miami, Florida. This setting for the new studio would offer, they hoped, an attractive lure to animators from across the country. That the location was also outside of the reach of the unions most likely aided their location decision as well. So it was that in 1938 boxes were packed and trucks were loaded as the studio headed south. And they weren't just heading to a new space; they were heading toward a new artistic horizon. Just a year earlier Disney had broken the industry open with *Snow White and the Seven Dwarfs* (1937), and now the Fleischers were ready to make their feature debut.

The studio's first full-length outing was an adaptation of Jonathan Swift's classic satire *Gulliver's Travels* (1939). In theory this pairing of story and studio should have worked, and yet the film suffered in its heavy use of rotoscoping, from which the characters came off as eerily wooden. Their second feature, *Mr. Bug Goes to Town* (1941), was looser but tried too hard, and there is a feeling as if they were trying to do Disney one better. While the brothers may have felt that going to full color and full length would elevate them in the eyes of the industry and the public, it is apparent in hindsight that it placed them in an uncomfortable position by asking them to become something which they were not. The results of both films were less than expected both artistically and commercially.

The move and financial setbacks played heavily on the already-thin relationship between Dave and Max until, unfortunately, they could stand each other no more.

In 1942 Max went to Paramount (who held their distribution contract) and demanded that Dave no longer be a part of the package. Paramount, perhaps tired of the brothers' increased bickering or their diminishing lack of returns, took this opportunity to call for the repayment of a loan that it had provided them for the establishment of the Miami studio. When the brothers couldn't come up with the money, they were unceremoniously let go.

In every divorce it is the child who suffers, and this case was no different. With the Fleischers off the lot, Paramount took total control of the studio, and, as soon as they could, they elevated some of Max and Dave's former employees into key management positions. They also changed the name of the animation division to Famous Studios and continued putting out shorts for another 25 years. The Fleischers were finally no more, in name at least. Their work, legacy, and influence, though, could not be erased or denied.

Next Steps

Dave headed to Columbia Studios, where he replaced Frank Tashlin as the head of their Screen Gems cartoon division. (Tashlin took the move in stride; for him every action he underwent was just moving him one step closer to his ultimate goal of working in live-action film.) Dave's stay at Columbia was not long, though, and he next found himself at Universal Studios. Tired of the animation game and looking for a new outlet for his talents, Dave took on the position of "General Troubleshooter." A close inspection of the credit-rolls of Universal films during this time finds Fleischer's name everywhere, as he assisted on any number of special effects and technical needs.

For his part, Max kicked around the industry, heading up animation divisions at other studios and offering research expertise, but he never again achieved the same level of innovation or acclaim.

What They Left

When one is considering the career of Max and Dave Fleischer, it is easy to find an initial point of entry through the technical innovations the two brought to the industry. A separate route into the conversation, and a point no less important, could be to examine how being based along the East Coast enabled them to integrate a significant on-screen attitudinal shift in the language and actions of the animated film. The Fleischers meant many things to the animation industry, but they never fully achieved the recognition nor rewards they deserved.

Across this look at the Fleischer Studio, we have continuously bounced across the country to the Disney Studio, because certain parallels can be drawn there. The thing about the Fleischers is that pound for pound their studio had the same technical prowess as Disney. What they lacked, though, was the intrinsic understanding of "America" as a whole — a place impressed by technology but tethered to the emotional pull of the story. And really, that's where the argument between the two sides lands.

Art. Science. Those opposite concepts frame the difference between the studios of Disney and Fleischer. In doing so the question stands — were they rivals or alternatives to each other? That one remains an industry powerhouse today while the other is largely forgotten should not tilt the argument to favor either approach to the medium.

HONORS

Max Fleischer: *The International Animated Film Society (AISFA),* Winsor McCay Award for Lifetime Achievement, 1972
Dave Fleischer: *The International Animated Film Society (AISFA),* Winsor McCay Award for Lifetime Achievement, 1972

SAMPLE FILM SELECTION

Out of the Inkwell (1919)
Minnie the Moocher (1932)
Popeye the Sailor Meets Sinbad the Sailor (1936)
Little Swee' Pea (1936)
Gulliver's Travels (1939)

THE INFLUENCERS

6. Frank Tashlin: Mr. Everything

"The better I know the cinema, the more I realize that it's an art which is dangerous to take too lightly."
— Frank Tashlin[1]

Frank Tashlin (2/19/13–5/5/72) was a true renaissance man — writer/director/cartoonist/designer and one of the most driven artists ever to work in animation. If there is any strong drawback to his work, it's that he didn't stay in animation long enough. He worked in animation during the first phase of his career and then lit out for a career in live-action filmmaking. During his short career at the drawing board, Tashlin helped to shape the language of animation. He was the first director who viewed animated films as *films* and framed their stories in much the same way one would with a live-action script. It's a common concept today, but at the time it was practically unheard of. As Michael Barrier states, "Tashlin was interested in animation not as an art form but as an exercise in cinematic technique."[2]

Up until Tashlin, animation directors treated their films like papier-mâché projects: a story structure was established, and then scenes were hung over this structure until everything was linearly covered in what was generally a straightforward telling of the tale. Tashlin had a different approach. It was almost as if he trained in live action and then came over into animation, rather than the opposite way around. Tashlin took framing pieces that were common across live-action film (close-ups, quick cuts, tracking shorts, etc.) and found a way to make them work in animation. The result brought more action, greater animation possibilities and a heightened sense of speed.

From the first time he sat in a theater and watched the images dance across the silver screen, Tashlin knew what he wanted to do with his life. He started work at the Fleischer Studios, where he ran errands, washed cels, and did essentially anything Max and Dave Fleischer asked him to. He was just happy to be in the industry and learn the business. From there he moved cross-town to the Van Beuren studios, where he finally had a chance to move behind the desk. While it gave him an opportunity to get hands on, perhaps the greater benefit was the wealth of material he cultivated and eventually poured into a comic strip called *Van Boring*. This comic, a series of short panel gags loosely based on his time at the studio, ran in the *Los Angeles Times* from 1934 through 1936. The series would eventually move from an off-hours pastime to a career generator.

Heading West

In 1933, Tashlin packed up his pens and headed west to take a position as an animator with Leon Schlesinger at Warner Brothers. He worked on some shorts but was still really settling into the process when he received his summons. It was 1935, and somehow Schlesinger finally discovered Tashlin was the creator of the *Van Boring* comic and felt that Tashlin should give him a cut. Tashlin (understandably) felt like this was an absurd request; Schlesinger pushed harder, and Tashlin, with no other recourse, quit. He took his stand on fairness, principle, and from an artistic standpoint. At that point, the comic was a constant for him; he could control every aspect, and he used it to begin to explore certain film qualities such as perspective, editing, and story-telling as he attempted not only to elicit a laugh but also to tell a fully realized story in the space of a few panels. Award-winning director Jean-Luc Godard felt he succeeded in that last of his goals: "The narrative technique in (his) strips is years advanced of most current ... films."[3]

He floated around a few places (writing for Max Roach and then for Ub Iwerks) before heading back to Warner Brothers in 1936. Tashlin would later explain, in an interview with Michael Barrier, that the reason for his return so quickly following his rough exit was easy — Schlesinger needed a director, and Tashlin needed the money. And so he found himself back at the studio but in a completely new position — director. His first credit came quickly with 1936's *Porky's Poultry Plant*. Tashlin wasted no time in trying out his ideas on camera placement and pacing, which he would continue to hone and develop, eventually redefining the conventional thoughts about what could be done within animation in terms of shot selection, camera placement, camera movement, and editing.

This film also presented Tashlin with his first opportunity to work with Porky Pig. It would become a partnership that would last his career, although not everyone was happy about it. "I hated him," Tashlin said about Porky. "I thought he was a terrible character.... You couldn't do anything with his body."[4] And yet he tried to make Porky work as a character by quickening the cartoon's pace, creating a manic energy. Tashlin understood, though, that there had to be more than just technical advancements in a film; otherwise people will bore easily. So he made sure that any "technical" components he wanted to play with not only fit within the script but also had a strong purpose for existing. If they helped to advance the action or, more simply, tell the story, they stayed.

While he may have hated working with Porky and felt that he didn't know what do to with him, there are those that feel his use of Porky, and other studio stars, was in perfect alignment with where they were as characters and where they could go. "Tashlin's cartoons are alive with a self-awareness of the form, its possibilities and materiality, and its explicit relation to live-action cinema. Not surprisingly, it is often in Tashlin cartoons that one most recognizes the 'genuine' star power of these animated characters."[5]

One of Tashlin's major influences over the cartoons released from Warners was in providing a continuing sense of speed. The quick cuts, carefully constructed montages, high and low camera angles, and MTV-style editing years before MTV was ever an idea all worked together to give the shorts a feeling of momentum, a forward progression. In a way he helped wrest the shorts from a linear, deliberately paced storytelling mode to something more akin to Mack Sennett. For example, in *Porky's Romance* (1937) Tashlin has cuts that last no more than four frames, and the effect is dizzying, particularly for the time. You can look also to the tracking shot in *Wholly Smoke* (1938), the simulated camera swings of *Little Pancho Villa* (1938), and the building montages of *Little Beau Porky* (1936). Tashlin used each of these techniques not to show off his skills, or up the "animation-quality" of the short, but for the purpose of plot exploration. For Tashlin it was also an opportunity to explore animation from a more holistic cinematic viewpoint. There was a drawback to Tashlin's "cinematic" approach, and that was that it didn't add much to a film in way of character development. While his directorial choices certainly aided in propelling the story, they didn't do much in terms of adding depth. Granted these were seven-minute cartoons, but the best ones (such as those that came from Michael Maltese and Chuck Jones) told a story and delivered the comedy by way of character or (as in the ones created by Tex Avery) eschewed all sense of character, were happy with that, and just ran to the finish line dropping jokes as they went. Tashlin's films seemed to sit in the middle. "I was always trying to do feature-type direction with these little animals."[6]

Tashlin's period at Warners was a relatively brief one (although it spanned three tours of duty), but his influence was far reaching. As one critic put it, "Tashlin cartooned cartoons."[7]

Along with his thoughts on animated films, Tashlin had another strong belief in, and passion for, artists' rights. In 1936 he was named VP of the Animators Unit. When the opportunity arose, he jumped to Disney, not to be a part of any artistic aesthetic, but to help establish a union presence there. He did so at great career and financial risk (his new salary became $50 a week, down significantly from the $150 he was making with Schlesinger), but he believed passionately in organizing Disney and accepted the sacrifice as necessary.

A Trip to Disney

From 1939 through 1941, Tashlin worked through a fruitless period at Disney. While he worked on the development of several shorts, none made it past the concept point. There was *Mountain Climbers*, a Donald/Mickey/Goofy follow-up to 1937's *Clock Cleaners* and *Pluto's Pal, Bobo*. He also worked on the premise for a film that seemed suited for his unique talents. *Museum Keepers* was a short set in an art museum that would have seen some of the great classics re-imagined with Donald as the key subject. The idea showed some promise, but the project seemed to bog down on the very idea that made it so intriguing — Donald taking part in classic art. Walt couldn't get past the idea and in story meetings seemed to spend more time on the merchandising and promotion opportunities behind the idea instead of extending out its story possibilities.

In many ways Tashlin's arrival at Disney was like a pilgrimage to the source of all, for as he has stated time and again, "...everything came from Disney's."[8] It's his contention that Disney provided the entire industry with inspiration, ideas and guidance of the both immediate and subconscious varieties. An example he cites is the Disney character known as Max Hare (from *The Tortoise and the Hare* [1935]), who was taken and morphed into Bugs Bunny while his laugh was pulled out and given to Woody Woodpecker; even the various mice characters (e.g., Sniffles at Warners), so prevalent at every studio, originated, according to Tashlin, at Disney. In fact, where Tashlin is widely credited with creating the blackout gag formula that was popularized by the Coyote and Road Runner series, among others, he actually credits the inspiration for that to Disney as well, although it's hard to find a permanent correlation between the two.

For all of his deep-seated appreciation for Disney, Tashlin was never really influenced by the "Disney aesthetic"; in fact an argument could be made that the work he would do after leaving the studio was in some way a direct refutation of Disney's push toward realism. His shift didn't occur in design, though; it happened through character, as his began to become more self-aware of their position and surroundings. In what would become a trademark of his, a Tashlin character would often break the fourth wall, something a Disney character, living in their completely realized environment, would never do.

> Tashlin's work exhibited an interesting combination of excess and discipline; while to some extent sharing manic sense of humor and fondness for social and sexual subtext of Clampett and Avery.[9]

In the midst of the 1941 studio strike, Tashlin departed Disney, his time there being marked by fits and starts. One has to wonder what this constantly revving-in-neutral process did to his mindset in terms of eventually leaving animation.

The Disney strike did more than achieve tactical equality amongst artists; it also freed artists to begin exploring other styles of animation, in effect taking off unstated restraints. "The Disney strike had HUGE industry effects on style, too," Tashlin later stated. "After the strike, people felt they could try anything [graphically] and they did."[10]

He left Disney partially because his goal of bringing the union in had been achieved and because Screen Gems at Columbia Studios had offered him a position of management. As he arrived at the new studio and was unpacking his equipment, he watched as a management shift happened before his eyes. Nearly everyone was let go, so while he was still finding his way around the building, Tashlin was given the responsibility of running the animation unit. His first act was to hire in many of the Disney strikers who could now continue their revolt on an artistic level. This was a serendipitous hiring decision, as not only did it allow him to harness some top-flight talent, but also this talent was either consciously, or due to the strike, subconsciously, against the style of animation that Disney had promoted and the industry had moved forward to accept. This anti–Disney attitude at Screen Gems resulted in an artistically modernistic group-think mentality. (In fact many of the artists here would meet again a few years later when they came together to form UPA [United Productions of America] which majored in modern design sensibilities.) "[Tashlin was] very streamlined, very of the time, ahead of the time really."[11]

The Artistic Front

While at Columbia, Tashlin performed two major contributions to further the art and concept of animation. The first was managerial — he assembled all of the right talent at the right time including John Hubley, Zack Schwartz, Emery Hawkins, Ray Patterson, Ted Parmelee, and John McLiesh and then had the good sense to let them explore their talents. Not every film was a winner, but what the artists were able to do was finally experiment with form and style in films such as *From Rags to Rags, He Can't Make It Stick* (1943), *Red Riding Hood Rides Again* (1941), and *Professor Small and Mr. Tall* (1943). Each had merits, but what they shared was a collective attempt at graphic expansion. And as the old adage goes, once the genie is out of the bottle.... "Under Tashlin we tried some very experimental things; none of them quite got off the ground, but there was a lot of ground broken. We were doing crazy things that were anti the classic Disney approach," said John Hubley of his time at Columbia with Tashlin.[12]

Tashlin's second contribution could be found in 1941's entry in the Fox and the Crow series — *The Fox and the Grapes*. The film took two established Columbia characters and re-imagined them in a series of fast paced blackout sequences (joke/break/joke/break). The movie would become a touchstone and inspire the modern-day chase film. While many give Tashlin all of the style credit here, he humbly passes on the credit to Disney: "This all came from Disney's — the whole idea of no story, of using a basic situation.... I cribbed what they had at Disney. You set up your problem: the cat is going to catch the mouse.... And there's a series of jokes, one after another [as the cat] keeps failing and failing."[13]

The Fox and the Grapes is a Tashlin film through and through; it's as if everything he had been working on and toward coalesced finally in one space. One can tell that right from the open, when we have a nearly 40-second sequence of the fox merrily loping through the woods. Tashlin films the scene from the side then head-on. That is followed by a top-down view, and finally we watch the fox from the back. In a cartoon of only seven minutes in length, it's surprising that so much time is spent on watching a character walk. It's an interesting narrative choice. Was Tashlin trying to establish some sense of character, or, before the action kicks in, was he telling the audience to take a break and catch their breath?

When the camera finally leaves the fox, it's only to track ahead of him forward and up through the trees, where we are finally introduced to the crow. The crow spies the fox (and even more importantly — his picnic basket) and heads down into the forest where, as he sets his trap, the camera pans back to the fox still happily skipping down the path. The entire sequence, just over a minute in length, is a virtuoso technical performance. While there are cuts to switch camera angles, their number is few, and they are executed so effortlessly as to be rendered all but imperceptible. In one instance, the camera trucks in on the crow, and once we, as the audience, understand that the focal point within the shot is the crow's eyes, the film jumps to a close-up of those eyes. The transition is effortless, though, because the cut just completes the connection the viewer has already made.

The other key thing this sequence does is establish a sense of space, which itself is unique in American animated shorts of this time period. Often with an animated short we have no real sense of the full world that the characters inhabit. Our knowledge of location is limited to the particular stage of action — a bullfighting ring, the inside of a clock, the ground between two spaceships on the Planet X. But where do those things reside, in the greater view? If there is any attempt to establish this, it is usually done through geographic shorthand, a term that originated on the blog *Animation: Hard to Find Films*.[14] Geographic shorthand refers to the attempt to link together locations by quick cuts, blurred zooms, and other similar devices. It is not essential in all cases that the viewer know the location and relationship between action stages, but it does help establish relationships, fill in detail on motivations, and strengthen the connection between viewer and character. Tashlin's shot choices here are unique in the way they expose the entire environment — we see everything at ground level, go up into the trees, and even drop through the soil into a mine. In all of these trips, the viewer isn't jarred by any quick edits, as everything takes place within the established camera work or through the relationship editing, as described above.

Once we are finally at the stage of action the back and forth between the fox and the crow over a bunch of grapes commences. One can see the seeds of the chase format, but it's interesting that Tashlin, known for injecting speed, leaves parts of these sequences somewhat drawn out. Still the ideas are in place and do add up to an enjoyable short.

Early in 1942 there was another shakeup at the studio, and Tashlin was asked to step down. Rather than take a demotion, he headed back to Warner Brothers, where he was named story director. After Director Norman McCabe left to join the Army, Tashlin was able to slide back into the director's chair. During this stop at the studio he directed 21 shorts including one that many people consider a minor masterpiece, 1943's *Scrap Happy Daffy*. Here the speed of Tashlin is on extreme display, beginning with Daffy Duck's Danny Kaye–like song recitation about what materials could be recycled. It's a funny bit in and of itself, but it's interrupted by an even funnier one, when Daffy returns to a drawing of a bathing beauty he had passed earlier, which at the time seemed to be nothing more than a throwaway gag based on its placement, and lets loose with the classic sound of a wolf whistle. The pace continues to grow when the action moves to Germany and the Third Reich declares all out war on Daffy's pile of scrap metal. From there the film mixes war propaganda with slapstick surprisingly well. Everything fits within the character and story, and one never feels like they are being preached at.

Like another Tashlin film, *Porky Pig's Feat* (1943), relies upon an imaginative and well-articulated appropriation of live-action technique (dissolves, expres-

sive camera angles, point-of-view shots, etc). The visual fields of Tashlin's cartoons are often extraordinarily imaginative and flamboyant; for example, the
in-flight passage of the hapless hotel manager through off-screen space is
reflected, in turn, within the eyes of both Porky and Daffy.[15]

Tashlin's disdain for the output at Disney (a viewpoint perhaps somewhat
skewed by the stalled time he spent there) was not a secret, and if it were, the
cat would have been out of the bag in 1943 with the release of *Corny Concerto*.
Made after Tashlin returned to Warners, it was technically Bob Clampett's
film, but he collaborated on it closely with Tashlin, who receives a "story"
credit. The film was an across-the-bow parody of *Fantasia* (1940), starring
Elmer Fudd, Porky Pig and Bugs Bunny. It succeeds in its irreverence as both
a pointed in-joke and a treatise on classical music.

In a 2006 *New York Times* article on Tashlin's live-action films, writer
Dave Kehr states (during a discussion of film comedy in the 1950s), "All of
those pioneering humorists and many others realized that the real world mat-
tered less to people than the sea of sounds and images that the ever more
powerful mass media were pumping into American Lives."[16] It's a theory of
satire that seems to suit not just Tashlin's live-action output but also many
of his animated shorts. Perhaps the ideas weren't fully realized for him yet
during this period, but he did play with the notion.

Tashlin's third go-round with Warners was short — by 1944 he was gone
again. He had made up his mind to pursue a career in live-action filming and
felt he needed to take the next steps to move closer to that. He took up with
the John Sutherland Studios, where he would work on stop-motion shorts.
He made the decision because it allowed him to learn about and experiment
with many of the technical aspects of the filmmaking process while relying
on his animation instincts in terms of story. He wasn't entirely out of the animated short business yet, though. During World War II, Tashlin did his part
by taking a post within the First Motion Picture Unit (FMPU). Here he
helped to create training films for servicemen and -women and directed a
number of the shorts starring Private SNAFU.

While it appears Tashlin was somewhat of a restless journeyman, he was
in reality putting himself down a path toward his ultimate goal of working
in live-action films. He tried to make each of his stops something that built
on his previous experiences and would provide an opportunity that would
help propel him forward. That push ahead had only one more stop, and it
was an interesting one that involved a partnership with the Lutheran Church.
The Rev. H.K. Rasbach was a Hollywood minister, friend to Cecile B. DeMille
and George Stevens, and pastor at a local church. The dropping of the atomic
bomb, closely followed by the birth of his son, gave Rasbach the impetus he
needed to pursue his dream of combining his interests. The result was a 20-

minute stop-motion animated short entitled *The Way of Peace*. Rasbach's goal with the $60,000 film was to create "a discussion on the church in the Atomic Age."[17] He used his connections to gather an impressive talent pool that included Academy Award–winner Gene Warren; animators Wah Ming Chang and Gene Warren; Lew Ayers; and Eddison von Ottenfeld. Whether it was the talent, the subtexted absurdity of the project or, more practically, money that motivated Tashlin, he came on board as a writer/director. The resulting film is a dark, moralistic tale that unfolds in a starkly straightforward manner. For an artist who was so closely associated with comedy, this was an interesting step outside, although some have noted the classic comedian juxtaposition — that anyone that happy and funny must have some latent disappointment. "As comic as Tashlin's movies are, they also reflect a deep unhappiness with the condition of the world."[18]

Many critics and reviewers have speculated about this place on Tashlin's career radar. None of his previous work had any suggestion of religious overtones, and yet here was a film by the church, for rentals and other churches. Was this farewell song to animation meant in any way to be a cautionary parable to the overall industry?

Moving On, Sort Of

Tashlin then finally made his move to live action. While he wasn't ashamed of his animation roots, and in fact often relied on the sensibilities he developed while working in the field, he simply decided that it was time to move on. "I spent a long time doing cartoons," he states. "I just lost interest in it."[19] It was a typically Tashlinesque statement and fit completely within his career trajectory.

Tashlin's live-action career is unique because he stayed within the genre of comedy. While his films (*Will Success Spoil Rock Hunter?* [1957]; *The Girl Can't Help It* [1956]) portrayed a potent social satire and dealt with "adult" topics, he never betrayed his animated ancestry. His past served him particularly well in the films he made with Jerry Lewis (*Cinderfella* [1960]; *It'$ Only Money* [1962]) and Bob Hope (*Son of Paleface* [1952]), wherein each comedian allowed himself to become a cipher, a sort of live action cartoon character.

In the end Tashlin was "interested in animation not as an art form but as an exercise in cinematic technique."[20] (He did continue that exercise but in a totally different format — print. He wrote and illustrated three children's books — *The World That Isn't; The Bear That Wasn't;* and *The Possum That Didn't,* where he could explore his thoughts on the world and in particular his ideas on institutions.)

What's interesting to note is that when you consider all of the media in which Tashlin participated — print, animation, radio, and live-action films — there is one glaring omission — television. Several of his live-action films, including *The Girl Can't Help It* (1956) and *Will Success Spoil Rock Hunter?* (1957), offered satirical slaps at the medium. Perhaps the reason that he didn't delve further into that medium can be found in a comment made in 1962 that hints at more than a technological preference: "I really hate television. It's no experience.... The audience doesn't participate — they just sit there and turn the dial and be critical."[21] This speaks as much to his disdain for television as it does to the passion that he put into each of his animated efforts. His attempts to change the language of the animated film were an attempt to bring the audience *into* the viewing experience to make them in many ways active participants. Not that they were going to run into the screen, but they would become more emotionally and tangentially invested in the action and by extension the story.

Throughout his career Tashlin was always looking forward to what the next big challenge would be. This is not to say, though, that he neglected what was in front of him. Rather, he used it as a stepping stone. In *Godard on Godard*, Jean Luc Godard argues that Tashlin's career was one of building. In his comic strip he worked out scene structure and cuts, which were techniques he transferred to his animated efforts, where he also learned the flow and, in a way, how to work with actors, a skill he carried into his move to live action.

In 1964, after a few years had passed since he last worked in animation, Tashlin could offer a more reflective view on his time there: "Cartoons are a very stimulating medium. For animators, the joke reigns supreme. But it's also a world of enslavement. The world of an animator, no matter how fertile his ideas may be, is in the end, a confined frame, a tiny glass cel where his creations come to life. It's as though the whole universe were reduced to a series of postcards. You spend your whole life splicing, flipping through cel sheets, drawing frame by frame. After a few years the whole thing becomes so debilitating that you lose all contact with the real world."[22]

His comments seem to be those of a man worn down not by the art or business of the medium but by the *process* of animation. "Cartoons are a very stimulating medium.... But it's also a world of enslavement.... You've got to get out of it. We live in fear. How many of my colleagues cling on to their jobs, just like bureaucrats, so that nothing ever changes. They get so caught up in their routine that they lose all desire to *break out*. You have to live with this fear, because insecurity is part of the life of anyone who devotes himself to comedy."[23]

Other directors were not perhaps envious of Tashlin but impressed by his career diversity. Tex Avery (who held slight live-action ambitions of his own) remarked with some envy, "He went much further in this gag business than we ever did."[24]

In *The New York Times*, Dave Kehr described how Tashlin's work on feature films called on the skills and instincts he developed at Warner Brothers, "Frames are organized with an artist's eye, with colors carefully coordinated to give even the most banal setting a bounce of stylish abstraction, and sequences are edited with an animator's absolute control over movement and rhythm."[25]

Director Charles Bitsch perhaps hit Tashlin's appeal spot on when he said, "A true movie nut, Tashlin is the first to have made films for other true movie nuts."[26] And there lies the base appeal of Tashlin's work to viewers everywhere — they all felt as if he made cartoons just for them.

SAMPLE FILM SELECTION

Wholly Smoke (1938)
The Fox and the Grapes (1941)
Scrap Happy Daffy (1943)
Corny Concerto (1943)

7. Matt Groening:
The Populist Hippie

It's easy to hate Matt Groening (b. 2/15/54). The print-cartoonist-turned-animation-mogul redefined television animation in the span of, if legend holds true, ten minutes.

The father of *The Simpsons,* Groening came up with what has become the quintessential American family in that quintessentially American way — a moment of panic with a deadline approaching. He did more than design the characters in that moment of fear; when things clicked and he knew exactly what the family looked like, he also knew exactly who they *were.* Like few others before him, Groening has an almost psychic connection into the collective American consciousness and pulled from that not what people want to see but who we really are. For what is *The Simpsons* if not a giant (yellow) mirror to America? This is the secret to Groening's lasting influence; whether through animation or comics, he can show us who we are in a way that we can both relate to and accept. There are no judgments made, no pronouncements given, no directions proclaimed, just a simple reflection of life in all of its absurd glories. Nowhere is this more evident than in Groening's panic-induced creation, *The Simpsons.* And while others now handle the day-to-day direction of that show, they are following in the pattern and process of observation first established by Matt Groening.

(It should be noted that the intent of this piece is not to present an overarching history/overview/analysis of *The Simpsons.* Instead we will focus on Groening as a creator and creative force of *The Simpsons* and others.)

Where Do You Start?

Groening has worked under a number of titles — artist, writer, producer — but his influence, it can be argued, comes from the unofficial titles under which he operates — thinker, observer, truth teller, prankster, storyteller.

From a very early age, Groening was interested in the idea of telling a story. In 1962, at the age of eight, he entered a writing contest sponsored by *Jack & Jill* magazine. The magazine presented a situation — a boy who hits his head in an attic — and readers were asked to spin a story from there. Groening's ending was inventively bleak — the boy died and became a ghost. This would be the first of Groening's many treatises about death and the human condition, and with it he won the contest. What makes Groening different than say a German philosopher in this discussion is that he would approach the topic not with fear and bleakness but with a matter-of-fact attitude, and ample helpings of humor.

Perhaps the biggest cultural influence he experienced was Jay Ward's influential 1960s series *The Adventures of Rocky and Bullwinkle* (aka *Rocky and His Friends*). He was initially taken because it was the only cartoon that his parents would watch with him. The more that he watched, the more he enjoyed it on multiple levels. He explained his interest in the show this way: "When I saw Rocky and Bullwinkle, I realized that you didn't necessarily have to be a great cartoonist or artist to make a great cartoon. All you needed was great writing."[1]

As he got older and rediscovered the show again, he was struck by how much it rewarded you for paying attention. It would be a trait he would carry over into *The Simpsons*. Groening paid homage to the series by giving his characters the middle initial J, the same that Rocky and Bullwinkle had, which they were given in honor of their creator Jay Ward.

Groening continued to write and draw for his own amusement until high school, when he had an opportunity to put everything together with a newspaper called *The Bilge Rat,* his first "publication." It consisted of the standard high school material save for one somewhat brilliant storytelling invention. He invented a group of thugs known as The Banana Gang, which he treated in the pages of the magazine as a very real group going around his Oregon town and terrorizing it. Incidents in the town would be described in news items in the paper as results of their activity, and fictitious letters to the editor would rail against their actions and call for help to end their reign of terror.

He would return to this technique of literary invention several years later when he was living in Los Angeles and at his first "real" job. He was hired at *The Los Angeles Reader* to do any number of things. Over time his duties expanded to include supplying an occasional comic and writing a weekly music column. Great gigs to be sure, but the problem was that he was never writing about the bands he was supposed to cover, and after a while he was not writing about music at all. It would have been okay, if not for all of those pesky, complaining readers who wanted their music information. And so, he slipped back to his high school days, and he simply made bands up. He concocted their playlists, wrote about what their concert was like, and described their album cover. The next week he thought more about it and wrote a retraction apologizing and promising to never do it again. And yet, the very next week....

This is an important moment in considering Groening's career. Where many writers take years to really find out who they are, Groening was ahead of the curve. He was a guy who wanted to have a little fun, to poke at convention, and never meant any harm by it.

Much of his day during this time was taken up working on a self-published comic called *Life in Hell*. The comic features a number of characters including the rabbits Binky and Bongo and the fez-wearing duo Akbar and Jeff, who started life as modified Charlie Browns. (Check out their familiar striped shirts.) More than just fashion sense, Akbar and Jeff shared with the Charles Schulz comic the worldview of an optimistic realist. One could imagine a typical exchange between the two happening between an older Linus and Charlie Brown. (Although the gay subtext in Groening's comics might be off-putting to Snoopy.)

In 1980 *The Los Angeles Reader* agreed to publish Groening's cartoon *Life in Hell*. It was a weekly opportunity for him to share, through his characters, the absurdities of life, particularly life in L.A.

Groening's cartoons were really just "picture words"—sparsely drawn panels where the focus is definitely on the text inside. His comics "were about language."[2] His sensibilities always leaned toward what was being said, not the medium in which they appeared, a trait that he would bring with him into animation.

As an artist, Groening's designs are recognizable and yet very simple. His cartoons particularly are often character drawings against a white background or, at the very most, simple sets.

America's First Family

> The Simpsons has become the new repository of the West's common metaphors, the wellspring of its most resonant quotes, the progenitor of its default tone ... the parlance of our times.[3]

In the mid–1980s, Emmy and Oscar–winning producer James L. Brooks was creating a show for the new Fox Television network. The program, *The Tracey Ullman Show*, would be a sketch comedy series, and Brooks was looking for something to run between the segments. One day he glanced at a framed print from a *Life in Hell* comic that had been given to him as a gift. That, he thought, could be the answer. And so Matt Groening found himself in the outer office of one of the most powerful men in Hollywood, and that was when he had a realization — Brooks liked *Life in Hell* and wanted to put it on TV, which was financially great, but Groening feared it would mean that he would lose control of his comic, which was something he never wanted to do. So with the clock ticking and Brooks due any moment, Groening grabbed some spare paper and quickly sketched out a family. This is what he pitched to Brooks — a series of shorts featuring a husband and wife and their three children. The family would be typically American — dysfunctional, sniping, frustrated, and full of love.

Groening named the Simpsons after members of his own family: his parents were Marge and Homer, and his sisters were Lisa and Maggie. He toyed with naming the boy Matt but felt that was a little too self-serving, so he settled on Bart, primarily because it was an anagram of brat. (Many of the names for the other characters on the show were taken from street names of Portland, Oregon, where he grew up.)

In terms of personalities, though, Groening looked outside of these familiar settings. Maggie, the youngest Simpson, was his take on a modern-day Sweetpea (from E.C. Segar's Popeye), while the others were given typical traits — frustrated father, caring mother, mischievous brother, and do-gooder sister. These stereotypes would be softened and shaded as the series continued to take shape.

As for their unique look, that was a mixture of design and chance. Groening had sketched out the initial designs for the family, but when it came time to give them their unique color, the studio hired Klasky-Csupo to do the animation, who chose yellow because of its boldness and because "it counterbalanced the simple design."[4] Groening realized that the stark coloration choice had an ulterior effect as well — it made the series instantly recognizable when viewers were skipping around channels on the television. It was a sentiment similar to the one that designer Ed Benedict had when designing the original Hanna-Barbera characters in the 1960s. He knew that great design could draw a viewer in, but keeping them engaged would be another story. Literally.

Before any of that, though, Brooks bought off on the concept. And, on April 5, 1987, in short 15-second segments, the world got its first look at *The Simpsons*. Because of the short time period, each segment had to be a self-contained piece, but the writers tried to fit those pieces together under a broad theme in each show. For example, in that very first show, each segment dealt with trying to get everyone to go to bed — Homer and Bart fought, and in the end segment Maggie fell out of a tree to the strains of Marge singing "Rock-a-Bye-Baby." The version of the Simpsons that first appeared was quite different than the one known today. They were rougher, both in look and mannerisms, sort of Ids run wild. And yet the audiences ate the segments up, so much so that Groening started to push Fox to take them out and give them their own series. It was a bold request, as there hadn't been an animated prime-time series on in years and not a successful one since *The Flintstones* debuted in 1961. But Fox, a new network desperate to make its mark, had really nothing to lose, and so on December 17, 1989, *The Simpsons* made its series debut.

Of course an entire creative production team was (and is) responsible for bringing the characters to life each week. For these early years, particular credit must be given to Sam Simon, who was really the driving force behind transforming the idea into a series. He took Groening's sensibility and social aesthetic and translated it out for a half hour of network television. Needless to say, the series was an immediate smash hit. Since its debut in 1987, the show "has permeated our vernacular ... the way we tell jokes, understand humor, and tell our stories."[5]

From the start, Groening was adamant that this was to be a world with clearly defined parameters. "Yes, crazy things could happen to the characters, but they had to react in the same way that a person would react in such a situation. When they hurt themselves, they really feel pain. This was my golden rule." Characters couldn't fall off a cliff and then just bounce back up; people couldn't perform unreasonable natural acts; there could be no Coyote/Roadrunner mayhem, without there also being a realization of the consequences of the action. It was somewhat of a limitation to the writers, but it also helped to bring the viewers into the show even further; there was a realization and a connection the viewer could make because the characters were operating in a world just like theirs.

The series has its moments of base, slapstick humor, but what has kept it running is its sophistication. The absolute undisputed key to the entire show is the writing. Some of the best scripts, such as "Mr. Plow" (season four) or "Marge vs. the Monorail" (season four) are absolute master classes in comedy writing. The situations are both real — starting a new business — and fantastical — buying a monorail from a travelling salesman — and are perfectly plotted and expertly paced. Both have some great jokes and fit in completely with Groening's thoughts on authority, friendship, leadership, and celebrity.

As seen in these two episodes alone, the humor on *The Simpsons* comes in many veins; none is given any preference over the other, and all are attached to their topics with the same gentle touch. Writer George Meyer explains, "We try not to attack something just for the thrill of watching it die."[6]

The Simpsons family has lasted for so long because they are able to find that careful balance between a hope for a better tomorrow and the realities of our daily life. And that doesn't mean wars and natural disasters but the hurdles that we have to face every day just to get by — crummy jobs, not enough money to pay the bills, family obligations. The show presents a hyper-realized version of daily life in any big small town in the country. Critic A.O. Scott says the series plays like "Raymond Carver stories optioned by Hanna-Barbera."[7]

The Simpsons is nothing if not a classic example of that old adage, "Don't judge a book by its cover." Here is a show that was heavily criticized when it first hit the air — it was called grotesque, rude, disrespectful, trashy, and it was even derided by a sitting U.S. president. In 1992 George H.W. Bush, at the Republican National Convention, declared, "We need a nation closer to the Waltons than the Simpsons." The *Simpsons* staff responded quickly and in their own special way. On their next episode, just two days later, in the opening sequence Bart was seen writing on the chalkboard, "Hey, we're just like the Waltons. We're praying for an end to the Depression too." It was an appropriate and incredibly fast response. Writing the line, animating it, getting it on film, editing it into the episode and then getting it to air in two days was no easy task; it just shows how much the president's line rankled the staff. (In the election that fall President Bush received an even worse rebuke when he was voted out of office.) Over time, those who first derided the show would come to celebrate its depiction of family, America, and even religion. Does any other television family go to church as regularly? The religious overtones of the series are one of the few places where it diverges with Groening, who is a proclaimed and committed atheist.

Of course the show, and Groening, in many ways courted controversy. When asked about his intentions with the show, he replied that he wanted to "create a sofa-centric sitcom about a typical American family and turn it upside down" with a message "that your moral authorities don't always have your best interests in mind. Teachers, principals, clergymen, politicians — for the Simpsons they're all goofballs, and I think that's a great message for kids."[8]

In 1996, the series was given a George Foster Peabody award, the first animated program to be so honored. The committee stated the award was for "providing exceptional animation and stinging social satire."

> The Simpsons *is the TV equivalent of Sgt. Pepper's Lonely Hearts Club Band.... After it came along, nothing was the same, and it established a generation's cultural references and sensibility. (Is there any situation without a suitable Simpsons quote?)*—*Time* magazine rankings[9]

Groening = Disney?

> *"When I came up with* The Simpsons, *that was a very deliberate attempt to follow in the footsteps of Walt Disney."*— Matt Groening[10]

There is a school of thought that posits that Groening has made himself into a modern-era version of Walt Disney.

This does not take a giant leap, but it does warrant some explanation. Both men were artists who held fast to their creations as they almost literally took on a life of their own and in many ways surpassed the importance of the artists who first gave them life.

The comparisons extend, though, as Groening, much like Disney before him, understood the importance of story to build success and then, once that success had been received, the need to capitalize on it. Across the 20-year run of the show, Groening has allowed a far-reaching range of products to be branded (t-shirts, books, pastas, candy, toys, air fresheners, clocks, Christmas stockings, magnets, games, telephones, bedding, towels, and more, so much more). If you had a product, chances are you would get the okay to brand it with someone from the show. It is estimated that since its inception, the series has made, through all of its episodes, licensing, and merchandising deals, over three billion dollars. Are there too many things, though? At what point does the brand become diluted? For his part, Groening claims to have a plan: "My secret goal has always been to entertain and subvert. To me it's all storytelling. *The Simpsons* lends itself to so many different media. There are the comic books and the books about the show, and the show itself, and the promotions, and the video games, and the movie and the amusement park ride."[11]

The reach of the show extends beyond physical tchotchke; it has even been a subject in, and of, universities. The University of California at Berkeley has a course on "The Simpsons: Sitcom as Political and Social Satire." They are not the only school with classes with a Simpson focus. Courses on the Simpsons and literature, satire, sociology, and folklore are taught at Columbia College Chicago, Fairleigh Dickinson University, Hofstra University, and University of Fraser Valley.

Groening, like Walt Disney, had an almost psychic connection with the psyche of America, but where Walt channeled his understanding into his theme parks, Groening channeled his connection into *The Simpsons*. (Although the characters *are* currently starring in a ride at Universal Studios in Orlando, Florida.)

In all of his work, Groening has a common thread of satire, parody, and an ironic hipness, but never has there been a full sense of malice or cynicism. His worldview has been heavily influenced by Akbar and Jeff's "cleaner" contemporaries.

> "I was excited by the casual cruelty and offhand humiliations at the heart of the strip. Peanuts *seemed emotionally real (and unlike anything else). Occasional sadness comes up (such as Charlie Brown's complaints that no one likes him, and Patty's unsympathetic explanations of why this is so), but this is offset*

by a friendly drawing style, great jokes and a sense of childhood exuberance that makes the discouragement of life seem a worthy price to pay." — Matt Groening on Peanuts[12]

Futurama

1999 saw another Groening series hit television — *Futurama*. The show was set 1000 years in the future so that he could overstep the laws of cartoon conventions that had been established for *The Simpsons* and just allow the characters to go off in any direction needed. If they needed a character to be able to, say, jump between two skyscrapers, they could have them do it thanks to some future invention. It was in *Futurama* that Groening moved away from the satirical sensibilities of Jay Ward and more toward the fast-paced, ACME Company, pure cartoon ideals unleashed by Warner Brothers in the 1940s. This future setting, though, robs the narrative of some of the attachment that viewers found so accessible in other Groening works.

Futurama hit the airwaves with high expectations that did not translate to ratings success. In fact the show was not a success until it was off the air and showing up steadily in reruns. When that happened the series started to gather the following it had deserved, which prompted Groening and Executive Producer David X. Cohen to bring the characters back in a series of direct-to-DVD movies. The success of these films prompted Comedy Central to order a new slate of episodes.

The Legacy

Looking at popular culture and modern entertainment today, one can definitely see traces of *The Simpsons*. What will be interesting is to look back in another 20 years, after the generations who have grown up with the series have their chance on the world stage, to see what the true effect was.

In each of his characters, Groening has created a fully realized alternative universe, and in doing so he's held a mirror up to America, for really we love his creations because when our guard is down, we see ourselves in them. "The Simpsons are our truest, best selves: stupid — maybe; lazy — you bet; suspicious of authority — always; willing to do anything about it — not really; but above all loyal to our spouses, our children, our little sisters, our friends, our hometowns, our bad haircuts, and our favorite brand of beer."[13]

A thousand years from now, if robot historians want to know what life was really like in late–twentieth-century America, they will look to *Life in Hell* and *The Simpsons*. No, there were no talking rabbits, and human hair was not sculpted into yellow spikes or blue pylons (well, not that often anyway). But everything else is pretty much accurate.[14]

When the question was asked of Jim Brooks as to what *The Simpsons* is ultimately about, he replied, "That you are not alone." "I can go along with that," Groening replied. While it fits the series it also covers most of Groening's work — from the print cartoons, to the modern family, to the space adventure — Groening is comforting each of us, telling us that no matter what happens (and crazy things will), we will make it through with each other. And for a man who makes his living with the jokes, he means this as a sincere statement of hope. I think.

HONORS

The Simpsons

Twenty-Five Emmy Awards
One Peabody Award
Twenty-Six Annie Awards
Six Genesis Awards
Six Writer's Guild of America Awards
Two British Comedy Awards
One American Comedy Award
Six ASCAP Awards
One GLAAD Media Award
A Prism Award
A Golden Reel
Named "The Best TV Show of the Past Twenty-Five Years" by *Entertainment Weekly*, 2008
Named "The Best Television Series of All Time" by *Time*, 1999

Futurama

Three Emmy Awards
Three Annie Awards
One Writer's Guild of America Award
One Environmental Media Award

GROENING

Ten Emmy Awards for *The Simpsons*
One Emmy Award for *Futurama*
National Cartoonist Society Reuben Award, 2002
British Comedy Award, 2004
Top 100 Living Geniuses as chosen by *The Daily Telegraph*. Ranked fourth (and is the highest-ranked American)

SAMPLE FILM SELECTION

Simpsons

Bart Gets an F (season two)
Mr. Plow (season four)
Marge vs. the Monorail (season four)
Treehouse of Horror (season six)
Homer's Phobia (season eight)

Futurama

Fry & the Slurm Factory (season one)
Amazon Women in the Mood (season three)
The Luck of the Fryrish (season three)

Print

The Huge Book of Hell, Matt Groening, 1997
School Is Hell, Matt Groening, 1987
Love Is Hell, Matt Groening, 1986

8. Ray Harryhausen: The Stop-Motion Master

"It was Ray Harryhausen who taught us all how to sing."
— Randall Willie Cook.[1]

As children, everyone draws — a picture of Mickey Mouse, a rainbow, a tree — but for most of us, we never tried to bring those drawings to life. Sure there was that kid in school who made a flip-book out of the corners of his science textbook, but he was more of the exception than the rule.

Stop-motion animation, though, is completely different — it's perhaps the one form of animation that each of us has performed, although often unintentionally. In fact it's been a part of human communication since people first started picking up objects to tell a story or re-enact the day's buffalo hunt. Granted this isn't *true* stop-motion animation, but one can argue that the basis for the art form is there. Because of this personal interaction, the medium of stop motion brings with it a level of familiarity to the viewer along with this instant connection and appreciation for both the intense, arduous process and for the "I've done that" connection.

More than any other animated format, stop motion also exudes an enormous amount of energy in what is seen on-screen. One of the true masters of the medium is Ray Harryhausen (b. 6/29/20). His work in the realm was ground-breaking, intensely influential, and completely captivating. Harryhausen found a way to take an inanimate object and give it life while making it *alive*. As Horatia Harrod exclaimed, "His creatures have presence. You can see the human hand at work in their movements, but it doesn't matter. It's as magical as if your toys awoke one day and began to walk around."[2]

First, a Giant Ape

With this long history as a human communication tool to begin with, it should be no surprise that as people were trying to figure out what to do with this new medium of film, stop motion quickly became the "go to" animation effect for films of a certain type. While it had been used as a tool since the end of the nineteenth century, the first time stop-motion animation and live-action filmmaking came together as a perfect marriage was in *King Kong* (1933) with stop-motion animation done by Willis O'Brien. When Harryhausen saw that film, it was as if everything suddenly coalesced in his being, and he completely and definitively knew what he was going to do with his life.

Harryhausen wasn't content just to admire the work from afar and dream; he became obsessed with learning everything he could about how the film was made. He asked questions, haunted the library, and flipped through every magazine with potential he could find. All of this research yielded surprisingly little in the way of hard, behind-the-scenes facts, but there was enough information that Ray could begin to understand the various techniques involved. One day he attended an exhibition at the Los Angeles County Museum that shared insight into the technical achievements of the making of *King Kong*. It was a Hallelujah moment, as he immediately knew what he wanted, what he *had*, to do with his life. He went home and set about creating small sets and models in his backyard, patiently practicing as he learned the ropes of his newfound life. Everything came to a head for him toward the end of the 1930s when he had an opportunity to meet Willis O'Brien. The seasoned veteran and the young wannabe spent a brief afternoon in conversation about the art of stop motion, where O'Brien said all of the right things — he was open, encouraging but not falsely so, suggestive, but not critical as he helped Harryhausen to see the potential he had and the promise the art form could offer.

All Under One Roof

The stop motion process provides a unique form of fantasy that is difficult to analyze because it provides an atmosphere of a dream.[3]

While Harryhausen's work is now the mark against which everything else is measured, during these early years he was not shy about admitting that he didn't have all of the answers, a rare trait in Hollywood, particularly for a young outsider looking to break into the business. What he could always propel himself forward on, though, was a strong level of confidence that this was what he was *supposed* to be doing.

After high school he finally had an opportunity to harness all of his natural talents and studious research and show others this was something he should be doing as well when he joined the only animator in Hollywood who was regularly pushing out stop-motion films — George Pal. Pal's *Puppetoons* were stop-motion animated shorts that featured strongly designed characters and relied heavily on a technique known as "Replacement Animation." This style, of which Pal was one of the pioneers, required that each character have several (or several hundred) various parts for use when animating a scene. During the shoot, rather than move the character for the action in the scene, the animator replaces the parts the character would use in order to simulate motion. In a simple example, if a character were bending their arm, a traditional stop-motion animator would perform that action movement-by-movement, while a replacement animator would work with six different arm types — a straight arm, an arm slightly bent, an arm at a 90-degree angle, an arm bent further, and finally an arm collapsed upon itself. During the shoot the animator disassembles and then reassembles the character based on the motion being performed. It is technically still animation, but it places a stronger focus on character design than on pure animation. While the *Puppetoons* were commercially and critically successful, even being nominated for several Academy Awards, the creative aspect and artistic freedom of the work was limited, and it was for this reason that Harryhausen left after working on roughly 13 of the films.

We should pause for a moment and note one truly key convergence that occurred during this time. While Harryhausen was working with Pal, they were briefly joined by Willis O'Brien. It was like an animator's version of The Million Dollar Quartet and something that the industry wouldn't see again until World War II forced the issue.

During the war, Harryhausen drew an assignment with the Army Signal Corps. Prior to his enlisting, though, he created a short entitled *How to Bridge a Gorge*, which, through a friend of a friend, found its way before Frank Capra. With his keen eye for talent, Capra assigned Harryhausen to work on the films in the *Why We Fight* series. Harryhausen also found himself doing some pre-work on the Private SNAFU series for the First Motion Picture Unit (FMPU). One has to believe that this was a completely ideal situation for a man who would go on to doing his best, and most famous, work by combining live action and animation. This opportunity to work among so many talented animators certainly had to have a strong effect, for although their techniques were quite different than his own, the theories that could be found in this community, particularly for an artist who had had such an insular career up to this point, would prove enlightening.

Yet Another Giant Ape

"There is an energy with stop motion that you can't even describe. It's got to do with giving things life."— Tim Burton[4]

After the war Harryhausen's career really took off, and again he had a gorilla to thank. Merian C. Cooper and Willis O'Brien were prepping a follow-up of sorts to their *King Kong* (1933) with *Mighty Joe Young* (1949). O'Brien called up Harryhausen and invited him to be a part of the production. Given a chance to work with his hero, doing the thing he loved, on a movie similar to the one that led him to his career, of course he leapt at the opportunity. He, along with animator Pete Peterson, worked alongside O'Brien during pre-production, and during the actual animating of the film the two younger men did the bulk of the work. Neither complained, though, as both recognized the special opportunity this was. Following the release of the film, O'Brien alone received an Academy Award for Best Special Effects. For Harryhausen the award had to be bittersweet — it was his work being recognized, and yet he was not. On the other hand, he felt deep admiration for O'Brien and realized that this was an award that was overdue by 16 years.

Harryhausen and O'Brien contemplated working on several other projects, but in the end Harryhausen sensed that it was time for him to step out from under the shadow of the great master. And that is what he did with *The Beast from 20,000 Fathoms* (1952). This film, featuring the now-standard plot of a monster attacking a city, is important because it introduced an early version of the Dynamation process, which would become Harryhausen's signature style. Dynamation was a whole new system of merging live-action footage with stop-motion animation. Previously this was accomplished with the use of mattes or through projecting across glass plates. While both helped achieve their desired effects, the time involved was intensive, and there were certain limitations in the interactions that could occur.

It was really Dynamation that Ray had been preparing for ever since he saw *King Kong*. That's because it involved everything he had been researching and experimenting with — animation, live-action film shoots, and acting. It was also the perfect fit for his even-handed, steady working style. As one comes to better understand the process, the question has to be raised — Did Ray invent Dynamation, or did Dynamation create Ray?

The name "Dynamation" was more for marketing than anything else, as it wasn't overly descriptive of the production process or final filmed result. During the 1950s when film studios tried anything they could to stem back the tide of television, they found that catchy names seemed to work in grabbing the attention of the public and cementing in their minds at least the *idea* that films had so much more to offer. Dynamation was one such name, amid others such as Vista-Vision, Cinerama, Emergo, and 3D.

Dynamation took the idea of shooting with mattes to accommodate animation and expanded upon it. To begin, every shot was detailed out and storyboarded as needed. When everything was ready, the live-action portion would be photographed on set. This footage was taken back to the animation studio, where it would be rear projected. (Rear projection involves placing a movie projector behind a special screen and then when the projector is turned on the image actually goes through this special screen, and can be seen on the front.) On the front side of this screen, Harryhausen placed a piece of glass, and then between these two components would be the animation table. On the glass Harryhausen would draw out his matte lines for the shot in production and then blacken out that space with paint. He would then animate the characters and film these actions. When the scene was animated he would remove the matte paint and run a second pass of the live-action footage. The result was an often-perfect marriage of live action and animation.

As if this wasn't complicated enough, there was an intense amount of planning and timing that had to be done to ensure the interactions were exact. For this, Harryhausen has no one to blame but himself, for with each of his films he kept raising the bar of audience expectation based on what he had previously delivered to them. In films like *20 Million Miles to Earth* (1957) and *The Beast from 20,000 Fathoms* (1953) what you have essentially is a monster running around a city. While the films were well executed, there are only so many times an audience can see that particular theme and get lost in the wonder and fantasy of it (particularly when there were so many others putting out similarly themed B pictures), and as an artist, Harryhausen needed an opportunity to stretch himself. (Quick side note—*Beast* was one of the first films to use television as an advertising outlet.)

So when a film like *The 7th Voyage of Sinbad* (1958) came along, Harryhausen took the opportunity to (borrowing a phrase from Disney Imagineers) "plus" the animation and get closer and more-detailed interaction with the animated characters and live-action actors. While there are many great sequences in this film, the sword fight between Sinbad and a skeleton is a standout (and, as we will see, a template). In the film the magician brings a skeleton to life and sends it after Sinbad. This two-minute sequence is centered on a Sinbad/Skeleton swordfight through a castle chamber, culminating on a winding stairway to nowhere. In the castle the fight is good but heavy on suggestion. Once it heads outside, though, the action is ratcheted up, and the entire sequence takes on new life. When they are on the stairs there is a very brief moment where Sinbad is pinned against a stone pillar by the skeleton, who takes the opportunity to cut in front of Sinbad and take the high position. It's an astounding sequence not only from a technical perspective in the way that the animation and live action have been matched but also from a dramatic standpoint. The skeleton moves with an evil swagger, and his head has the bob and sway of a prize fighter. The effect is that you are left quite unsure as to exactly what it plans to do, which tightens the suspense and helps sell the overall dramatic feel of the movie. This dramatic touch elevates the film from creature feature to taught thriller. The entire sequence is a masterful use of stop motion and shows Harryhausen's emerging mastery of the form.

In a promotional reel for the film entitled *This Is Dynamation*, the audience is given a very brief look behind the scenes at the work that went into this scene. It really helps to illustrate just how detailed everything needed to be in order to achieve the intended result. In countless interviews Harryhausen has echoed this theme of *planning*, in one form or another, as the key to his success. Given the intense complexity of the animation he was undertaking, he needed to do more than just storyboard out a sequence; he had to pre-plan his work step by step, frame by frame to ensure that every component would line up to portray a seamless action line. As a true testament to his talents, though, even though the action was planned and prepared for down to the smallest detail, his animation does not feel robotic or staged; there is an overall organic feel to the movement of the characters; their actions seem to be coming from them, not manipulating them from afar.

A concern with a Harryhausen film is that the creatures and animation have the potential to overrun the story, but to his credit, he is always able to make his animation work as *part* of the overall plot of the film, so that while people may be drawn to the film for the effects, what they get is a comprehensive and cohesive story. It's a point that he understands completely, as he'll often refer to himself as "a 'technician' who had the fortune to 'author his films.'"[5]

The Animated Auteur

> "[I love] the early [Ray] Harryhausen, Jason and the Argonauts in particular. I also love the Seventh Voyage, the best Cyclops that will ever be done. There was just this wonderful sense that Harryhausen's monsters were real. Despite the sort of lurching quality they had, they had an undeniable reality to them."— Henry Selick[6]

As Harryhausen moved further out from under the shadow of O'Brien, he undeniably started to assume the position of auteur on his films, a description generally reserved for directors. It's nearly unheard of, particularly during this period, that someone from the effects department, an animator even, would have this type of artistic control over a live-action film. His output wasn't just part of the film, though; in reality it *was* the film — what Harryhausen created gave the film a reason for existing. His overall involvement extended far beyond his responsibilities as an animator — he storyboarded shots, in some cases acted as a sort of autonomous second unit director, wrote script treatments, and even held the titles (and fulfilled the duties) of producer and associate producer. And so, even though his name was not above the title, these truly were "Harryhausen Films."

Although he had been achieving great success, as he had throughout his career, Harryhausen continued to experiment and study. The culmination of this work can be seen in 1963's *Jason and the Argonauts*, arguably Harryhausen's masterpiece. The story is a mixture of Greek mythology, albeit seen through the lens of twentieth-century Hollywood. In a movie filled with show-stopping sequences, two very opposite scenes stand out. The first features the massive bronze statue Talos. This original character, inspired by the ancient statue of the Colossus of Rhodes, attempts to stop Jason and his crew from passing on their ship. What makes the sequence work so well is the way that Harryhausen restrains his natural inclination to imbue his characters with fluid movements. Harryhausen was able to capture perfectly the leaden way (we assume) a giant bronze statue would move. And while the statue has no facial features through which any direct personality may be conveyed, there is something in his herky-jerky motions that conveys a sense of doom.

The second touchstone sequence occurs near the end of the film. Jason has possession of the princess and the Golden Fleece and now just wants to get home. Standing in his way — "The Children of the Teeth." Harryhausen started the design of this sequence with a quick sketch of Jason and a crew member on a plinth fighting a skeleton army. It was a cool image, he thought; little did he realize that it would become a moment in one of the all-time iconic film sequences. That image spoke to him because it immediately got to the dramatic aspects of the entire sequence. It's one of the things that makes his work so riveting, so lasting, and so influential. Action is great, and master shots have their place, but drama is the linchpin that drives the story, any story, and gives it a purpose. He understood this intrinsically and imbued each of his films with these little dramatic moments, such as the one mentioned a moment ago, that help frame the action.

Of course for many, this is *the* stop-motion sequence — three lone warriors and seven skeletons in a battle to the end. It takes what he did with Sinbad and amps it up and over. One of the chief bits of praise lavished on Harryhausen consistently is that his work exhibits an amazing amount of personality. When you consider the somewhat piecemeal way in which he needs to create a sequence, it's impressive how much "acting" he can derive from his models. This sequence is the epitome of personality animation. Just watch as the skeletons slowly approach Jason and his men. The skeletons don't just lumber forward as one might expect; they crouch slightly into an attack position and then methodically move forward. Harryhausen has given them this sort of skip-step, which gives them a cagey swagger. Suddenly the skeletons stop, and the men brace for the attack, when there is a scream, and the skeletons charge. What Harryhausen does is have the skeletons raise their weapons and slightly contort their faces as they chase the men to their plinth "fortress." It's a primal sequence, one in which the skeletons seem very self-aware; it's as if they realize they are skeletons and try to use the fear they produce to their advantage. This is all married to a perfectly matched Bernard Herrmann score, which heightens the drama and helps to propel the viewer past the effects and straight into the conflict.

Precision Control

This film, like all that Harryhausen has worked on, has the potential to slide into self-parody or some sad grade–Z monster movie. To avoid this, he has worked with one guiding principle — "No cheap laughs or gothic frights, it's (all) pure fantasy dread."[7]

The thing about stop motion, and it's one of the components that makes Harryhausen's work so much more impressive, is that yes it's tactile, yes it's very precise, but it's also so unknown; because of the time involved and the process it envelopes, an animator could complete an entire sequence, and only when it was all projected together find out that a model had shifted and caused a jump in the action. When Harryhausen was at his peak output, unlike hand-drawn animation, there was no frame-by-frame comparison during the shoot and no way to insert additional drawings, or add a quick insert cover shot to adjust for a mistake. If you made a mistake during stop motion, you were going back to the beginning.

Look at the numbers of the skeleton sequence in *Jason*, as mentioned earlier. It runs just over 4 minutes and 30 seconds and yet took 4½ months to film. Broken down even further, this amounted to 184,800 individual movements. Every one of those movements held the potential for a complete re-shoot. When you consider this, his subject choice becomes all the more ambitious and his talents all the more impressive.

The other thing about stop-motion animation is that it is also in many respects a very egotistical art form (an argument that could be made for *all* art really). The strong, self-confident animators realize this, though, and use it to their advantage, as Harryhausen hinted in a rather tongue-in-cheek way:

QUESTIONER: What drove your stop motion passion?
RAY: A Zeus complex. I had control over these little figures.[8]

DIY

One of the things that people latch onto with Harryhausen is that he is essentially self-taught. Granted, this "education" only works because he had the natural abilities and talents to make it work. He pursued an art form that had a relatively small practicing professional field at a time when little was known and written about the talented performers behind the camera, and he was able to not only master that art but also elevate it to a point where his work is seen as the definitive example. With a strong personal drive but surprisingly non-existent ego, Harryhausen studied and experimented and practiced and failed and tried again until he not only knew what he was doing but also knew the best way to do it. For example, his first models were made of wood, but he soon discovered that he was not able to move them as fluidly as he would have liked (and they had a tendency not to hold their poses). So he knew he would need another material to use as his base. On a whim he took a quick trip to the auto parts store, where he picked up some rearview mirrors. Back in his shop, he took those apart and used the ball-and-socket connector of the mirror as the basis for his next series of model tests. These worked exponentially better. Following his meeting with his idol, Willis O'Brien, Harryhausen understood that a drawing or series of drawings made before a scene is shot, before any sets are built even, can greatly help to convey the mood, feeling, and texture of a scene, and so he soon started taking art classes at night (focusing on anatomy) at Los Angeles City College. This also opened him up to other artistic opportunities not even as much through classes but in conversations and almost by osmosis within this environment.

As the technical pieces of the model work started to fall into place, in his mind a new gap of knowledge came to light, so he did the only thing he knew how to do — he set out for answers. He started classes at the University of Southern California (USC) on the technical basics of filmmaking including editing, photography, art direction, and so on.

He was taking all of this knowledge and pouring it into the experiments he was shooting in his garage whenever he could. While he was making technical advancements, he felt that the movements of his characters still tended to be stiff. This was remedied, though, by following the lead of Disney artists and heading to the zoo to study the movements of animals. While many of Harryhausen's creatures were based more in fantasy, he always tried to find some modern-day animal that he could use as inspiration or a connecting point in terms of motion.

He plied all of this knowledge into a very specific system of character movement, which he took from his time with O'Brien and improved upon.

A Harryhausen set was built on a type of peg-board, and each of his models had holes in their feet. What this meant was that each character could be locked down into place to avoid any unintentional bumps along the animation path. These models were built early in his career by his father (for his early home experiments, his mother would contribute by sewing costumes), and it's interesting to note that even up through pre-production on *Jason and the Argonauts*, the elder Harryhausen was making models for his son's efforts.

If Harryhausen's on-screen efforts weren't enough to endear him to film fans the world over, his rise to the top would certainly do the trick. His story holds a promise of success — if you love something and you apply yourself, you can reach that which once seemed unattainable. This ethos combined with his attitude of exploration and personal education place him at the forefront of the DIY/Independent film model. It's been said before, but it certainly bears mention here — it's rare that an animator would seem to be in such a position, but it's wholly justified. On his films, Harryhausen took on such great technical and creative responsibility it was almost at times as if the animating itself would fall to the background. This would not be a purposeful decision, and one gets the sense that if he had the choice he would have had an opportunity to truly reach the smoothness in the animation that he strived for. Although his results would, at times, be imperfect, there was a charm in that.

> *"While Ray Harryhausen was going for perfectly smooth animation, it is the unavoidable imperfections in his work that give it soul and make it memorable."*— Henry Selick[9]

Perception

> *"There's still a great love of traditional techniques. I think people can relate to it more, somehow. With some CGI I think the brain slightly perceives that things aren't real. There's no gravity, the light's not quite real, the shadows aren't quite real."*— Nick Park[10]

For all of his artistry and influence, there are a couple of "bumps" in Harryhausen's career. For one, by the very nature of the way that he went about practicing his art — being involved in every aspect from his involvement in everything from storyboards to shooting — Harryhausen is sometimes seen as more of a technician than an animator or artist. It's actually a description he has used for himself from time to time as well, which doesn't help his cause. While there is a truth in this term as a description, it only scratches the surface. While he should justly be recognized for his technical expertise, it should not come at the expense of the creativity or artistry he has proffered his craft. "His technological innovations improved the looks of animated films and brought down production costs considerably. The latter influence enabled Harryhausen to amaze and entertain audiences for nearly thirty years."[11]

The second issue, perhaps harder to argue, is the extent to which Harryhausen influenced other filmmakers. A wide range of successful motion-picture professionals, in a number of areas, state emphatically that Harryhausen was a guiding influence in their work. They include Steven Spielberg, George Lucas, Peter Jackson, Henry Selick, Nick Park, and Tim Burton. Harryhausen, though, at some level dismisses the connection because of his view of the state of stop motion today. He has stated on numerous occasions that stop-motion animated films should be graded on a much softer scale since they are more "entertainment," while he views his work in mixing stop motion and live action as having greater dramatic depth and therefore implied importance because they were components of a larger live-action story. Additionally he has a mixed view of computers (partially because they have taken over the work he at one time performed so well). He sees computers as a supporting tool in the animation process but scoffs at the idea that they would ever completely replace the solitary hand of a stop-motion animator. While one wishes that he could more clearly see the connection, it's hard to hold this short-sightedness against him.

The Fairy Tales

Harryhausen's feature career was bookended by films that were practical, personal, and perhaps a little unexpected given his penchant for fierce creatures and fantasy animals — fairy tales.

His "Fairy Tale Series" (which stretched in completion between 1946 and 2002) consists of fairly straightforward re-tellings of their source material. Were they completed by any other animator, they might be remembered only in the back of the DVD bin, but as they stand, they can be considered minor works by an artistic master. Looking at these films through that lens, one can find some interesting contrasts. The first thought that comes to mind when viewing these films is surprise at the softness in the animation. There is a playfulness in the characters that is lighter than what can be found in Harryhausen's other work. This extends to (or comes from) the character design, which has more in common with lavishly watercolored children's storybooks than any of his other work.

The fairy tale series, which includes (among others) *The Tortoise and the Hare* (2002), *The Story of Hansel and Gretel* (1951), *The Story of Rapunzel*

(1951), and *The Story of King Midas* (1953), came about in large part due to an accident, but it is one that provides an early insight into Harryhausen's deep desire to work in film and his DIY ethos.

Fresh out of the service and looking for a way to kick-start his career, he remembered the prize he had obtained during a dumpster-diving exhibition at a local Navy office — roughly 1000 feet of undeveloped 16mm color film stock. He decided that the best use would be to visualize stories that he had loved since early childhood — classic fairy tales. When he completed his first set, in 1946, he strung them together under the banner of *The Mother Goose Stories* and took them around to area schools, where he offered to project them to classrooms for a slight fee. While the return he achieved financially was modest, the personal and artistic recoupment was great. He had proven to himself (and others) that he could take a project from start through completion and do so to the amusement of an audience. That was something that he never overlooked; no matter what amount of work he put into a project, what technical achievements he made, if it wasn't acknowledged by an audience, it was all so much of an exercise in futility, but this reaction was little expected, as Harryhausen, like Walt Disney before him, had an innate understanding of his audience. He was able to tie into their fantasies and fears and give them the perfect stories for the time.

Believable Magic

Part of Harryhausen's legacy, ranking slightly behind his technical and artistic achievements, lies in his admittedly spotty historical teachings. Some of his films were brand-new stories, while others were tales made from the parts of others. One of the reasons that he choose Sinbad as a hero was because he was recognizable, yet not so well-known as to prevent Harryhausen from grafting onto that perceived persona a number of separate, but tangentially related, old world myths and in turn creating a new series of mythic stories for the modern age.

Ray Harryhausen was quoted once saying something along the lines of "We are born to the time we are supposed to be in." Coming from someone else this may reek of pseudo-psychology, but with Ray there is a very real truth in this. One might amend this quote, though, to say that "We are *working* in the time that we are supposed to be," for he entered the film industry at a moment when an art form was teetering on becoming obsolete or only an end to a means and elevated it to be something like the subjects he covered — otherworldly. "I think that's the power of Ray Harryhausen. When it's done beautifully, you feel somebody's energy."[12]

HONORS

Gordon E. Sawyer Lifetime Achievement Award, The Academy of Motion Picture
   Arts and Sciences, 1991
Winsor McCay Award, International Animated Film Association, 1991
Annie Award, Outstanding Achievement in an Animated Short Subject for *The Story
   of the Tortoise & the Hare*, 2002
Inspiration Award, Empire Awards, 2004
George Pal Memorial Award, Academy of Science Fiction, Fantasy & Horror Films,
   2006

SELECTED CREDIT LIST

The Storybook Review (1946)
Mighty Joe Young (1949)
The 7th Voyage of Sinbad (1958)
Jason and the Argonauts (1963)
The Golden Voyage of Sinbad (1974)
Clash of the Titans (1981)

9. Ed Benedict:
The Reluctant Influencer

"Animation is an expressive and not purely mechanical medium."
— Bill Melendez[1]

If you want to watch a cartoon today, the simple fact is that you can. There are cable channels devoted to the medium, as well as DVDs, videos on demand, theatrical releases, and of course the Internet. Cartoons have even found their way to mobile devices. Of course there was a time when you had only two ways to watch a cartoon — movie theaters and network television. And even within that distribution framework, you weren't always getting the freshest product, as some of the cartoons on television were only re-packaged (often slightly edited) theatrical shorts. Within this system, there was little originality and more focus on filling space than on creating something unique for the viewer's consumption. Cartoons were time fillers, hoping to hold an audience's attention from one product sponsorship to the next. The hold that animation had on the public at large was diluted by the introduction of television and the general push into the suburbs of 1950s America. Animation had truly become the medium for children and studios played to the lowest common denominator of that group.

(This is not to say that there wasn't "mature" animation programming at this time. Jay Ward was producing *Crusader Rabbit* in a pre–Bullwinkle style, while Bob Clampett had both a puppet and later animated version of *Beany and Cecil*, which counted a fan base that included Groucho Marx and Albert Einstein.)

This was the landscape into which Ed Benedict (8/23/12–8/28/2006) carried his pencil and, with a few designs, changed the relationship between the viewer and the animated image. Benedict's designs and layouts were wholly original; they hinted at the animated shorts of the past while leaning toward the future. His characters had character; there was an emotion in his work and a personality, even when the characters were in a position of rest.

Viewers immediately connected with a Benedict design; they took notice, and they found a renewed interest in the medium and a type of visceral excitement. This wasn't creating a jump-for-joy moment at the sheer sight of Auggie Doggie but more of a subconscious connection with the character on the screen, which elicited an immediate interest and an excitement about where they were going to take you.

A native of Cleveland, Ohio, Benedict was a workhorse artist who worried less about trends and more about drawing what was right. He was of the rare breed who intuitively understood what animation was about. He realized that a cartoon was a medium where anything could happen, but he thought that the "anything" should be done with style and control.

Benedict's designs permeated the airwaves and were responsible for creating the house style at Hanna-Barbera. He joined with the studio during its formative years and through his designs helped to establish not just individual characters but an overarching style and attitude.

Benedict, who downplayed his importance to the point that he often disparaged his own artistic output, styled the look and environments for nearly every key character for a generation plus one. His work, particularly his late 1950s and early 1960s designs for *The Flintstones*, *Yogi Bear*, *Snagglepuss*, *Jinksey*, *Magilla Gorilla*, and *Quick Draw McGraw* (just to name a spare few), set the tone for American television animation. In fact, his work held unprecedented sway over popular culture during the latter half of the twentieth century, from finding its way into our vernacular, to acting as a cultural touchstone, to finding a place on everything imaginable including toys, books, movies, games, blankets, and more. In fact, an argument could be made that his work on *The Flintstones* alone kept a generation healthy. Would Flintstones vitamins hold a 55 percent market share if they didn't look like, well, the Flintstones?[2]

An Early, Curly Path

When he started, Benedict initially took the path of a journeyman artist. He started working for Disney in 1930, and by 1933 he had migrated to the Walter Lantz studio (which was based at Universal), where he, in a weird twist of coincidence, worked on shorts starring the Disney-bred *Oswald the Lucky Rabbit*. He didn't stay long, though (hopefully he kept his pencils in an easy-to-pack case) as he headed from there to Columbia for a year and then back to Universal before circling around to Disney, where he took a position as a layout artist. Some of his work from this second go-round with Disney can be seen in the *Willie the Whale* segment of the 1946 film *Make Mine Music*.

His whirlwind tour around the industry was not entirely uncommon for the time period; while it kept him hustling, it was certainly educational, as it exposed him to, and gave him experience with, a wide range of house styles that would eventually coagulate together in his Hanna-Barbera designs.

At the end of 1946 he was on the move again, being named head designer for Cartoon Films. Up until this point, Ed had been primarily an animator, but Cartoon Films was a new outfit, and Ed had been hired to help give it a distinct style. He had tired of animation as a day in, day out job and looked forward to this new challenge. "It takes so long to get anything done (in animation)," Benedict has said. "It's like blowing a horn, you expect the notes to come out on the other end, you don't want to wait until next week for them."[3] While Benedict was the lead designer there, and found some interest in the work he was doing, the studio head Paul Fennell was a brilliant micromanager whose constant "let me show you how to do it" style eventually drove Benedict away.

He didn't leave without a plan, though. He was heading to MGM to help his friend Tex Avery modernize his films. It was 1952, and Avery had three films in various stages of production, and Benedict created the layouts and character designs for each of them. There was a caveman story, *First Bad Man* (1955), which Benedict would later return to for inspiration when designing *The Flintstones*. Another film was *Deputy Droopy* (1955), for which Benedict created some simple, modern sets for Avery's bang-bang-bang-like gag-filled story of two bandits trying desperately not to wake a sleeping sheriff so they could properly rob him. This was Avery's bread-and-butter plot structure, as he had used a variation of it previously in *Rock-a-Bye Bear* (1952) and would return to it when working for Walter Lantz with *The Legend of Rock-a-Bye-Point* (1955). Of the three, the Droopy version stands out because the character of Droopy is perfectly suited to this kind of action and because of Benedict's layouts, which place the action in this slightly skewed version of the real world. The whole film is designed around angles, from the Sheriff's basic body structure to the town buildings. These are not German expressionist angles but slight shifts in what would otherwise be a "standard" old West setting. This tilted effect puts us into this definitive cartoon reality where the viewer knows from the beginning that they aren't going to be seeing some character study but a *cartoon*.

Their last coupling at MGM was *Cellbound* (1955), whose story concerns a criminal trying to escape jail but ending up inside of a television set. It's a curious film, typical Avery gag after gag, but it lacks the energy and feel of excitement of something like the Droopy picture.

Benedict's designs for these shorts are visually pleasing and conceptually tight. When you are working on an Avery cartoon, you have to give him the space to work in, and that's exactly what Benedict provided. His designs are modern but not stylistically limiting, yet they still offer a new perspective to each of the characters.

Some of this is Benedict's natural pessimism toward his work, because the result of his collaboration with Avery is a solid mix of the two styles, with *Deputy Droopy* particularly standing out.

Avery never got to see things all the way through, though, as during the production cycle, he accepted a job at Cascade Pictures. Benedict (somewhat surprisingly given his penchant for career jumps) stayed at MGM but agreed to moonlight for Avery, which is somewhat surprising considering that Benedict would later share a slight disappointment in the collaboration explaining that Avery's desire to fit in any gag he could was a hindrance to his design style: "I had to create the background around the stuff that Tex had laid out. I couldn't design a layout."[4]

Making His Mark

Despite his reservations, something about Avery clicked with Benedict as he worked alongside him as long as he could. For Cascade, Benedict worked on spots for the newly burgeoning industry of television commercials along with various industrial films for Avery, and others, until 1957, when MGM shuttered the animation division. First out of the building when the doors were closing were MGM producers, directors, and all-around animation stalwarts Bill Hanna and Joe Barbera. Hanna and Barbera lit out and formed their own studio, taking many of their former MGM animation staff members with them. Top on the list of recruits (and not just alphabetically) was Ed Benedict. Benedict was brought on as a designer to give each character, prop, and environment a distinctive yet appropriate look and feel. What made this assignment different from all of the previous ones was that the Hanna-Barbera Studio would be creating animation for television, and that provided an interesting challenge for Benedict. While this didn't change the basics of what was needed or what the process was, it did inspire one to spin a new thought into their creative process in order to meet the demands of this new delivery format both technically and from a storytelling perspective.

Designing for television brought about an entirely new series of rules and necessitated a new understanding of the audience. For example, television increased the importance of instant design credibility in animation. Previously, animators had the luxury of a captive theater audience and a linear time progression to tell their stories, so designs could be unveiled to a certain degree; their meaning (within and without) could be revealed as the story dictated and based on the needs of each individual character. In the theatrical arena, design was important but perhaps slightly under story, particularly during animation's Golden Age. People were more apt to remember a great gag than an interesting-looking short (that is until UPA came along and taught the audience differently). Television radically changed all of that in a number of ways — longer time frames, commercial segmentation, and of course more immediate competition. If someone didn't like what they were watching, with a flick of the dial they could find something else. The pressure on the artist grew exponentially to create something that was visually stimulating and appealing to immediately capture an audience and then keep them tuned in.

Up until this time Benedict had a very distinct, although of-the-time, approach to design. His work at Cascade for instance looks just as you'd expect a 1950s industrial cartoon to look, which makes his design and layout for the newly independent Hanna-Barbera shows all the more impressive. It's important to remember that during this time period Hanna-Barbera *was* television animation. There were other studios producing a cartoon or two for after school or Saturday morning, but none had the reach or volume of Hanna-Barbera. That is not to say that the studio achieved success based solely on volume, for there had to be a reason that people wanted to watch and continued to return to these shows. Animation historian Jerry Beck believes that the success can be traced back to one place, or person. "It would not be an exaggeration to say that a large part of Hanna-Barbera's success ... is owed to Benedict's incredibly appealing and fun character designs."[5]

Why Does *It Work So Well?*

So what makes a Benedict design work so well? It's like asking what's so special about the Mona Lisa: it just is. Still, there are some traits in a Benedict design that may hold some answers. Benedict always worked with a conscious thought of his medium, and for that his characters exhibit a cartooniness without being too much of a cartoon (no wiggling rubber-hose arms and popped eyes, for example). A 1950s modern stylization shows in some of the angular aspects of his designs, yet they still retain a classic, Golden Age look. He counted Disney and UPA among his artistic influences, and it shows. His designs show a unique understanding of the delivery medium and the viewer's relationship with it, and he was able to use this understanding to infuse his design with a style that created an instant connection with a viewer. With a Benedict-designed character, you immediately can see that this is someone you want to spend a little time with. His characters work from a design perspective in that they follow all of the classic principles of symmetry, angles, shapes, and curves. This sort of textbook approach does not rob them, though, of one of their key traits — personality. His designs are case studies in personality. One look at his Yogi and you can immediately see the innocent mischievousness, while Boo Boo carries a starry-eyed servitude; his Fred Flintstone (before the series was hijacked by runaway popularity — a popularity engineered to an extent by the initial designs of Benedict — and the designs softened) had a victim-of-the-world aura while Barney appeared to be a guy who was just happy to be here. To view Benedict's designs is to remember why we were attracted to and fell in love with these shows to begin with.

Benedict designed each character with just the scantest bit of information, so the look that he created really helped inform their overall personality. As he explained, "Joe (Barbera) would just tell me what he wanted. He made the voices. I guess he described what the bear would be doing ... very brief.... So I would just do bears (in the case of Yogi) until I got a few of them that I thought might fit the bill ... and then I would take them up."[6]

What's remarkable is the speed with which Benedict worked out his designs. He had an amazing ability to process character, personality, and graphic style in a free-form way right at the drawing board. He has stated that the design of characters like Yogi Bear and Fred Flintstone took "maybe half an hour, couple of hours."[7] The process packed into that time was not one of hard research or animal studies either but one of time on and time off: "I might work a little bit on it and get up and have a cup of coffee and a cigarette or something and come back.... I might go out and the garage and polish the car or something, come back in and work on it some more."[8] *Speed* might be considered a key word for Benedict: he works quickly and isn't prone to much discussion or art introspection. This working process was most likely the result of a quick artistic impulse and a "disdain" for the longevity that could be found in the creation of an animated short: "It (the process of animation) snuck up on you so slowly that there was nothing shocking about it, sort of like watching grass grow."[9] His push toward speed translates over into his designs, particularly his work at Hanna-Barbera. A Benedict design didn't want to force you to overthink character type and details; it wanted to speed that process up for the viewer and provide, upon immediate sight, a basic understanding of the character type. Just consider Huckleberry Hound, Quick Draw McGraw, or Snagglepuss. This was done not just through character design but in designing the props and backgrounds as well. Through his work, he also helped Hanna-Barbera define who they were in the eyes of the viewer and as a studio.

To fully appreciate Ed's brilliance, consideration must be given to other animation designers of the time. There are designers such as Tom Oreb, who brought a strong, stylized appearance to much of his work; providing a similar feel to his characters was Mordi Gerstein, who, along with Sterling Sturtevant, worked for a long time with UPA. Each of these designers had a great design style, but their work was more technical and stylized for the sake of the art; where Benedict added stylization, it was done to strengthen the character. Where their work differs from Benedict's is that his accented the cartooniness of the designs more openly. There was no mistaking that these were from an animated film. The other differing point is that, outside of dedicated design circles, Benedict's work has survived the test of time and continues to be referred to, to inspire, and to remain relevant. Granted, his initial character designs have been deviated from over the years by other artists, but one may argue that this only reinforces his relevancy.

The designs and layouts proffered by Benedict straddled the age of pure animation and the time of design as an animated element. He embraced both viewpoints and where appropriate melded them into his own unique style. An example can be seen in *Tough Little Termite* (1959). This Huckleberry Hound story opens with our hero on the way home. His neighborhood consists of exactly one house surrounded by color blocks representing the other "houses" in the area. The skill Benedict provided, though, is in presenting this concept as a modernist cartoon convention and not a stylistic artistic design.

Contrast this with the work of Iwao Takamoto, who succeeded Benedict at Hanna-Barbera and eventually reached the position of vice president of creative design. Takamoto led the studio toward a more "realistic" approach to design, which gave us several uniquely styled characters including Penelope Pitstop and Scooby Doo's Fred and Velma. He also took Benedict's characters and changed their designs to give them a softer appearance, which robbed them of much of their personality. There is no distinctness in any of these; they could be from any show anywhere. We really only know them because we have a history with these characters and their shows, but if you step back from that for a critical moment, you see that they lack any real definition and style and act less as characters and more as vapid ciphers onto which a story could be grafted.

A trait that found its way into Benedict's work, particularly through the light angles and attitudes, was a grown-up sensibility. The angles of the design, the slightly uneven posturing, the understated weariness all give his characters an almost worldly feeling to them. If you could forget everything you knew about Yogi Bear and you were seeing him on Benedict's boards for the first time, you wouldn't be surprised to see him walking the streets of New York City.

"Benedict's skill lay not only in designing memorable characters ... but in placing them in memorable settings as a layout designer."— Steve Holland[10]

The design and layouts he created for *The Flintstones* are perhaps his most widely known work. Not only did he do character design and background layouts, but he also worked on the look of a number of the show's "modern devices," which include the pterodactyl airplane, the baby woolly mammoth vacuum cleaner, and the warthog garbage disposal. It should be noted that Hanna and Barbera had conceived the Flintstone characters and then asked artist Dan Gordon to provide some early concept sketches. Benedict took this information and used it as the basis for his final designs.

The Creator as Critic

Today Ed's work is revered for the intelligent way that it evokes character, its immediate humor, the emotion held in its poses, and the modernly classic styling that has helped it maintain a popular longevity. Even though his work, particularly what was done during his Hanna-Barbera period, has been universally acclaimed, Benedict openly dismissed his achievements. Take this exchange between Benedict and animator John Kricfalusi (discussing the pilot episode for *The Flintstones*):

> KRICFALUSI: What did you think of it?
> BENEDICT: I thought it stunk.... I just didn't like the appearance of the whole damn thing.... As a matter of fact, I didn't like any of the future ones either."[11]

What's not clear, though, is why he had this negative perspective of his work. His time, particularly at Hanna-Barbera, seemed to be filled with fun opportunities that presented him with a series of interesting advancements and challenges. Did he feel slighted at working in television? Was he somewhat embarrassed for the riches his designs wrought? Was it his Cleveland-born "we just do what we need to" pride? His death in 2006 means we may never know. And in some ways his negativity only heightens the attractiveness of the work. We want to like what we're told we shouldn't.

> He's a master of asymmetry. If you look at the left side of the face on one of his characters, it's different from the right. Look at the original Yogi Bear. Everything about him is asymmetrical, one hip is higher than the other, etc.... Asymmetrical ... makes things look alive.[12]

The importance and influence of Ed Benedict's work cannot be overstated. As we work to dissect how he did what he did, perhaps we are overlooking a simple reasoning for the strength of his drawings — Ed understood that at their core, cartoons have to be visual. Visually appealing. Visually telling their story. Visually presenting their ideas. And he worked to create characters and locations that did just that.

A particular disciple of the Benedict style is animator John Kricfalusi (*Ren & Stimpy*). John K (as he is commonly known) may have seen in Benedict a type of kindred, artistically equal soul, and he was smart enough to engage Benedict and learn at his feet.

When reviewing the career of this unassuming artist, an argument could be made that the designs of Ed Benedict made television a viable medium for animation. To begin, he worked on some of the key early animated programs like *Ruff and Reddy* (1957) and the aforementioned first original primetime animated series *The Flintstones*, and the success of those shows allowed the momentum of animation to continue forward. Granted, he was not the only member of the teams creating those shows, but he did play an intensely critical part, for as much as what is said about the importance of story in any medium, animation is so dependent on the visual aesthetic. If the look of a series doesn't immediately engage you, then the chance of building and maintaining an audience is practically nonexistent.

> *"His Hanna/Barbera look became one of the defining styles of an age of animation and is still being drawn from today — is there a single show on Cartoon Network or Nickelodeon that doesn't owe a huge debt to his shapes?"* — John Kricfaulsi[13]

HONORS

The International Animated Film Society (AISFA), Winsor McCay Award for Lifetime Achievement, 1994
Motion Picture Screen Cartoonists Awards, Golden Award, 1985

SAMPLE FILM SELECTION

Deputy Droopy (1955)
The Flintstones, season one (1960)
Top Cat, season one (1961)
Boo Boo Runs Wild (1999)

THE TRAILBLAZERS

10. Lotte Reiniger: Shadowplayer

"I believe in the truth of fairytales more than I believe in the truth in the newspaper."

— Lotte Reiniger[1]

There are originals in the animation industry, there are trailblazers, and then there are those who defy categorization. In that latter group would be German-born animator Lotte Reiniger (6/2/1899–6/19/81), who has the distinction of having produced, directed, and animated the world's oldest-surviving (and perhaps first) full-length animated feature film. That she did it nearly a decade before Disney's *Snow White and the Seven Dwarfs* (1937) and that she was a woman in what was primarily a man's industry makes her achievements all the more impressive. From everything that she could have been labeled, Reiniger would most likely have favored the term *artist*, for that is what truly drove her.

A native of Germany, Reiniger broke out on the world stage in a huge way. One has to wonder how her career would have changed if the German political climate had been different and she could have focused more on her work and less on seeking asylum in neighboring countries. For her "debut," she chose a classic story but one that had enough versions to provide her the artistic freedom she desired. *The Adventures of Prince Achmed* (started in 1923; released in 1926) is based on the tales of the Arabian Nights. (Note: The release date indicates the initial German release. Copyright and clearance issues held back the American release until 1942, which probably did not help its historical arguments over who was truly first to bring an animated film to the market.) It has been described as "a brilliant feature, a wonderful film full of charming comedy, lyrical romance, vigorous and exciting battles, eerie magic, and truly sinister, frightening evil."[2]

Achmed was not the first story that Reiniger committed to film; by the time that she got to that story she had already completed six one-reel shorts. Even before she touched upon film, though, she was working with the same basic elements, putting on shadow-puppet plays for family and friends. She had even constructed a small theater, which she used to put on shows for her family. She was enthralled with the concepts of shadow theater, being particularly inspired by Thai Nang puppets, and becoming a strong advocate for it throughout her life.

This knowledge coupled with the "trials" she underwent in the short film processes combined to give her the opportunity to refine her craft and better understand the process of filmmaking. The result allows *Achmed* to be more technically advanced than it had a right to be, but the film that sits on the screen makes it feel as if this were the 100th feature from the artists and not their first. Creatively *Achmed* leaned hard on the mood and "aesthetic intensity" of German expressionism, which was so prevalent at the time; artistically the color tints and ornamental character design helped to set an otherworldly mood, which matched the magic so central to the film's story; and technically there is a clever use of special effects, and a multiplane camera adds depth years before Disney's celebrated version.

The Centerpiece

To get a sense of the interplay of these elements, one should watch one of the more celebrated sequences in the film — the "wizard's battle." It's an astounding bit of animation depicting the back-and-forth spell-casting fight between the villainous sorcerer and the good witch. In an attempt to capture a magic lamp, which is central to the story, they throw spells and transform into different animals as the battle rages on against a tumultuous background. Many see echoes of this sequence in Disney's *The Sword in the Stone* (1963). There are two components that make this sequence function so energetically. One is the character movement Reiniger injects. While we are aware that these are relatively small, flat characters, their fluidity and nimbleness help break down any viewing bias and bring the characters to become more fully realized. The sequence is also helped forward by some masterful special effects as prepared by Reiniger and her three-man crew (in particular, animation effects artist Walter Ruttman), who used a number of tricks including painted glass sheets, scrims, and gauzes — all strategically placed between the light and the glass on the light table to create any number of effects. The sequence is a technical masterpiece with the film being double exposed. First the fight was staged and captured, and then the backgrounds composed and added in. The resulting sequence is more than what Reiniger herself described as "satisfactory."[3]

In fact the film is filled with special effects that were far ahead of their time. While Reiniger worked on the main sequences, her assistants Bertold Bartosch and Walter Ruttmann worked on the effects animation. Part of the reason that the effects are so potent was that the two had the fortunate luxury of a backer/patron for the project and an unhurried production schedule. They utilized paint, sand, paper, pin pricked back-boards, soap, and double exposures to create their scenes. Ruttman had some specific ideas for the climactic duel, and so he contracted famed animator Oskar Fischinger (*Color Rhythm* [1942]; *Spirals* [1926]) to create a wax-slicing machine to obtain the sizes and shapes this sequence needed.

While the mid–1920s were still definitely the domain of silent film, Reiniger and her team decided to work toward a sound-based finished product. She hired composer Wolfgang Zeller to compose a music score and a separate piece filled with sound effects. Zeller broke down his composition beat by beat, which allowed Reiniger and her team to animate to the soundtrack. When the film was played, a live orchestra was encouraged to accompany the film with the combination being a reportedly dazzling effect.

Careful attention must be paid not to simply lump Reiniger into the "Firsts" category of animation, for in doing so there can be a tendency to overlook the delicate artistry of her work. And that is where the true influence of Reiniger lies, for if she had made the 42nd animated film, she would still be a key figure within the art form. Had she only ever made *Achmed*, it could still be argued that she was a master artist, but she continued honing her craft so that over the course of a career, this style was the only style of film she made. In retrospect, as Phillip Kemp at the British Film Institute states, "No one else has taken a specific animation technique and made it so utterly her own."[4]

A Mastery of Technique

Reiniger's technical mastery becomes all the more impressive when you consider that with each character, she was working with anywhere between 25 to 50 separate pieces held together by fine lead wire, which enabled her to get precise and complex movements. Reiniger understood the characters so well because not only did she animate them, but she also designed each of the characters in her films, doing meticulous research to choose clothing and architectural styles that could translate both the story and the character, in silhouette. After a design had been chosen, the character would be cut from black paper. Each key piece would be cut separately and then assembled with lead-covered wire (to keep the figures from warping under the lights). The last step was to roll the figures flat. This kept each part malleable but still retained the needed flexibility required for the animation. And this was the "standard" Reiniger format; over time, though, she would substitute a cardboard and metal mix in place of the black paper for stronger and longer-lasting characters.

This technique had been used earlier by animator J.S. Blackton in the early 1900s and then a few years later, more extensively, by animator Emile Cohl. Cohl used the technique of cardboard cutouts as a way to supplement the hand-drawn animation process and the quotas with which he was tasked. His cutouts had none of the precision and drama that Reiniger could put into hers. Viewing Cohl's creations, and he was a talented filmmaker in his own right, only solidifies Reiniger's position at the top of her craft; her skills with scissors were unparalleled.

Where Reiniger's films differ from a straight-ahead film version of one of her beloved shadow-puppet plays is through the use of camera angles. She was comfortable cutting between long and medium shots and close-ups, which, from a technical perspective, meant that she needed two sets of "actors." Artistically this second set of characters had to have the detail to work in close-up, but they also had to be manipulated with precision and confidence, for at that size, any small jump is magnified. Two sets of each actor also provides the film with a fluidity that was unseen in even many of the live-action films of the day. The actors in a Reiniger film were not combined to one stage and not limited to one directional movement (which truly would have rendered them as flat). Instead they have this free mobility, which, on top of expanding the field of action, also provides the characters with a stronger definition of character.

The "stage" where the performance of these actors was captured had a very DIY aesthetic to it. Her initial camera frame and light table that she worked on were made of metal, but she eventually switched to an all-wood rigging because she found it easier to "forgive" the wood (for the twists and settling that happened during the course of production). She herself seemed to marvel at the actual simplicity of it all, as she would encourage people to make their own films and start by cutting a hole in their kitchen tables, covering it with a plane of glass, and then adding a light underneath. Perhaps her belief that "anyone can do it" (or at least try) subconsciously prompted her to make *her* process difficult. It was as if she enjoyed the challenge. For example in 1923 she built a camera rig in the only space her financial backer had available — in an attic. This placement forced her to kneel to work. She would later say it was a preferred method of animating.

The Achievement

After three years in production, during which she shot over 250,000 frames of film (of which she used over 100,000 frames), the question must be asked — *was* this film first? Was *Achmed* the first full-length animated film?

Unfortunately there is no definitive answer, and there may very well never be. For years the Disney promotion machine willed the title to *Snow White and the Seven Dwarfs* (1937), but a resurgence of interest in Reiniger's work and the advent of a more readily accessible global film base has caused scholars to re-evaluate the rankings. A film from Argentina — *El Apostol* (1917) — has its own argument for the position at the top of the list, but all known copies of it have been lost to time, and so the argument stands on memory and fuzzy history alone. Others cite early films of J.R. Bray and Max and Dave Fleischer. While there is some question as to who deserves the ranking of number one, there is no dispute that Reiniger's work is near (or at) the top of the list and that she deserves a special spot for being the first female animator and director to break through the walls surrounding this male-dominated art.

It's safe to say that Reiniger didn't make *Achmed* to secure any place in the record books. In all of her later interviews and even her own book, *Shadow Puppets, Shadow Theatres, and Shadow Films* (1970), she doesn't address the issue with much fanfare, just a passing comment and nothing more. It leads one to believe that she made *Achmed* for the simple reason that she had to — it was the only way to tell the story that she needed to tell. And what a way she did it. The reviewer for *Forward* said of the film, "A miracle is done here."[5] It is certainly like no other film that came before it. In fact it was so new and "unusual" that theaters across Berlin at first refused to screen it. Undaunted, Reiniger and her cohorts established a space in Volksbuhne to house the first public screening. The film's next major milestone was Paris, and then back to Berlin (finally), and then on to the rest of the world.

Reiniger could have very well rested on her laurels (and deservedly so), but that was not in her nature. In 1928 her next film, *Dr. Doolittle*, was released. (It's interesting to note that after this she never again made a feature-length film; everything going forward was a short.) To challenge herself (a typical Reiniger decision) this film had a strongly pedigreed musical score created by Paul Dessau, Kurt Weill (*The Threepenny Opera*, Tony Award winner), and Paul Hindemith (Balzan Prize winner).

"She was born with magic hands."— Jean Renoir[6]

In 1929 she took her one, and only, shot at directing a live-action feature — *The Pursuit of Happiness*. Although the medium was different, the content played straight into her wheelhouse — the film told the story of people who ran a shadow-puppet theater in a carnival. The film starred Jean Renoir and Bertold Bartosch. Unfortunately, it started as a silent film, and an attempt midway through production to transition to the emerging sound technology did the film no good. Reiniger took the hint and, ever forward, poured her energies into creating shadow films.

The Move from Germany

Unfortunately, the Nazis, making their way to power, had a different opinion of her films, which was okay because she had a different opinion of the Nazis as well. As the Nazis rose further into power, Reiniger sensed that it was time, and she and her husband/camera operator, Carl Koch, fled the country. After some false starts, the couple landed in England, where they settled and lived out their lives.

During this nomadic period, though, they somehow managed to turn out 12 films including *Carmen* (1933) and *Papageno* (1935). They lived on the road until 1949, when they finally had the opportunity to move to London. Reiniger hardly noticed, though, as she remained extremely busy. She would maintain an upbeat production pace for the next 30 years thanks in part to advertising work and a commission from Primrose Productions for a series of fairy tales for the BBC. For her it was the continuation of a study she had spent the majority of her career on.

Throughout her career Reiniger never achieved the acclaim afforded many of her peers. This could have been due to her medium and the public's misperception about it; it could have been gender based; or it could have been due to her reliance on fairy tales as source material. Time and again, she returned to the stories of the Brothers Grimm, Hans Christian Andersen, and others to serve as the basis for her films.

Reiniger did not do a verbatim retelling of the familiar tales; she would inject a modern sensibility into the story through the actions of the characters. Where others see fairy tales as a children's storytelling device, she thought differently. "Reiniger did not see her work in film in opposition to past traditions, but a way to revitalize them, using a new form, as when she used stop-motion photography to dramatize a tale from *The Arabian Nights*. A modern, existential condition is visible in the construction of her silhouettes: fragmented pieces of paper bolted together at various joints, moving mechanically from frame to frame."[7]

If the stories were originally for children, though, that was okay with her, too. As she explained, in many ways they were her core audience. "I love working for children, because they are a very critical and very thankful public." And why wouldn't they be thankful? They were witnessing, as Jean Renoir, a close friend and passionate admirer of her work, declared, a "visual expression of Mozart's music."[8]

In addition to her technical and artistic talents, Reiniger was also an astute study of movement. She was known to have spent long hours at the zoo studying the animals for upcoming films. She would also walk through the house, acting out scenes to "get the movement into my own bones."[9]

Without the advantage of having a visible face on her characters, she needed to get the expression of every emotion across through the movement of the body.

It is one thing for an animator to have at her disposal the character's face so that certain moods can be conveyed. It's entirely a different affair when that face and the entire character are rendered in silhouette profile, and yet this never detracts from Reiniger's shorts; the viewer still walks away entertained, enlightened, and enriched.

The films that Reiniger created could be linked through technique and tone to Terry Gilliam. Both had a nimble cutting technique, which imparted an extraordinary amount of life into their animated figures. One could even argue that there is a deeper common thread that runs through their work. Where Gilliam used the artwork of old masters to upend society, Reiniger chose classic stories (*Cinderella, Snow White and Rose Red, Sleeping Beauty*) that she could imbue with a modern, often feministic bent. On a much simpler level her influence carries on through films like *The Mysterious Geographic Exploration of Jasper Morello* (2005) and in the work of artists Alex Budkowsky and Kara Walker.

Lotte Reiniger continued working up until she passed away. Her last film, *The Four Seasons*, was released in 1980. A year later she would be gone.

Her place in the history books is tied to *Prince Achmed*, but her legacy stems from her artistic abilities and natural determination. She had a number of factors working against her, and yet she created exquisitely crafted animated films that showcased a deft touch.

HONORS

The Gallant Little Tailor, Silver Dolphin, Venice Biennale, 1955
Filmband in Gold, West Germany, for service to German cinema, 1972
Verdienst Kreuz, West Germany, 1978
The Adventures of Prince Achmed—100 Best Full-Length Animated Films of All Time, Online Film Critics Society, 2003 (the only German animated film on the list)
The Adventures of Prince Achmed— One of the "100 Most Important Films," German Film Archives, 1995

SAMPLE FILM LIST (ENGLISH TITLES)

The Ornament of the Heart in Love (1919)
The Flying Trunk (1921)
The Star of Bethlehem (1921)
Cinderella (1922)

Sleeping Beauty (1922)
The Adventures of Prince Achmed (1926)
Carmen (1933)
Puss in Boots (1936)
Jack and the Beanstalk (1955)

WRITING

Shadow Puppets, Shadow Theatres, and Shadow Films, by Lotte Reiniger, 1970

11. Lillian Friedman: The Patient Trailblazer

Lillian Friedman (birth date and death date unknown) is an important figure in animation, both for what she did and for what she did not do. The first full-time, fully credited, female animator at an American animation studio, Friedman fought to be equal in a system that valued her more by gender than by skill. In the end she made a courageous move and decided not to play the studio game. By that point, though, she had already done what she needed to in "the business that I loved to hate."[1]

To understand Friedman's importance, one must have a sense of the relationship of women and animation, particularly in the first half of the twentieth century. This is a complicated subject, as it encompasses not just the structure of an industry but the political and sociological structure of the country. We can, though, explore from a broad perspective the role that gender played in the title of "animator."

While one might think that animation, an arts-based medium, would have a somewhat more liberal attitude in regards to things like gender, unfortunately, this was not the case. The animation industry was no different than any other American industry during this time period — work was viewed as a temporary stopping point for women on their way to a more permanent career as a wife/homemaker. While there were women within the industry, the vast majority (98 percent) were not viewed as "serious" artists. Women that worked at a studio held the "traditional" role of secretary, or those with stronger artistic ambition could find work in the ink and paint department. The only other place where one might find a woman in any place of prominence was as a "checker" or "supervisor" reviewing the animators' drawings as they came through to make sure poses matched up. Over time women found themselves with some expanded opportunities as background painters and inbetweeners, but their numbers fell far below those of men in those positions.

This is not to say that women were not active members of the animation community; it's just that they had no power or long-term career options. Some women, like Sadie Bodin at the Van Buren Studios, tried to overcome these obstacles and make their own opportunities, while others, like Lillian Friedman, stood purely on their artistic abilities, and a little luck — being in the right place at the right time.

Friedman got her start in animation in 1930 at a small New York studio, where she did ink and color work on *Mendelssohn's Spring Song*, a short made as a showcase for the Brewster Color process, which was a competitor to Technicolor film processing. Brewster couldn't make any Hollywood headway, and so the company stopped the promotion of it, which meant that Friedman was out looking for a new job. She bounced around for a bit before finding herself in 1931 at the Fleischer Studios working as an inbetweener.

A Big Break

After about a year, her natural abilities caught the eye of animator Shamus Culhane, who had her promoted as his assistant animator. Unfortunately for Friedman, shortly thereafter Culhane departed the studio, and she was demoted to her old inbetweener position. Her artistic talent was unmistakable, though, and many inside the studio had taken notice of her. One of her most fervent admirers was Nelly Sanborn, who was working as a "timing supervisor," checking each animator's work to ensure that all of the needed pieces were in place. This put her in a unique position in that she could review and, in effect evaluate, the work of each of the studio's animators. One day Sanborn pulled Friedman aside with a proposition — Friedman would draw a scene of Betty Boop. Sanborn would then present it to Max and Dave Fleischer as the work of a "new artist." The goal in effect was to take the gender politics away from the artistic abilities.

When the brothers saw the finished sequence, the intended effect occurred — they wanted to hire that artist to animate for the studio. When it was revealed that the artist already worked there and that it was a "she," the Fleischers were taken aback but undeterred.

And so it was that in 1933 yet another barrier in Hollywood was crossed. This newfound "equality," though, decidedly had its limits. Not only was she continually under pressure to prove herself, but she was also paid less to do it. Her starting salary ($40 a week) was just a third of what the average male animators earned in a week ($125).

Friedman was happy in her new role, though, and worked hard to prove she was up to the challenge. She had the exact temperament needed for this position, where she was expected to lead and yet follow, to produce and yet not overproduce, to make the Fleischers look good for their decision but not appear that she was their "pawn." It was a thick maze to navigate, and yet she seemingly did it with little complication.

The Clouds Roll In

Across the board things were good and generally happy, but like so many other times those words are used, trouble was right around the corner. That trouble spilled over in 1937 when the studio became the site of the first major labor strike in the animation industry. The walkout by many of her colleagues put Friedman in a completely unwinnable position — she was pro-union but also understood that, in many respects, she was part of some grand gender experiment, and the wrong step could not only send her back down the corporate ladder but also make that ladder increasingly difficult for those coming behind her.

Weighing all available options, she decided it was in her best interest to remain on the inside, deciding perhaps that it was more advantageous to be in with management regardless of the outcome of the strike. When the strike was settled, the union came out on top, a fact that her fellow animators, those who had joined the strike, never let her forget.

In 1938 the Fleischers made the surprising decision to move the studio to Miami. Friedman was invited to be a part of the move. She attempted it but in the end returned to New York. Eventually the constant badgering about her union choice and her gender created a work environment that was counterproductive, and so she decided to return to New York and seek work elsewhere. Unfortunately she quickly discovered that other studios were not as progressive in their role definitions as the Fleischer brothers.

As an aside, it is interesting to note that the Fleischer studio was also home to one of the most progressive animated female characters of this (or any) period — Betty Boop. While other studios had female characters, they were often sidekicks and portrayed for simpler, comic effects. Betty was a sexually charged young woman who spoke to the modern sensibilities of the day and showed the progressive thought patterns pervasive at the Fleischer studios. Eventually the Production Code would step in and effectively mute her style, but not before she had made her mark.

An Industry Blockade

In 1939, Friedman tried to make the transition to Disney and was told, in no uncertain terms: "Women do not do any of the creative work in connection with preparing the cartoons for the screen, as that work is performed entirely by young men. For this reason girls are not considered for the training school."[2]

Two years earlier another artist, Jessie Lamberson, had tried to break the gender barrier at Disney but had met with a similar rejection: "Upon closer inspection of your application, we note that you listed your occupation as 'housekeeper.' We assume, therefore, that you are a woman. If this is the case it will be impossible for us to further consider your application inasmuch as we employ only men in our animation department."[3]

This is not to imply that Disney had *no* women working at the studio. In the 1930s there were roughly 200 women working in the Ink and Paint Department. This number fluctuated across the years, with a significant population of females remaining on the workforce, but they always were given the "behind the scenes" jobs.[4] Similar arrangements could be found at other studios as well. Things were starting to change, though.

Friedman's accession to fully fledged animator did not break open wide the glass ceiling, but it certainly cracked it. Over the next few years more women succeeded in becoming full animators. Following Friedman at the Fleischers' studio was Edith Vernick, while over at the Walter Lantz studio, LaVerne Harding started animating regularly in 1935. At Disney, Retta Scott became the first woman at that studio to receive an on-screen credit, in *Bambi* (1942). Others to come were Retta Davidson, Beth Case Zwicker, Nancy Stapp, and Eva Schneider. Not everyone was promoted to the "top"; many became inbetweeners or assistant animators, but for the first time a promotion to the position of animator was a very real option. For some this "possibility" was still not good enough, but for an industry that was relatively unchanged for 30 years, it was a rather positive step.

As more and more women entered the industry, more opportunities opened to them (albeit at a sometimes glacial pace). In 1985 *The Care Bears Movie* was directed by Arna Selznick, marking the first time a major Hollywood animated film saw a woman behind the lens. Nearly 10 years later, in 1994, Brenda Chapman became the first female head of story for a major animated film when she oversaw *The Lion King*.

Unfortunately, Friedman would not be around to see these advancements. Unable to find any steady work, in 1939 she retired to upstate New York to take on a second career — that of a wife.

A Path Left to Follow

Looking back at the surviving pieces of Friedman's work, one sees a competent, extremely capable animator. Had she had an opportunity to work longer, and particularly at other studios, it would have been interesting to see how her style changed and if it got any stronger. Based on what we have, it is a safe conclusion to say that Friedman stands out not through her pencil (directly) but through who she was as a person.

Friedman's career was short lived and yet long lasting. Her roughly five years as an animator were enough to prove to an industry that women had the artistic talent, temperament, work ethic and (with the strike leaning heavily in the minds of studio chiefs everywhere) loyalty to be animators.

While one cannot fault her ultimate decision to retire, there is some slight disappointment at her decision to leave her art behind so early.

Friedman is fascinating in her career choices — she had reached the pinnacle in her profession, and, rather than slide back down the ladder, she gracefully bowed out. There was a certain peace she made with an industry that built her up and then essentially locked her out. Rather than give them the satisfaction of her taking some/any job, she said, "Thank you," and headed off to start her next life chapter.

HONORS

Golden Awards, Motion Picture Screen Cartoonists Guild, 1987
ASIFA Award, The International Animated Film Society, 1988

SAMPLE FILM SELECTION

Can You Take It (1934)

THE TELLER OF TALES

12. Henry Selick:
Sharing Hope Through
the Darkside of the Story

Henry Selick (b. 11/30/52) is in many ways a throwback — his talent is in stop-motion animation, which, in this digitally cultivated world, is somewhat quaint. He has shown great proficiency as a writer, director, and animator, but perhaps his greatest mark is that he has reminded us that it is okay to scare children.

Selick's movies, commercially successful and artistically lauded, have played into our primal instincts of inquisitiveness and cultivation of fear. Not that he is a shockmaster, an animated William Castle or Wes Craven, but instead Selick has used his talent to tell stories that look back to ancient campfires and cowboys travelling along the open prairies at dusk — his stories are not necessarily ghost stories but atmospheric tales of things that go bump in the night. They are children's stories for people who understand that children don't need to be coddled.

In a time when theaters are overrun with sequels and nearly every animated feature has a computer generated sheen to it, Selick's films provide something quite the opposite — originality and darkness (of the Penny Dreadful/ Brothers Grimm fairy tale variety). He gravitates toward the tales told in the darkness because he understands it is only then that the light is the brightest.

This is all not meant to make it appear as if Selick's films are without an upside, for the promise of that is what makes his movies work so well. No matter his setting, his stories are about investigating the proverbial steps toward the "dark before it gets light." With Selick things tend to start bleak and then get darker, but in the end there is hope. His genius lies in the way that his films cover this spectrum — artfully and intelligently. They invite the viewer into a particularly unique world and then put them on the path for the story to unfold. It's an unusual strategy in an increasingly "show me" entertainment outland.

"There's an inherent charm as well as a certain reality [in stop-motion] that you can't get any other way. Real materials, real cloth, real puppets are there on the screen bathed in real light."— Henry Selick[1]

Selick's films are modern fairy tales seen through a lens darkened by reality. In this way he pulls a direct line from the Brothers Grimm. With this penchant for the dark corners of a story there is some small level of humor in the fact that he got his start in the industry in a place not well known (at the time for sure) for its independence and tolerance for anything but being "The Happiest Place on Earth."

Finding His Way

While Selick has made a name for himself in stop-motion, this has been only his current medium of choice. He has worked in hand-drawn images, computer animation, and cut-outs.

Selick's fascination with animation came at a young age, when he first saw both Lotte Reiniger's stop-motion movie *The Adventures of Prince Achmed* (1926) and the animated creatures of *The 7th Voyage of Sinbad* by Ray Harryhausen.

He pursued this interest into college with the results being that two films he created at California Institute of the Arts—*Phases* and *Tube Tales*—were nominated for Student Academy Awards from the Academy of Motion Picture Arts and Sciences. (In a nice turn Selick was asked to present the Student Academy Awards for 2010.)

Following graduation Selick went to the Walt Disney Studios, which even during this period (the late 1970s) was still *the* place to be. Under the tutelage of one of Walt's original animators, Eric Larson, and new star animator Glen Keane, Selick learned the business while contributing to films like *Pete's Dragon* (1977) and *The Small One* (1977).

In 1979 he took a short absence from the company to work on several of his own projects with backing from the American Film Institute. One of these shorts, *Seepage*, became a critical success, winning multiple awards. In *Seepage,* Selick used stop motion and watercolor animation to bring to life the story of two people talking while sitting next to a pool. Full of acclaim and more importantly confidence, Selick returned to Disney, where he was immediately put to work on *The Fox and the Hound* (1981). While it had several interesting passages, working on the picture failed to satisfy his creative urgings, and so he again took leave from the studio, this time on a permanent basis.

He picked up enough side work that by 1986 he had his own production company, Selick Projects. He did work for Pillsbury, Ritz Crackers, and MTV. It was for this last organization that he also found an opportunity to re-explore using his talents in a narrative format.

Slow Bob in the Lower Dimensions was a series Selick pursued for MTV in the early 1990s. If the pilot (1991) is any example, the series would have been a Selickian mix of atmosphere and art. A mixture of stop motion and live action, the short features Siamese twins, a man who sleeps on walls, a talking lizard, and the shadow of an eerie old man in a rocking chair. It's as if Tim Burton and David Lynch had collaborated.

The dimensional world he has created, with its picture-chasing scissors and use of found images, feels the strong influence of Terry Gilliam, but Selick's piece plays more as homage than as derivative outtake. If there is a drawback to the short, it's the music track by The Residents, which feels thin and forced, and one hopes it was meant to be more of a temp track than a final piece.

Perhaps more importantly, though, this was the film that brought classmates and former Disney compadres Tim Burton and Henry Selick together again.

Then There Was Jack

"There's something very emotional about the process when it's handmade."
— Tim Burton[2]

Selick came into the film that would eventually be called *Tim Burton's Nightmare Before Christmas* with a challenge: to take stop-motion animation where it had never been before. Burton, now an accomplished live-action film director, had his start in the industry at Disney as well. While there he and the similarly minded Selick hit it off almost immediately, so years later, when Burton had the opportunity to bring a poem he had written during his time at the studio to life, he leapt at the opportunity and immediately thought of Selick as the perfect artist to realize his vision. The idea was to take this incredibly original story and present it in a way that had never been seen before while still, particularly important because of the "off-ness" of the story, maintaining some level of familiarity for the audience.

To meet this challenge Selick established a separate production unit at Disney. Skellington Productions was filled with hand-chosen artists and technicians who collaborated together perfectly to advance this form of animation. Working in tandem was key particularly given the enormity of the shooting location. All told, the crew took up over 40,000 square feet in warehouse space, which was spread across 20 sound stages filled with every set, prop, and device available. Many of the sets were extremely complicated, with parts that slid back and forth, while others were simply massive, with animators camping under them and popping up to manipulate their actors as needed. *Nightmare* took three years from start to finish (*Coraline* would take four). This speaks both to the amount of labor a stop-motion film takes as well as to the level of detail that Selick injects into his films.

This is all meant to spotlight the technical challenges that Selick faced on a daily basis, not to mention the artistic and dramatic decisions. That he is able to juggle everything and walk away with a film like this is an impressive act and a testament to his skill and artistry. While he used a number of cutting-edge effects, Selick is not just an innovator; he also has a sweet spot for nostalgia, which is why he requested that the film be shot using a Mitchell 35mm camera, the same camera type that helped bring King Kong to life.

Production went smoothly, with the only "hiccup," if you will, coming at the end, when the title was officially changed to include Tim Burton's name. With his name above the title, Burton became, in the mind of the public at least, the sole creator of the film. One could reasonably make the argument of course that Burton's name was the bigger box office draw, but the decision did in many ways diminish Selick's contribution from a public perspective.

Who?

While those in the industry understood who the driving force behind the film was, the public was not as educated, and after the success of the film the easily conditioned viewing public turned to Tim Burton for more. No one was clamoring for a "Henry Selick Film."

> "But the director of the film, a veteran stop-action master named Henry Selick, is the person who has made it all work. And his achievement is enormous. Working with gifted artists and designers, he has made a world here that is as completely new as the worlds we saw for the first time in such films as Metropolis, The Cabinet of Dr. Caligari, and Star Wars."— Roger Ebert[3]

He stayed with Disney for his next project — the adaptation of *James and the Giant Peach* by Roald Dahl. Dahl had always been leery of Hollywood and was reluctant to turn his stories over to them, but with the promise by Disney of Selick at the helm and Burton in a producing role, the Dahl family relented, and James was on his way.

Selick's second feature was no less dramatically complicated than his first. It told the story of James and his attempt to flee his evil aunts. Through a magical twist he lands inside a giant peach, where he meets a number of insects that journey along with him. Even at this still-early stage in his career it was simple to see that Selick was not looking for the easy way out in terms of topics or presentation. This was his "singing animals in an animated film" film, but he doesn't use "convention" as an excuse; instead he pushes against it, using the preconceived ideas of the audience against them.

Selick's original plan for the film was to shoot James as a live-action boy and have him interact with stop-motion creations through the entire story. When that became too cost-prohibitive, he explored making every element stop motion. Disney balked at the cost, and so a compromise was reached, the beginning and end of the story are told in live action, while the center, James' time in the peach, became an animated feast. While stop motion is the main form of animation used in the film, hand-drawn images, cut-outs, and paintings were all integrated into the stop-motion action.

Two sequences here are particularly worth noting: the underwater sequence where James, Centipede, and Miss Spider try and retrieve a compass from a shipwreck inhabited by skeleton pirates starts with a hint of Harryhausen yet skews a little slapsticky. Based on Selick's other works, one has to wonder if the dread in this sequence was turned down by Disney. Technically it's a sharp animated sequence, and it does serve the story, but as it plays out you can feel the potential in it, and one is left to wish that it had been explored further.

The second sequence occurs earlier in the film. James has ingested too much of his magic peach and falls into a type of fever dream, which is a cut-out animated sequence that perhaps more than anything else in the film plays to Selick's natural inclinations. It's the most terrifyingly vivid "reaction" sequence since Dumbo got drunk.

Following the release of *James,* Selick took up some smaller personal projects before returning to the silver screen with *Monkeybone* (2001), a live-action/animation mix that was an adaptation of an underground comic book of the same name. One of the central characters of the film, Monkeybone, is an animal closer to a sock monkey than a real primate, and so rather than go the hand-drawn animation route to bring Monkeybone to life (à la Roger Rabbit), Selick choose to have the creature live as a stop-motion puppet interacting with other actors because "[stop motion] has a great textural quality that CG doesn't quite achieve. The wrinkles there are real and by it being handmade ... it's a performance. An actual performance with incredible charm."[4]

Even though it had a wildly distinctive look and the animation and live-action interaction was cutting edge, *Monkeybone* failed to ignite the box office. Selick's next film would not suffer the same fate.

Coraline

In 2004 Selick set up shop at LAIKA. It was through this studio that he completed what could be considered his magnum opus. In fact, if Selick directed no other films, his mark in animation, in film really, would have been made with 2009's instant classic — the Academy Award–nominated (Best Animated Feature Film of the Year) *Coraline* (2009).

This film, the first full-length, stop-motion animated film to be completed in 3D, is a beautifully told story of a family that moves into the "house at the end of the lane" and the life that the title character, a young girl, both finds and creates there. The film was adapted (by Selick) from a book by Neil Gaiman, and it was a true example of the perfect marriage of artist and material.

The film's ability to take mystery and turn it to wonder while passing through dread, the commentary on success in families, and the way that it captures the angst of growing up all work with perfectly timed and designed animation to make the film an instant classic. The story is told in two very distinct locales, the "real" world and the "other" world, and in following this convention *Coraline* follows along the lines of another family classic — *The Wizard of Oz* (1939) — in that you are left wondering if what you just saw was real or (character-) imagined.

The Wizard of Oz shares a number of thematic elements with *Coraline* including the above-mentioned ideas of places real and imagined; a young woman's place in society and family; the journey of self and place through worlds that are strange with characters both helpful and darkly cunning. Selick also chose to make some conscious aesthetic comparisons as well: "One of the most amazing things in *The Wizard of Oz*, especially when it first came out, was this fantasy world Dorothy wakes up in is in color. She comes from the black and white world on the farm to this world full of magic."[5] In *Coraline* there is a similar distinction between the real world, muted and drab, and the world of the Other Mother, which is filled with color and has a particular, if offsetting, buoyancy about it.

As he has throughout his career, Selick uses technology (in this case 3D) judiciously in service of the overall story. While the entire film utilizes 3D to create a sense of space, it is only during the Other World scenes when it is used to at first create a sense of wonder and then, as the world begins to crumble, an enveloping sense of dread.

Throughout the film Selick and his team of artists are able to capture in perfect detail the differences between what Coraline has and what she wants and how the desire for the latter can have unintended consequences.

The Audience?

The question is raised — are Selick's films appropriate for children? Unfortunately audiences too often hear that a film is animated and immediately conjure up the idea that it will be glossy, musical, funny, and adventurous yet safe. In other words, what is now considered the "Disney Style." Disney is a good place to find a parallel to what Selick has done, just not their current slate of films. People forget that the early Disney films were filled with vile villains and rather shocking acts against the characters — the witch wishing to have Snow White's heart in a box in *Snow White*, the whale swallowing Geppetto in *Pinocchio*. (Looking even further, the source material for many Disney films, and in turn childhood stories — the Brothers Grimm — have an extremely dark streak running through them, and yet they are loved by children the world over.) Selick has maintained that connection with his childhood self and remembers that children enjoy (to a point) being scared. It's part of their intrinsic makeup and their rite-of-passage world discovery. So when the question is asked — are his films appropriate for children? — the answer is an emphatic yes.

The Journey

Selick's films have a common element across them — one character crossing through a portal into an alternative world. In *Nightmare* Jack tumbles through the door he finds in the trees in the forest; in *James* the journey starts when James crawls through a hole in the peach; in *Coraline* there is a hidden door in the new house; Stu and the Monkey travel into the parallel world via a "portal" under Stu's hospital bed in *Monkeybone*. The passageway, or portal, is an ancient storytelling device, and Selick puts it to good dramatic use. It's a way of not only triggering the action of the story (for none of the stories truly begin until the character has been "awakened" by their journey) but also alerting the audience that we are about to step outside of reality.

The characters in a Selick film are willing to take this journey because they all share a longing for something better. In this way, even though they are a skeleton or a little girl or a boy inside of a peach, they are no different than any other archetypical hero. It's one of the things that helps these films resonate with audiences so well: the audience undergoes a certain amount of self-projection and affirmation, as they can walk away with a very clear "moral" — no matter how different from society you seem to be, you can live the life you want and make a difference in your corner of the world.

A "Selick" Film

Selick, like his friend Burton and in some ways the cartoonist Charles Addams, has the ability to make a dark topic feel mainstream and safe. Surprisingly, *charm* is a key word in Selick's film vocabulary, and it's a conscientious decision as he turns to it often to describe what he does. In a Selick film the audience knows there will be trouble but that there is also an acceptable end.

In his three major solo animated works, Selick is interested in exploring the other side of a life being lived. It's important to note that this is not the *underside* of life, but an alternate way of the world. This is made clear by having the key action occur in a separate space. This allows the rules to be different (grasshoppers can sing, fathers live with button eyes) while leveraging the bookended reality in the story to highlight the changes and choices the characters make.

These separate, or parallel, spaces allow Selick to play with the ideas of cause and effect and personal choice in a narratively subtle way. The adventures of each main character, while often confined to that parallel universe, have repercussions in our/their (or the real) world. The actions taken don't directly affect things like a timeline or physical space, but, more importantly, they affect a character's attitude and general understanding of self. Coraline will never be the same after her time in the Other World, but that's not a negative thing; by her newfound appreciation of her own world she will affect and change it but that change will occur by what she does going forward, not what she did while absent. It's a slight distinction but an important one because it shows us a very important philosophical conclusion that Selick has chosen to champion — we are the masters of our own destiny, a destiny that can shape our decisions and thereby our path forward, if we let it.

On a more surface level, Selick's films have a particular aesthetic appeal, which is drawn out through the intricately designed characters and sets. A character in one of his films has an unmistakable uniqueness about them, and the sets have an impressively rich amount of detail woven across them. As a viewer it's wonderful because it only better helps to realize the world being created, but as an artist there has to be a slight trepidation due to the challenges of hand-animating a character in such a fully realized space.

The Tactile Medium

If you work hard and put your whole heart into a film, it will be timeless and stand up to repeat viewing. We're trying for something handmade, with a wealth of detail, that vibrates with the energy and humanity of the artists who brought it to life.[6]

Stop-motion animation is a very tactile medium, which is one of its joys for both the animator and the viewer. For as beautiful as a computer-rendered film can be or for all of the artistry that goes into hand drawn animation, stop motion combines the best of both of those techniques with a backreaching connection — it hearkens back to two cavemen re-enacting the day's hunt with some modified pine cones. Through all of his films, Selick has used an art form primarily known for its use in special effects and holiday specials and proved it can be a viable long-form storytelling option.

Selick, who has made use of some of the digital storytelling options currently available, nevertheless does lament some of the technological advancements of modern filmmaking — "Now you can shoot the whole scene and play it back while you animate. This assists the animator but actually slows down the process because they keep checking it every time they shoot a new frame. Computers have slowed down what is already a time-consuming process."[7]

> I do think there's a part of everyone that likes to see handmade stuff. That's what we offer. It's never going to be the dominant filmmaking style. It's always going to be the cousin off to the side. You know, the more eccentric relative of yours that some of the kids like.[8]

Next

In 2010, Selick went full circle in a way as he signed a multi-year deal to create films for the Walt Disney Studios. Perhaps with both parties somewhat older and wiser and better understanding of the strengths each side can offer, Selick will be able to build on *Coraline* while, at a time when the immediate Hollywood reaction is to go digital, continue to show that there is still magic and imagination in one of the oldest filmmaking practices.

> *"Henry is an artist. He has a vision.... He understands something people often forget— that children love to be scared. Kids love to see cool stuff."*
> — Neil Gaiman[9]

Although Selick's films are not consistent blockbusters, they are among the most interesting and innovative animated efforts being created. Each feature has completely different tones and stories, but they share a commonality in their depth and complexity. Each film to this point in his career survives on a number of emotional and technical layers that add a personal tone, as well as an audience connection point, to each production.

> I've done a lot of soul searching over the years. What are the strengths of stop-motion? What should we try to hold on to? There are a lot of strengths: it's touched by the hand of the artist — you can feel that. You can sense that

life force, but it's imperfect. It can't be done perfectly — that's what CG can do. And I'm trying to get people to embrace that: if it pops, if cloth shifts a little, if the hair is buzzing. It's like this electricity of life.[10]

HONORS

Annie Award, Best Individual Achievement for Creative Supervision in the Field of Animation, *The Nightmare Before Christmas,* 1994

Annecy International Animated Film Festival Grand Prix Best for Animated Feature Film, *James and the Giant Peach,* 1997

Annecy International Animated Film Festival Grand Prix Best for Animated Feature Film, *Coraline,* 2009

British Academy of Film and Television Arts (BAFTA) Children's Award for Best Feature Film, *Coraline,* 2009

SAMPLE FILM SELECTION

The Nightmare Before Christmas (1993)
James and the Giant Peach (1996)
Monkeybone (2001)
The Life Aquatic with Steve Zissou (2004) (visual effects: underwater scenes)
Coraline (2009)

THE TEACHERS

13. George Newall
and Tom Yohe:
The Entertaining Educators

"I fully believe the animated picture will emerge as one of the greatest mediums not only of entertainment but also of education."
— Walt Disney[1]

Walt Disney had an eerie way of seeing into the future. While he saw
the potential, and truth be told he was one of many who did (others included
animation pioneers J.R. Bray and Max and Dave Fleischer), it took several
years and the combined creative power of a group from outside the animation
industry to bring that premonition of animation as a broad educational tool
to fruition. That group, led by George Newall (b. 6/17/34) and Tom Yohe
(4/26/37–12/21/2000), brought us the 1970s–1980s series *Schoolhouse Rock*,
which taught millions of children (and their parents) multiplication facts, sci-
entific equations, and American history while permanently lodging songs into
their brains.

Schoolhouse Rock wasn't the first time that animation was used for educational efforts, but it *was* a defining moment when all of the techniques were
perfected. Just as it's a case study for using the medium to teach, it's also a
perfect example of smart management because the producers knew how to
hire in the right people and then step back and let them work. There is something telling in the fact that this series, so immensely popular that it continues
to be utilized and celebrated decades after its initial airing, was created by a
bunch of advertising executives and musicians. Had this been an animation
studio production, one has to wonder how the standard committee processes
would have worn away the charm and creativity from each episode. As it is,
the series thrived perhaps in part because Newall and Yohe didn't know that
it shouldn't.

In the 1970s, Saturday morning television was a vast wasteland of inter-
changeable shows from Hanna-Barbera, Filmation's bland outputs, and

DePatie-Freleng's not-so-super superhero stories. Tucked in between was a three-minute show, airing five times a day with an aim of teaching kids things such as what an interjection is. Not a very promising position to be in, particularly when your goal was to teach, but that didn't stop anyone involved. *Schoolhouse Rock* didn't disguise the fact that it was trying to teach its audience something (it's right in the name), and the audience didn't care. Rather than use that time for a bathroom break or to refill the cereal bowl, viewers actively sought the shows out. They were even listed in *TV Guide* (perhaps the shortest programs ever to appear there), and more than one Saturday morning zombie used "The Guide" to plot their program-watching to catch multiple viewings of some of the episodes. The most astute channel-changer could plot a viewing course that would enable them to catch the episode multiple times. And that is the genius of George Newall and Tom Yohe. They put out three minutes of school every Saturday, and people actively sought it out. The two men, with no background in animation, went about creating one of the most influential animated series of recent times.

The Rolling Stones Started It All

David McCall, a principal at McCaffrey & McCall advertising agency, had returned from a family vacation and was regaling George Newall, the agency's co-creative director, with some of the experiences he had with his son. McCall lamented that his son could sing every Rolling Stones song but struggled through his multiplication tables. Always thinking forward, McCall wondered if perhaps they couldn't create an album with math-focused songs. The two decided to explore the concept, and Newall, a long-time jazzman, commissioned a fellow musician, Bob Dorough, to create a song. Dorough, known for his somewhat quirky lyrics, grabbed at the idea with excited determination. He took every math book he could find and locked himself away with his piano, and when he emerged, he carried the music and lyrics to what would become the first *Schoolhouse Rock* song, and one of the most famous — "Three Is a Magic Number." It was at this point that co–creative director of the agency Tom Yohe, a man whose co-workers described as "entirely more talented than he needed to be," became interested and involved in the project.[2]

As Yohe listened to Dorough's demo he started sketching, and suddenly everything clicked. Newall, Yohe, and McCall realized what they had was not a record but an animated series. In one of those fortuitous events, Radford Stone, an account executive at the agency, had as a client ABC Television. He knew that they were looking for new animated series, so he set up a meeting between Newall and Yohe and ABC Children's Programming executive, Michael Eisner (later to run the Disney Corporation). Eisner listened to the song, reviewed the storyboards/sketches, considered the concept, and then turned to advice from a special guest he had invited. Without a moment's hesitation Chuck Jones said quite simply to Eisner, "Buy it." And then he turned his gaze to Yohe and added, "But only if *he* designs them."[3]

Concept, design, broadcast time, and music (at least the first song) were all now in place. The only piece missing was finding someone to animate the thing. Because they were in advertising those were the people they knew, and so they turned to Focus Presentation, where Phil Kimmelman was creating animated commercials. Phil liked the concept and without hesitation came aboard. It should be noted, though, that Kimmelman would eventually split the animation responsibilities with Kim/Gifford Productions due to an increasing workload of advertising clients. When the series was "re-commissioned" for a short run in 1992, the producers asked J.J. Sedelmaier (JJSP) to provide the animation. Three episodes were produced over the following year: *Busy P's*, *Mr. Morton*, and *Dollars and Sense*. Since then, JJSP has produced two parodies, "Conspiracy Theory Rock" for *Saturday Night Live*, and "Midterm Elections" for *The Daily Show with Jon Stewart*, which allowed many of the original artists and animators to have a little fun with their creation.

Hitting the Air

Schoolhouse Rock premiered on January 6, 1973, with "Three Is a Magic Number." The feedback from that first episode was clamorously positive. Although the series had *Rock* in its name, its primary influence and musical style was jazz. No one seemed to mind or care, though, as the episodes continued to roll out. That the series was so rooted in the timeless, free-form nature of jazz played a big part in its cross-generational/crosscultural appeal and continued interest.

One reason for the popularity of the series was that it was ubiquitous, airing five times a day on Saturday and twice on Sunday. It was one of the few shows that people truly couldn't miss.

While everyone has their favorite *Schoolhouse Rock* song, with "Conjunction Junction" (1973) and "I'm Just a Bill" (1975) often topping the list in public polls, for Newall and Yohe the definitive song for the show was "Three Is a Magic Number" (1973). Bob Dorough's mournful interpretation of his own music and lyrics not only helped secure the series' production but also set the overarching tone. It was the moment when idea, concept, and talent merged perfectly.

Production on each episode lasted about three to four months, with Newall and Yohe helping where needed. As executive producers they oversaw all aspects of the show. A musician through passion and background, Newall worked with the musical elements, while Yohe stood on the design side, the two men either doing the work themselves or overseeing guest designers and musicians such as Jack Sidebotham, Rowland Wilson, Bob Eggers, Lynn Ahrens and Dave Frishberg.

Behind the Scenes

Newall has stated that the production process could have been shortened, but they took the time they needed to get things right, and that is one of the keys to the series' success.[4] There was never a rush or anything other than self-imposed stress to complete the updates. After all, this was for them a side project in reality, and the safety inherent in the knowledge of that gave them the freedom to work as they wanted to and needed to.

One reason for the popularity of *Schoolhouse Rock*, particularly when it was first aired, was that you never knew exactly what you were going to get. While there was a general thematic and overarching design link across each entry, the music styles, topic focus, and look differed from piece to piece. This, coupled by a conscious decision to not include any recurring characters, freed the thoughts of the creative team, which kept each episode unique.

So how did they do it? How did this team of non-animation professionals come to set the gold standard for utilizing animation in education? Newall put it as succinctly as anyone could: "We had good people and we stood back and let them work."[5]

> *"I don't think you realize that Schoolhouse Rock defined my generation."*
> — A Harvard student to Tom Yohe[6]

In 1976 *Schoolhouse Rock* was up for a Daytime Emmy Award (Outstanding Children's Instructional Series). Their competition —*Sesame Street* and *Mr. Rogers*— put the team in awe, and in some respects they were humbled to even have their names written down on the same piece of paper. No one expected anything more than that; after all, "Who beats *Sesame Street?*"[7] and yet when the envelope was opened, to nearly everyone's surprise (but also their pleased acclaim), Yohe and Radford Stone found themselves at the podium. Newall should have been there as well, but he had missed a few recording sessions during production, so (as a joke) Yohe had him listed in the credits as "Occasional Contributor." With the Emmy only given to officially listed "producers," Newall would have to wait until 1978, when the show won its next Emmy, to get a statue of his own. The series would pick up additional Emmys in 1979 and 1980.

Newall and Yohe had an uncanny ability to spot talent in unlikely places. They also had the rare ability to trust those instincts and let the talent go in the direction it needed to. Take the story of the "discovery" of Lynn Ahrens. She was working as a receptionist in the agency and would often bring her guitar to work to play around on during her free time. One day Newall approached her and asked if she might be interested in coming up with some songs for *Schoolhouse Rock*. Ahrens jumped at the chance for what she felt was an audition. It turns out, though, that she had been auditioning during her lunch break practice sessions all along, as the song she came up with — "The Preamble" — went straight into production. She would go on to write a number of other songs for the series including "Interplanet Janet," "Interjections!," and "Telegraph Line." (Ahrens would eventually transition to a successful career as a Broadway lyricist, eventually winning a Tony Award for her work on *Ragtime*.)

The series flourished under the rare convergence of all of the exact right talent together at the right time. It's important to remember, though, that great talent has been assembled in other endeavors, and the results have been less than stellar. What might have made this group so special was their status as animation "outsiders." They weren't ingrained in the industry and didn't know what they "could" and "couldn't" do, so they did what they wanted. As Newall explained: "We were a bunch of advertising guys, this was just something we did on the side. Tom [Yohe] used to design on the train coming to work. I would write at nights."[8] "We had good paying day jobs and didn't worry about whether or not the shows would be picked up for the next season."[9]

Given that the creative team was rooted in the advertising agency, one would expect that, particularly as the series grew in popularity and acclaim, there would have been a whiteboard hanging on the wall of an office somewhere detailing out audience surveys and popular topics all tied to a tactical strategy working toward a master marketing plan. The fact that none of this existed must have been extremely attractive to the creative participants. What they did have was a rough general theme for a season — multiplication, American history, and so on. Songwriters would go off, put some thought into topics, kick the idea around with Newall and the series educational consultant, and a topic would emerge.

Showcasing that free-flowing, organic process, Newall shared this story: "A crosstown ad agency called us up. They wanted to talk about *Schoolhouse*. So we said sure and they came over, we all got into this conference room and these guys started asking us about our formula for success. They figured the show was doing well and we must have a blueprint or formula or some A-B-C plan. I looked at them and said, 'Sure we've got a formula — it's Bob Dorough, that's your formula.'"[10] Such was the importance of the musician in the production process.

Next Steps

In 1978 Newall and Yohe decided to pursue animation as a full-time endeavor and started Newall & Yohe, Inc. David McCall, their now-former boss, warned them that *Schoolhouse Rock* was that once-in-a-lifetime experience and it would be next to impossible to capture lightning in a bottle twice. McCall, being the man that he was, agreed to allow Newall and Yohe to continue to work for and produce *Schoolhouse Rock* through their new shingle. This proved to be an immensely generous opportunity for them personally, but it was also an extremely important decision for the integrity of the show, as it kept the core creative team intact and ensured that the direction would not be altered, as would inevitably have occurred were new producers brought in.

After a few years, Newall and Yohe shuttered their company and returned to advertising as a full-time endeavor (while still leaving time to work on *Schoolhouse Rock*). At their studio they had undertaken several initiatives, the largest of which may have been *The Metric Marvels*, a series that intended to do for the metric system what *Schoolhouse Rock* did for, well, everything else. Unfortunately, the American public had a fierce backlash against the metric initiative, and the intended national conversion never took hold. It was a scenario the seasoned ad men were familiar with — with nothing to push, there was no need for a series, either, and so after just seven outings, the characters were retired. They also worked on the short-lived mixed animation/live-action series *Drawing Power*. Somewhat successful, it was awarded an Emmy in 1980 for Outstanding Achievement in Children's Programming — Graphics and Animation Design for Yohe, Paul Kim, and Lew Gifford.

By the mid–1980s *Schoolhouse Rock* was nearing the end of its course, although it continued to run on the air in reruns and sporadic new episodes. The last big push for the series came in 2009, when the old gang reunited behind *Earth Rock*, which was the latest set in the *Schoolhouse Rock* series (behind *Grammar Rock*, *Science Rock*, *America Rock*, *Multiplication Rock*, *Computer Rock*, and *Money Rock*.) Unfortunately, not everyone came back. In 1999 the inspiration behind the series, David McCall, passed away suddenly while doing charity work. Sadly the year 2000 saw the loss of another key creative member when Tom Yohe passed away at the age of 63. There was some level of continuity preserved, though, because the design responsibilities were taken over by Tom Yohe, Jr. It made perfect sense, as he was an artist himself and had watched his father design the original series at their kitchen table on weeknights after work.

You Saw It Where?

In 1993 the series made the very logical jump from the television screen to the stage. The project was the work of several lifelong fans who saw the theatrical potential in creating what is known as a "jukebox musical." What seemed like a fun idea quickly caught fire, and after winning awards and playing to sold-out houses for months, the show moved to New York. The book and music are now available for local productions, and the show averages 500 performances a year. The series always had a very delicate balance of education and entertainment. When transferred to the stage, much of the education value gets diluted, as you're caught with personalities, performances, and actor interpretations; on the other side, the entertainment value and camp curiosity go up.

From the very beginning the education community embraced the series and did their best to institute it into the classroom environment. Each episode performed a teacher's dream — it got children excited about learning, and, even better, they *actually* learned. The show had an on-staff educational consultant to ensure that their concepts were sound, but the consultant didn't try to guide the topics; they just helped keep things on track. Where at first the episodes were used as standalone teaching devices, over time teachers have developed curricula surrounding the various topics. Shared lessons on topic points, craft ideas, supplemental reading, and discussion topics are circulated and used by teachers looking to use the series both as a tool and as a way to open a larger discussion with their students.

The relationship between the *Schoolhouse Rock* production team and the educational system really reached its peak with the release of *Earth Rock* (2009). This DVD was created, in part, because Newall wanted to find a way to create "teacher friendly education."[11] The idea for the series actually had come about several years earlier, when Newall and Yohe began to outline a series of environmentally based *Schoolhouse Rock* broadcast spots. Unfortunately they could not drum up much interest, and so the project was shelved until the 2002 release of the 30th Anniversary DVD, which saw an intense outpouring of admiration for, and interest in, the original series. With those DVDs flying off of the shelves, the time seemed right to add another segment to the series, and so Newall pulled down those environmental ideas and reordered them for the new national attitude on the environment.

The Legacy

What is the legacy of *Schoolhouse Rock*? It has won awards and critical acclaim; the Museum of Television & Radio held a retrospective on the series in 1995. Its songs have been remixed and covered by independent rockers like Moby, The Lemonheads, and Buffalo Tom. Thirty years after its first episode, the series may be more popular than ever. While the accolades and attention are nice, Newall and Yohe would perhaps be happy with something simpler — that the series accomplished what it set out to do. A generation of children picked up the fundamentals of grammar and how the world works from the animated three-minute segments of *Schoolhouse Rock*, squeezed in among ABC's Saturday morning cartoon shows.

From its inception *Schoolhouse Rock* was able to use the marriage of music and animation as an educational tool in a way that had never been done before. Before the popularization of VHS recorders, the production offices were continually overrun with phone calls from schools asking for a copy of a particular episode. The most popular request was for *The Telegraph Line* (1979), which told all about the nervous system. The organizations that most frequently requested this show were medical schools. Today Newall and Dorough, along with educational consultant Dr. Odvard Dyrli, give lectures on using the series as an educational tool. When they spoke at the educational conference EduComm in 2009, they were treated like rock stars.

"Who knew?" Yohe told the *Dallas Morning News*. "We were just having fun doing it, and it had an impact on a generation."[12]

Newall and Yohe were the rarest breed of animation producers — egoless, talented, and tuned in. They started the series to see if they could solve a problem, and this, as Newall proclaims, "labor of love"[13] did just that. And so much more.

"Darn, that's the end."— Interjections!, music and lyrics by Lynn Aherns, 1974

HONORS

Yohe

Emmy Award, *Schoolhouse Rock*, Outstanding Children's Instructional Programming — Series and Specials, 1976

Emmy Award, *Drawing Power*, Outstanding Achievement in Children's Programming — Graphics and Animation Design, 1980

Newall and Yohe

Emmy Award, *Schoolhouse Rock*, Outstanding Children's Instructional Programming — Series and Specials, 1978

Emmy Award, *Schoolhouse Rock*, Outstanding Children's Instructional Programming — Series and Specials, 1979

Emmy Award, *Schoolhouse Rock*, Outstanding Children's Instructional Programming — Series and Specials, 1980

Action for Children's Television Act Award for Cartoons with a Conscience

Fifty Greatest Cartoons Ever, *TV Guide Magazine*

SAMPLE FILM SELECTION

Newall

I'm Gonna Send Your Vote to College (2002)
Report from the North Pole (2009)

Newall and Yohe

Three Is a Magic Number (1973)
My Hero, Zero (1973)
Unpack Your Adjectives (1975)
The Energy Blues (1978)
Meet Meter Man (1978)

14. The FMPU: Animating Our Way to Victory (and Education)

During World War II the entire country pulled together, and no trick was left untried in the American effort to propel the Allied forces to victory. In a shuttered silent movie studio in Hollywood, California, a group of talented and dedicated film creatives and production personnel applied their talents to the war effort. Their contribution, a film series, not only was instrumental in preparing servicemen and women for the fight ahead but also helped to inform the educational system.

This was the First Motion Picture Unit, or FMPU (1942–1945), which created a number of live-action and animated training shorts during the war. These films were played for recruits and soldiers in the field with a purpose of providing training on key techniques, themes, and attitudes. The films, particularly the animated ones, offered a mix of education and entertainment in their attempts to train.

Animated Education

The FMPU represented the first mass-scale, popular use of animation as a complement to, or supplemental tool within, the education system. Animators had previously used the medium as an informational/educational tool — in 1918 Winsor McCay recreated *The Sinking of the Lusitania*, J.R. Bray set up shop at West Point and created animated training films during World War I, and Max and Dave Fleischer spent 1923 producing *The Einstein Theory of Relativity* (1923) and *Darwin's Theory of Evolution* (1923). So what the FMPU was doing wasn't revolutionary; where they stood out, though, was in their output and influence.

The unit was started in April of 1942 when United States Army Air Force General Henry Arnold provided military commissions to Warner Brothers'

Jack Warner (as a lieutenant colonel) and producer and writer Owen Crump (as a captain). He also provided them with a very succinct mission — create training films. The two newly commissioned officers set out to find space and people. Because Hollywood was still producing entertainment during the war, the FMPU would need to find a location that was convenient to the film community but still outside so it would not disrupt the day-to-day business of movie production.

The location was easy — famed silent-film producer Hal Roach had been pressed into active military service, and when he left, he shut his studio down. Warner and Crump knew the location would be perfect, and they were able to lease it from Roach for the princely sum of a dollar a year.

Gathering talent proved to be slightly more difficult but not impossible. Working with military recruiters and draft agents, they were able to gather an impressive collection of animators, editors, writers, technicians, actors, actresses, and below-the-line staff. This commissioned group mixed with some contractors to make up the core of this new "studio."

Leading the Troops

One of their key "recruits" was Academy Award–winning director/producer Frank Capra (now adding Major to his impressive list of titles). What Capra provided was more than just an impressive knowledge of the technical side of film production; his great contribution was his innate sense of story. He understood that while some of the films being produced (particularly the live-action ones) were technical "Put tab A in slot B" productions, others (particularly the animated efforts) needed a lighter touch, and he tried to instill that throughout. These were still serious affairs, though; Martha Sigall remembers that workers in the ink-and-paint department were only allowed to have ten cels from any one film at a time, lest someone see some top-secret plans.[1]

The speed of war meant that training needed to be fast, portable, and consistent. With such a diverse audience, the training also had to be accessible; it needed to speak to the enlisted men and women in a manner that they would relate and react to. This was an important factor because 37 percent of the U.S. fighting forces had less than a high school education.

The government quickly realized that it had a secondary problem on its hands as well — they were facing what psychologists were calling a "better" form of propaganda, a more overt form. The best way to combat that, the powers that be felt, was through animation, and so Rudolph Ising was commissioned into the studio.

While the unit made a number of successful live-action and animated films, the focus here will be of course on the animated efforts. These animated shorts were not afterthoughts or relegated to B material; they were looked upon with equal importance and covered some very important subjects.

The Language of the Animated Film

> We have found that the medium of animation has become a new language. It is no longer the vaudeville world of pigs and bunnies. Nor is it the mechanical diagram, the photographed charts of the old "training film." It has encompassed the whole field of visual images, including the photograph. We have found that line, shape, color, and symbols in movement can represent the essence of an idea, can express it humorously, with force, with clarity. The method is only dependent upon the idea to be expressed. And a suitable form can be found for any idea.[2]

The use of animation as a training tool was a good one because it allowed for a consistent message to be continuously delivered, it would be more engaging and entertaining than a live speaker, it was portable, and it was commonly accepted. It also allowed for certain economies of detail because the viewing audience (all military personnel only) had literally grown up on cartoons, so the directors could take advantage of this knowledge and rely on visual shorthand when appropriate to carry ideas and or action across.

Animation, particularly hand-drawn, also allowed for the presentation of *concepts*. Where live-action film (and to an extent stop-motion animation) could cover techniques and certain skills, hand-drawn animation could explore the importance of understanding that technique or skill. For example a live-action film might explain to the viewer the importance of not spilling secrets, but the SNAFU film *Spies* (1943) could carry that idea out further and show the consequences of an action such as that; another live-action piece might explain the proper care and handling techniques for a soldier's gas mask, but the SNAFU short *Gas* (1944) illustrated the danger of a devil-may-care attitude with a gas mask (and equipment in general), showing the havoc and destruction that could be wrought.

Other films in the SNAFU series, such as *Gripes* (1943), attempted not to provide step-by-step instructions on a particular action but to propagate a sense of order and building morale and togetherness.

SNAFU

The star of the majority of the animated efforts produced by the FMPU was an everyman named Private SNAFU. (SNAFU was a popular military acronym for Situation Normal All Fxxxed Up.) SNAFU was created to be the worst soldier that ever put on a uniform. From his attitude to his actions, everything that he did was wrong, and the bulk of each picture showed both him and the audience how these bad acts could have a major impact.

What made SNAFU so popular and made his stories work so well was that he was not an idiot nor was he belligerent; he was just incompetent, portrayed as a base element, an easygoing guy who did what he needed to but time and again needed reminding about what was right. In other words, SNAFU worked as a funnel for a particular film's message because he was so relatable. This trait carried over in that the production team treated SNAFU in a way they had never handled a series character before — he got sick, he screwed things up, there were consequences, and he even died, multiple times. From 1943 through 1945 there were 26 three- to four-minute SNAFU films overseen by a stable of top directors who had honed their skills with Leon Schlesinger. The names at the top included Frank Tashlin, Chuck Jones, Friz Freleng, and Bob Clampett. The preference for one studio over another was due to a combination of enlisted "participants" and government contracts. The absence of any large number of Disney artists from the unit's rolls did not portend any direct bias. The Disney studio was essentially "overtaken" during the war and had a separate, specific set of U.S. Government contracts for other films.

It was not only Warners directors on the job, though; further evidence of the Warners influence could be found in the series entries entitled *Gas* (1944) and *Three Brothers* (1944), which featured a cameo from Bugs Bunny himself.

These directors (and co-star) were not the only "big name" talents to spend time with SNAFU. Nearly every name in the industry contributed something to the production of these films. In fact, the shorts were like mini–All Star Games. While it's great to have all of this talent together, it would have been very interesting to see what they could have created with fewer content constraints. Regardless, among the other artists working were vocal talent Mel Blanc, musical director Carl Stalling, Ben Washam, Robert Cannon, Hank Ketcham, P. D. Eastman, Bill Scott, Ken Harris, Phil Monroe, Manuel Perez, and Virgil Ross. There was also Theodor Geisel, who was one of the chief architects of the series. Of course he is better known by his pen name — Dr. Seuss.

Geisel had wanted to join the war effort and was able to parlay his background as a cartoonist for *PM Magazine* into a commission with the FMPU. Geisel fell into a strong working relationship immediately with Frank Capra, who gave the whimsical writer one piece of advice that he always referred to: "The first thing you have to do in writing, is find out if you're saying anything."[3] Geisel appreciated the opportunity to work under the storytelling master. "He taught me conciseness, and I learned a lot of juxtaposition of words and visual images."[4]

SNAFU, it can be said, had a lot of fathers, but Geisel and P.D. Eastman were two of the stronger presences, along with some spark of creation from Frank Capra. They imbued their creation with a rugged quality that attempted to portray in a realistic (if exaggerated) manner some of the greater concerns of the day. A SNAFU cartoon was permitted to have a mild amount of swearing, off-color humor, and even some slight nudity (of the cartoon variety), the thought being, if we're going to send them out into combat, we might as well give them something to smile about, too. With a locked audience consisting of military personnel only, it provided the production team an extra level of freedom in what they could and could not do.

Geisel was the primary pen behind many of the scripts for the series, and his work shows through. Familiar in many of the shorts is Geisel's rhyming patter, here taking on more abrupt, purposeful delivery. The humor in those scripts was one of the strong points of the series. The stories eschewed topical references for more schoolyard humor — the bra of a female German spy holds a tape-recording device; SNAFU, after a typically egregious error, morphs into the backside of a horse; nuts (lug nuts) fall off of a Jeep in winter; in an extreme close-up, SNAFU's bare backside and a mosquito meet friendly. It's all part of what made this series so immediately popular — "slang, irreverence, humor, and an occasional bit of titillation."[5]

Graphically, the SNAFU films look very much like other animated efforts produced during this time, although they tend to have a strong Warner Brothers flavoring. Continuing on the theme of making SNAFU a relatable character, the stories take place in every location where a soldier might be — Africa, Europe, the Pacific front, bases on U.S. soil.

In many of the films, SNAFU is guided by the Technical Fairy First Class, a gruff, built, cigar-chomping, five-inch-tall, winged fairy. Full of magic and direction, the Technical Fairy acts as the figure of reason and authority and, in some cases, oracle, such as in the 1943 short *Gripes*, where the Technical Fairy shows SNAFU "what might be" if he didn't have around him all of those things he so hotly complains about.

The FMPU production teams worked in close harmony with U.S. Military staff to ensure accuracy of the subject at hand. By the end of the run, the two groups were in perfect symbiotic form — So much so that a film called *Coming Home* (1945) had to be shelved because it dealt with the use of an American secret weapon that bore an eerie resemblance to the soon-to-be-released atomic bomb.

The SNAFU films were great peer-to-peer communication tools. They had these young male animators speaking (through the films) to a young, primarily male armed forces audience. They knew what the others wanted to hear and see and found ways to speak in that language.

The SNAFU shorts played at the end of a weekly bill known as the Army-Navy Screen Magazine. The placement there was practical, as often there would be sustained cries to rewind the film and show it again, and tactical: "Their place at the end, serves to lock in the meaning of any one film bill. That is, the SNAFU cartoons act as a sort of ideological exclamation point to many of these collections."[6]

The films were extremely popular because they were entertaining. Viewers learned without being hit over the head and being told to "learn!" They were also professionally produced, which made a stark difference in their acceptance and the lasting value. As animation historian Jerry Beck said, "These had all of the bells and whistles of a standard Looney Tunes cartoon."[7]

The SNAFU films worked on multiple levels; they didn't just teach their lessons but also promoted, subtly, the basic tenants of Army life — hierarchy, discipline, structure. This may have been one of their biggest benefits because SNAFU was able to teach intangible but very vital skills. And he could do so for an estimated four million uniformed viewers a week.

> Thus, the Private Snafu cartoons ... not only incised indoctrinational and informational material but attempted to excise any attachments the soldier might have that could impair his single-minded attention to fighting and winning the war. The informational success of the series may be judged ... by the length and regularity of the series. And the army must have felt that the Snafu series also was serving its indoctrinational purposes, because a new Snafu cartoon appeared about once a month until the end of the war.[8]

Other "Teachers"

While SNAFU may have been the most popular character, he was not the only one at the unit's disposal. Seaman Hook did for the Navy what SNAFU did for the Army. Hook, created by Hank Ketcham (who would eventually also sire *Dennis the Menace*), was a sort of SNAFU-lite, and his films, some of which were directed by Robert McKimson, lacked the vibrant energy of his Army counterpart. Hook also suffered from a lack of a strong design. Where SNAFU has a leaner, more general appearance, Hook is squat with an over-exaggerated pug nose. It's hard to know why that particular design choice was made. What we do know is the effect, which is rather off-putting.

Yehudi was another character who showed up in separate films. A chameleon, he attempted to extol the virtue of proper camouflage techniques.

A huge problem the Air Force faced was with pilots "flat-hatting," or essentially buzzing people on the ground. On top of the fact that it scared people to death, several pilots were lost. In order to combat this practice, in 1944 FMPU created an animated short called *Flat-Hatting*. Directed by John Hubley, the film proved to have a near-immediate effect in almost stopping the practice by pilots.

The FMPU also proved to be an important outlet for the work of Ray Harryhausen, who would go on to widespread acclaim for his stop-motion animation work in films such as *Clash of the Titans* (1981), *Jason and the Argonauts* (1963) and *The Golden Voyage of Sinbad* (1974). During the war his talents were used in training films to animate equipment that was not readily available to be filmed with a live-action camera.

After the war, Harryhausen took what he learned and put it into a series of shorts depicting popular fairy tales. Following the war more and more schools started to adopt 16mm films as a viable teaching tool. Harryhausen saw an opportunity here, and so he started to solicit local schools to discover what types of films might best suit their curriculum. The overwhelming cry was for shorts that could help associate words with actions, and this spurred him into creating *The Storybook Review* (1946), *Little Red Riding Hood* (1949), *Rapunzel* (1951), *Hansel and Gretel* (1951) (TV), and *The Story of King Midas* (1953).

The animated output of the FMPU was widely popular and very effective. "The reaction to the animated 'Snafu series' was greater than the reaction to any of the live-action films. The Air Forces Psychological Test Film Unit undertook a study of how much was learned through use of an animated training film as compared with how much through oral and written instruction on the same subject matter. The superiority of the film, both for learning and retention, was particularly clear *when full use was made of the unique possibilities inherent in the medium.*"[9]

The War Is Over

During its short existence, the FMPU produced more film footage than any other Hollywood studio during the same time period. The influence of the animation created here had lasting effects in a number of areas.

While people in the animation industry would move from studio to studio in their civilian life, this was the first time that a large number of people from the industry were mixed together. It gave people a chance to exchange ideas, share theories, and develop like-minded associations. The friendships developed at the FMPU would directly affect later collaborations at studios such as UPA.

Some of the stylistic techniques used in these films, such as the limited backgrounds in *Flat-Hatting*, could be seen as a trial run for the later run of graphic stylization and "limited animation" movement of the 1950s. An additional contribution can be seen in the visual sparseness of the shorts, which could have been deemed an artistic necessity. In order not to complicate the message being given, the animators kept the action on screen to only the basics and then found ways to play creatively within that space.

Animation was popularized and accepted as a viable educational outlet. The films of the FMPU provided many men and women with their first broad exposure to education through animation. Because of the quality and effectiveness of the shorts, it is only natural that these soldiers, when becoming civilians, would look again to this format as an effective way to teach and be taught.

The animated classroom filmstrips of the 1950s, *Sesame Street*'s animated segments in the 1960s, *Schoolhouse Rock* in the 1970s, the animated afterschool specials of the 1980s, and the computer-based animated training from the 1990s through the present all owe some part of their origins to the output of the FMPU.

SAMPLE FILM SELECTION

The Good Egg (1945)
Hot Spot (1945)
The Return of Mr. Hook (1945)
Three Brothers (1944)
Censored (1944)
Gas (1944)
Booby Traps (1944)
The Goldbrick (1943)
Spies (1943)
Gripes (1943)

THE STORYTELLERS

15. Joe Grant: The Constant

I've never seen an artist whose work is as fresh,
as exciting, and as invigorating.[1]

Joe Grant's (5/15/08–5/6/2005) story is one of determination, longevity, artistic confidence, loyalty, studio politics, influence and forgiveness. Grant would be notable alone for the span of his involvement within the industry, but there is a greater importance to his story. What's key about Grant is what he was able to do during that time. Grant was handpicked by Walt Disney and from that beginning rose to a position of unparalleled power, influencing the direction of the most influential animation studio in the world and, in a way, animation art as a whole.

To really understand Joe Grant and his importance to the animation industry, we can start in the middle of his story, for it is here where he unguardedly lets his pure passion for his work come through. Up until this point Grant was often viewed as a heady artist and calculating businessman, but this display of pure emotion helps to frame those two competing opinions and see what was truly driving him during this period. After a meteorically successful career at Disney, Grant was on his way out. The choice to leave was his, and yet one gets the feeling that he didn't really want to leave. His resignation letter is coated in disillusionment but carries passion and bares the artistic rage still burning inside of him.

> Goodbye to Pixie Land—
> Some of the pixies, in a fit of mournfulness, have laid the hands of violence upon themselves. Some laughed themselves to death with broken hearts. Some perished of pernicious ennui. Many fled in time. Others were expelled, kicked out by the royal boot. Some stayed on to the end and watched the slow disintegration of a fabulous and phony fairyland. I am one of the latter.[2]

It's a striking letter to read, as you can hear not the aggrievements of a bitter employee but the dripping heartbreak of a man whose dream was taken and who had played a part in its own death. What is it that drives a man to such soul-crushing despair, and how do you rise from that?

How It Began

Joe Grant was a happily employed newspaper cartoonist for the *Los Angeles Record* when he got "The Call" out of the blue one Monday. Walt Disney wanted to see him. Disney was working on a Mickey Mouse short —*Mickey's Gala Premier* (1933). He had seen the caricatures that Grant had drawn in the paper of Hollywood stars, and Walt wanted Grant to come do the same for him. Grant, a former child actor, visited the studio and was smitten. He was a well educated, well read, versed in the world artist, and the opportunity to be in this type of creative environment spoke deeply to him. "I was enthusiastic as Hell about that business. I thought it was the greatest thing! I couldn't think of anything beyond it…. I had fallen in love with the idea."[3]

Grant came onboard and immediately offered caricature designs for the film. Joining Mickey was a veritable who's who of 1930s Hollywood including Wallace Beery, Marie Dressler, Ethel Barrymore, John Barrymore, Lionel Barrymore, Laurel and Hardy, The Marx Brothers, Maurice Chevalier, Eddie Cantor, Jimmy Durante, Jean Harlow, Joan Crawford, Bette Davis, John Gilbert, Sid Graumann, Edward G. Robinson, William Powell, Monty Hale, Rudy Vallee, Adolphe Menjou, Janet Gaynor, Buster Keaton, Douglas Fairbanks, Joe E. Brown, Greta Garbo, Charlie Chaplin, Clark Gable, Mae West, Harold Lloyd, and Marlene Dietrich. With the success of those caricatures, he was asked to take on additional responsibilities including writing (with newly assigned partner William Cottrell) scripts for the shorts *Pluto's Judgment Day* (1935), *Who Killed Cock Robin* (1935), and the winner of the 1935 Academy Award for Best Short Subject, Cartoons, *Three Orphan Kittens*. Separately Grant started to teach caricature classes, at Walt's behest, to any interested artists through the Chouinard Art Institute.

The Grant/Cottrell partnership was a rising success when Walt broke the team up. He did offer Grant, as a sort of "consolation prize," the opportunity to work on the designs for the Wicked Queen in the feature currently under development —*Snow White and the Seven Dwarves* (1937). This allowed Grant to revisit his caricature studies, and he went at the assignment with abandon. The result was a terrifying creation who exuded pure fear yet in an elegant way. A key part of the character is the transformation of the Queen into the old woman, an idea that Grant took from observing an aged neighbor picking apples. This real-world grounding only served to make the character even more frightening.

This was typical of what Grant brought to the creative process. With his real-world experiences and art history understanding, he was able to effortlessly draw on a number of outside influences to shape his work. While he was most certainly not the only one at the studio during this time calling on an understanding of the works of Paolo Veronese, he was the one with the highest-profile results in doing so. Grant was incredibly ambitious and confident enough to believe that he could meet the high goals he had in mind for himself. While working on his assigned duties, he often had ideas that he lacked time to explore or that needed a different form of expression. Rather than file those away, he would go home and work them out with colored pastels and then bring them back to the studio for discussion. There was a brashness in this, for sure, but one can also see a clever calculation, as, sure enough, other artists started to follow suit. What this proceeded to do was create a particular mindset around the studio and set Grant at the center.

Grant's Influence Grows

Following the success of *Snow White*, Walt found another use for Grant's prodigious talents and asked him to head the newly created Character Modeling Department. This elite group would be responsible for the Disney style, as they were charged with story research and development along with designing model sheets. This became an intensely unique and powerful position, for every other animation studio was working to match or counter what was being created at Disney. Any deviation by Grant and his group would send ripple effects throughout the industry, so in many ways Grant was not just overseeing the house style of the studio but influencing an entire industry.

This was a position that Walt had been eyeing Grant for as far back as 1935. According to internal memos when discussing the addition of adding a layer in the animation process that would focus solely on character design, he stated, "I think we should utilize the talents of Joe Grant."[4]

Disney was contemplating the need for a new department within the studio that could keep watch on the disparate projects floating around. It was a role Grant would later successfully fill.

> *"Grant brought articulate erudition and visual sophistication to the studio."*
> — Robin Allan[5]

The work being done by Grant's team was far reaching. They were not just designing characters (as if that is an easy thing to do on its own); they were also enhancing the story ideas those characters would be part of. "We write graphically," Joe Grant has said. "The first steps are to get the big things.... We try with writers to get a story line strong enough to hang gags and ideas on. That's the principle."[6]

To ensure the high level of consistency and artistic expression now expected from the department, before any model sheet could leave the department it had to be given the stamp "OK, J.G." It was the symbolic Touch of God that for some ensured artistic integrity, but others would come to resent those four letters.

After the department had been up and running for a while, Grant found a way to expand their reach further. He got Walt to see the benefit in having three-dimensional models of the characters and even some key props. These plaster castings would help animators by providing them with a comprehensive view of their character and help to instill an additional level of realism into the work. Charles Cristondoro, Ted Kline, Duke Russell, and Lorna Soderstrom were all brought in at Grant's bequest to begin sculpting models.

Grant saw himself somewhat outside of the day-to-day studio processes. He was, in his mind at least, an instigator — "The drawings I make are not storyboard drawings, they are *inspirational* drawings."[7] Even when Grant was charged with the development of a more traditional story outline, he went about the project in a sideways, teasing manner. Starting in 1939 Grant and Dick Huemer worked on the development of *Dumbo*. The idea for the story had existed in the form of a very short print story, and it was thought that it might make an interesting short film, but as Grant and Huemer worked on it, it became apparent that there was more there than initially thought. (They wouldn't need that much more time, though, as the finished film came in at just 64 minutes in length, making it one of the shortest features the studio ever produced.) Grant and Huemer worked through the story elements, but then, instead of holding a traditional storyboard session, they parsed the story out to Walt bit by bit, day by day (they would eventually have an initial 102-page script). They knew that this Dickensian technique would be a way to keep Walt, who was increasingly being pulled in different directions, focused and make him more invested in the story. Instead of just providing page details every day, they even went so far as to frame the chapters in a large storytelling context. For example one "episode" of the treatment began, "Dear Reader, if you are at all fainthearted, or impressionable, we earnestly advise you to stop right here. Read no further! Do something else! Go to the movies — or to bed — anything; but skip the rest of this chapter."[8]

At the time that they were writing the script, the studio was in the throes of a serious internal discourse on labor relations and unionization that would culminate in a heated walkout and strike in May of 1941. Grant and Huemer sided with the studio and placed their feelings into the *Dumbo* script by caricaturing some of the strikers as the drunken clowns in the picture who grumble about the boss and then storm off to demand a raise.

While an underlying effect of this was to maintain a level of control, and certainly some level of "studio" power, the stated reasoning for delivering the story in this manner was to build excitement and anticipation. The end result of this exercise was seeing their story make it to the screen, and so one is left to wonder why they didn't try this exercise with future scripts. The answer could be that Grant was always looking for a way to innovate artistically, and perhaps he felt that "repeating himself" would be to go against his ideals.

Partners

Huemer and Grant worked well together, perhaps seeing in the other a kindred spirit of the world. It didn't take them long to become partners in the truest sense of the word. A gag sketch from this time shows one head made up of half of Grant's face and half of Huemer's. It was both a humorous manifestation of a solid working relationship and the show of solidarity of artistic thought. Prior to their work on *Dumbo* they offered assistance of a different sort on *Fantasia* (1940). The two were instrumental in the development of the film, as they were responsible for selecting the songs and helping to streamline concepts. To prepare for this Grant and Huemer accompanied Walt and conductor Leopold Stokowski on a retreat to discuss musical themes for the film. Upon their return, Grant and Huemer locked themselves in a room and listened to records over and over again. They had to find pieces that fit stylistically within the broader film, that were musically interesting, and that had a certain visual component to them. They would make selections and take them to Walt and Stokowski to analyze and discuss, and on the process went. The final playlist is heavy on popular composers (perhaps a subconscious attempt to make the film feel more accessible to certain audience types) including Beethoven (*Symphony No. 6 in F, Op.68 "Pastorale"*); Stravinsky (*The Rite of Spring*); Tchaikovsky (*Nutcracker Suite Op. 71a*); Bach (*Toccata and Fugue in D Minor*); and Schubert (*Ave Maria*). Works by Dukas, Mussorgsky, and Ponchielle rounded out the bill.

Grant and Huemer would continue working together to shape a wide variety of films for the studio. They placed Donald up against the Nazis in *Der Fuehrer's Face* (1942); helped to frame the South American based, friendship-baiting, cultural education and celebration film *Saludos Amigos* (1942); and returned to Donald to showcase the ease and importance of the income-tax process in *The New Spirit* (1942), which was commissioned by the U.S. Treasury Department. On the feature side, they were part of a team that attempted to bring some order to *Alice in Wonderland* (1951).

While people saw in Grant and Huemer a productive, creative friendship, there was another friendship that would cause Grant more trouble. Through the back and forth of the creative discussions, Grant and Walt built up a strong friendship that allowed Grant to control his projected studio persona and helped his department to achieve a high level of independence.

As might be expected, not everyone looked upon Grant as the answer to everything. The animators working straight on films didn't like that they were given quotas they had to meet on a daily basis while the artists in Grant's department worked under a much more relaxed atmosphere. They could work at their own pace, do research, discuss ideas, and be more of the true ideal of an artist. Perhaps even more than that, though, they resented the Grant/Walt relationship. Grant and Walt had developed an easy rapport (one that was not repeated by many); they often sat in Walt's office after hours having drinks and discussing the news of the day. It was a somewhat odd pairing — the driven studio chief and the idealistic artist — but there was a connection between the two men. Perhaps each saw in the other an alternative version of himself. Regardless, their connection was particularly evident during story meetings, when Walt would call on Grant for an opinion or, more often the case, Grant would produce a "surprise" drawing or sketch or idea at a key moment in the discussion. The effect of this gave Grant greater leverage in the discussion at hand, but it disheartened the artists and storymen whose session was essentially hijacked. Through this Grant was seen as opportunistic, power hungry, Machiavellian. What were his true motivations, though? It's a question not easily answered. Did he aspire to succeed Walt? He already had nearly unfettered artistic control throughout the studio; he had to have known that he would have lost that if he was running the day-to-day operations. Was it that he saw in Walt a way to better connect with the objects, people, and places that he had only read about? More than likely he had an honest friend-ship with a man whom he considered an "equal." Perhaps a clue can be found with Grant, who said he felt that Walt saw in the model department a room of kindred souls. "He was part of it," Grant said of Walt. "He wasn't an ani-mator, he was an idea man, and a storyman."[9]

It was around this time that Grant came up with the idea for what would become *Lady and the Tramp* (1955). He had been watching his wife's cocker spaniel and started to formulate the story; unfortunately for him he would not see it come to total fruition.

The Sad Middle Section

The friendship between Walt and Grant would be strained in 1941 when the great labor strike ran through the Disney Studio. Walt was particularly stung by the actions of the strikers, many of whom had been loyal employees. He always had this ideal that the studio was one large family, and now he didn't know whom he could really trust. Once the strike started, nothing would ever be the same at the studio.

Following the strike, World War II, the headway being made in live-action films and on television, and with the plans for Disneyland pushing forward, the Character Model Department was disbanded. Grant hung around for a few years more, but in 1949 the situation had deteriorated to such a point that he walked away. The exact cause of his departure has been wildly speculated on as being a fight with Walt, but perhaps the reason isn't as important as what he did when he left. What is immensely fascinating is that although he harbored ill feelings toward the studio, he didn't leave and go somewhere else. A lesser man might have moved across town somewhere with the vindictive desire to get a job at a rival studio and "show Disney a thing or two." This was not how Grant operated. Whatever his feelings, wherever his anger was directed, he didn't let it get the best of him; he simply walked away. Now a counter-argument could be made that this was in some ways a worse decision because it deprived audiences and the industry of his gifted talents. His decision, though, like all of Grant's decisions, was well calculated. When deciding to leave I think he surveyed the industry landscape, reviewed his own interests, and found that an exit would be a better option than hanging on too long.

If the story were to end here, it would be bittersweet, like the breakup of two people you know belong together who just can't make it work anymore. Thankfully Hollywood loves a second act, although this one doesn't start for 40 years.

Grant left the Disney, and for all intents and purposes he retired from filmmaking. He took up with his wife in her pottery business and was, by all accounts, happy with his new life and got his fill of the animation game from old friends who had stayed active.

The Happy Next Chapter

In 1989, one of these friends — Jack Kinney — asked Grant to sit in on a meeting with Charlie Fink, who was Disney Feature Animation's Vice President of Creative Affairs. Charlie was looking for some fresh ideas and thought it would be interesting to get the opinions of some who were there at the beginning.

Fink was more than impressed with Grant, and upon returning to the studio searched for a way to bring him in on a permanent basis. A short time later, Grant got the call — would he come back? It was a daunting question: the industry had changed, the culture had changed, all of the players had changed. But Grant understood that the basics he dealt with when he first started at the studio in 1933 were still the core values being followed — story, character relationships, character design — and so he packed up his pencils and drawing pads and headed back to Disney. There is also the question, though, of how a man who so sadly left would be able to return. Was it that enough time had passed; was it that the key players had changed; or was it simply the youthful wish of an aging man to matter again?

Whatever his internal motive, Joe Grant was back. His return provided an unprecedented level of continuity, as here was the artist who helped select the songs for *Fantasia*, actively participating in a story meeting on a computer-generated feature. He would be quick to state, though, that really not that much was different from when he first walked through the doors.

"What's the real difference between 1940 and today?" Grant reflected rhetorically. "Ah, much is the same. Same deadlines, same politics, people drew better back then."[10]

Among some of Grant's contributions during his second stint at the studio include the ideas for Abu in *Aladdin*; Mrs. Potts in *Beauty and the Beast*; and Meeko in *Pocohontas*. He also worked with the relationships within *The Lion King* and helped to christen the film *Monsters, Inc* (2001). The director of that film, Pete Docter, developed a strong relationship with Grant, which ended up influencing the character of Carl in *Up* (2009). Grant also was provided with an opportunity to develop several of his own concepts, one of which, *Lorenzo* (1994), was nominated and won an Annie Award for Best Animated Short Subject.

Perhaps the most interesting project that Grant took part in was *Fantasia 2000*. Working on the development of this piece really helped to close the loop on a career that had come full circle. This film retains the *Sorcerer's Apprentice* segment of the original feature, which Grant worked on, and it features a new sequence based on a story by Grant. Set to *The Carnival of the Animals*, "Finale," by Camille Saint-Saëns, the viewer finds a battle of conformity between six strait-laced flamingos and one that just wants to play with his yo-yo. It's a funny concept and is executed perfectly with a great sense of pace by director Eric Goldberg.

To say that Joe Grant loved what he did would be an understatement, so it is somewhat comforting to know that he did it until the end, as he passed away at his drawing desk, pencil in hand, on May 6, 2005.

"My personal belief is it's not the destination, it's the journey," Joe Grant once said.[11]

That's a phrase that you hear often, especially from creative individuals. In fact it runs the risk of cliché, but in Grant's case it's hard not to argue that there is a strong amount of truth in that. One of the great legacies of Grant's career, particularly during his first term at Disney, was this inclusion of a creative process in story and character development. The encouragement to look to other disciplines, to have a broader experimentation period, to explore art theory and find ways to use it were all incubated in the Character Modeling Department. Of course those are ideal situations, and even during his time at the studio that process didn't last completely in its most idealized state. They did, though, carry on in the mindset of artists, writers, directors, and producers who would continue with the processes, carry them on, adapt with them, pass them on.

Unlike many artists, Joe Grant's career cannot by summarized in any one particular film. We can't point to any specific style of filmmaking and peg it to Grant, nor can we capture his overall contribution through his words. This is because Grant's role in the history of animation was much more broadly woven. Perhaps above all else, Grant was the great influencer. His ideas and decisions shaped the artistic mindsets at the most influential animated film studio in the world. As others based their work on Disney's output, they were unknowingly providing a response to the artistic proclivities of Joe Grant.

Joe's decision to leave the studio and then later return sets a benchmark for employee dedication (in any field) and helped to put some historical weight behind a bevy of modern-age films. His return also helped, along with the studio's separate reconciliation with strike leader Art Babbitt, to repair some great cosmic rift caused by the labor issues of 1941.

Across his entire career with Disney, Joe Grant showed that creativity knows no bounds.

HONORS

The Walt Disney Company, Disney Legend, 1992
National Cartoonists Society, Rueben Award, 1996

SAMPLE FILM LIST

Mickey's Gala Premier (1933)
Fantasia (1940)
Dumbo (1941)
Lady and the Tramp (1955)
Mulan (1998)
Lorenzo (2004)

16. Bill Scott: Writer and Moose Advocate

"Bill Scott was probably the most all-around gifted story man that animation has ever produced."

— Bill Hurtz[1]

Writer, producer, animator, vocal talent — the animation world has rarely seen someone like Bill Scott (8/2/20–11/29/85), whose work has provided entertainment and inspiration for generations of television viewers. Many artists and entertainers sustain a few years of creative output under the public's watchful eye before they burn out or simply run dry, but Bill Scott was one of those remarkable talents who, across a 40-year career, hit it out of the park nearly every time he was up.

The key to Scott's success was something that at first doesn't even make sense — in a visual medium Scott saw things in *words*. His gift was to inherently understand the story being told. It sounds simple, to be sure, but when you stop to think about how many hours have been wasted on poor animation, on things that look great but have no emotional link within the story *or* no story at all, you realize that Scott's gift is a special one. Across his career, he also had an uncanny populist sensibility — he was hard-wired into the popular American temperament. Not only that, but he was also able to channel this knowledge into creating better work and, in a cyclical turn, using that work to direct the sentiment of the culture.

For all of his talent and influence, though, Scott may have wanted most to be remembered as someone who made us laugh. Scott's legacy comes as much from the way that he made us smile as from his effect in refocusing animation toward a cerebral, cohesive and engaging expanded narrative.

The Path of the Writer or *Pen the Beginning*

To fully understand and appreciate Scott's impact on the animation community, one has to understand the role of the writer in this medium historically. At the risk of not giving this important topic enough attention, we'll place a "Cliffs Notes" history here.

In the beginning, no one "wrote" a cartoon. Sure they had something resembling a story, but more often than not it was just a loose plot structure onto which gags could be hung. In fact writers were first known as "Gag Men," as their primary responsibility was in creating jokes for a short. (Writers were not the only ones on the low end; at this point the animation production structure was such that only a select few key parties would receive any on-screen credits.) These gag men were just tools at the directors' disposal. Animators knew where they were starting and where they had to end and they plowed through between the two points. Only occasionally would they turn to others for a joke or idea. It didn't take long for the animators to discover who in the office had the best gags, and they increasingly relied on them to provide comedic support. These gag men contributed more and more, and soon they were creating whole stories. As their function changed, so did their title, to "Story by..." and eventually "Story Man." Scott despised the way he and his peers were viewed. Writer-producer John Cawley remembers how proud Scott was of his work: "Bill disliked the terms 'gag man' and 'story man.'" He says, "Having written for theatrical cartoons, as well as the Jay Ward shows, Bill was adamant that he had been a writer. 'We created stories, characters and dialogue,' he would tell me."[2]

This is not to imply that there were no writers of note during this time. People like Michael Maltese and Tedd Pierce were pushing the field in terms of story structure and a writer's involvement in an animation unit. But for there to be a full-scale shift in respect and importance, something, or someone, more was needed.

Where Did You Come From? or *The Bill Is Healthia Story*

Bill Scott had the textbook, inauspicious beginning. Born in Philadelphia in 1920, his family moved to New York when he was five. It was here that he discovered the movies and, in doing so, sealed his future. He was immediately overcome by the allure of the silver screen; the cartoons particularly enraptured him. (The first cartoon he recalled seeing was a *Felix the Cat* short.)[3] Whenever he could scrape the money together he would head to the theater, not caring what was playing, just wanting to see *something*, wanting to be transported.

As he watched everything he could, he began to hone his tastes. Soon he was making decisions on what feature to see based on what cartoons were playing with it. While many considered the animated shorts a side attraction, to him they were the main event. He wouldn't just watch them, though; Scott studied them with a particular reverence, paying close attention to how they were constructed, listening intently to audience reactions, gauging what was and wasn't working. He would even memorize the names of everyone who brought those pictures to life.

Scott spent a great deal of his time in the dark, but it didn't stop him from making friends. In fact he ended up in a valuable friendship with a boy who even out-geeked him — a kid who was so deep into animation that he rigged up a small "studio" in his garage. Scott was ecstatic; now he could take the step from casual fan to participant in the process. The friends labored long and hard; the works they created were rudimentary at best, but they gave Scott a chance to get his hands dirty. Eventually he took some of these films around town to the various local theaters in an attempt to drum up some actual work. Even at this early age Scott showed promise, and several of the theaters hired him to produce title cards. It was uneventful work (creating new ways to say "please be quiet"), but he was happy to be working and, in some way, "in the business."

While Scott continued this work as he went into college, he considered it a temporary occupation and prepared to move into a "respectable" career. Following graduation this meant teaching English and Drama. Scott would later recall this time and the importance it had on his career development: "Join a drama group. Be in a play. Get up on stage. Get in front of an audience. Say something. Do something. Feel what they give you back. Watch them watch you, as I'm watching you watch me. Know at what point you're reaching and at what point you're not reaching people. It's invaluable.... I count every moment I spent in drama classes and in production classes and in public speaking classes as a boon."[4]

Scott was the type of person who threw himself completely into his work. With his personality and drive, he might have gone on to an illustrious career as a teacher had it not been for Adolf Hitler.

You're in the Army Now, or *The Lion, the Witch and the War, Dope*

In 1942 Bill Scott, like many young men, signed up for service in the Army. Through a series of happy coincidences, he found himself assigned to the FMPU — First Motion Picture Unit. The Army (wisely) decided to take full advantage of the large numbers of movie stars, producers, directors, technical personal and production artists who joined during this time. They placed these people in the FMPU, where their directive was to make training and promotional films. One of the units in the building was animation focused.

Scott could not believe his luck; he was now walking the same halls as the men whose names he had memorized as he sat in the theater every Saturday morning.

Determined to seize this opportunity, Scott mustered everything he had and approached his commander, to whom he spun story after story about how he was an animation artist (greatly exaggerating the size and importance of the garage studio he came from). Eventually through talk and perseverance, he got re-assigned to the Animation Division. The group of veterans in the unit saw in Scott another starry-eyed kid and set about to put him in his place by giving him the absolute lowest job possible in animation — cel washer. Scott was not to be derailed, though, and he applied himself fully. Scott quickly progressed through the ranks until he landed in the production department, where he was charged with writing story treatments. At the end of the war he may not have become the perfect soldier, but he had been tutored in the art of animation.

Creating a Career or *Great Scott!*

Now that he had spent some time "in the business," Scott decided to try and make a living in animation, so after the war he called on some of his FMPU friends and applied for a position at Warner Brothers. And so it was that in 1946 he came to fulfill his dream, working in a full-fledged animation studio.

There he would be under the watchful eyes of writers Michael Maltese and Tedd Pierce. Each brought a strong sense of story and an irreverent style of humor to their work, and Scott absorbed all of it. While at Warners, Scott wrote the story or script for a number of shorts including: *Doggone Cats* (1947), *What Makes Daffy Duck* (1948), *Bone Sweet Bone* (1948), *The Stupor Salesman* (1948), *Riff Raffy Daffy* (1948), *Two Gophers from Texas* (1948) and *Bowery Bugs* (1949).

Scott's stint at Warner Brothers was short, and after leaving, he set up space at Ajax Studios. It was during this time that he reconnected with another former Warner Brothers veteran — Bob Clampett, who was producing a daily 15-minute puppet show called *Time for Beany. Beany* was a topical, smart series that spoke to audiences on a variety of levels. The show was a critical and cultural smash and quickly moved from being broadcast solely in L.A. to hitting televisions across the country. It had a passionate, diverse fanbase including Groucho Marx and Albert Einstein. The satire-driven stories had a fresh, anything-goes feeling; their tempo was quick, the humor across the board, and the characters accessible. Much of this could be credited to Scott's writing.

In 1950 Scott took his collected knowledge to United Productions of America (UPA) studios. At this time UPA was producing fairly standard theatrical shorts for Columbia but was pushing to do more. The year that Scott got there, they found the story they had been waiting for when a fellow former FMPU member, Theodor Geisel, came calling with a story he felt would make an ideal animated short. Geisel, better known as Dr. Seuss, had just written *Gerald McBoing Boing*—the story of a boy who only speaks in sounds. Scott and Phil Eastman (who would later, as P.D. Eastman, become a famous author of children's books himself) teamed up to transform this book into a script.

The resulting short was a seven-minute animated revolution. Its innovative use of stylized design and limited animation, the perfect integration of sound effects and its unique and tender story combined into something completely new. Each of the pieces was put together with an artist's eye and driven by an understanding of the prevailing popular culture sentiment. The short was a critical, cultural, and industry (it won the Academy Award for best animated short) success and proved that the public was not only accepting of new forms of animation but also craving it, and suddenly every other animation studio found themselves scrambling to meet this new style. For their part, UPA continued to experiment with the medium and in turn continued to soar to new heights.

Many look at UPA and consider it a graphical revolution, but really, without their strength in story the reliance on strong designs would hold interest for a picture or two but would lose appeal over time. The UPA writers understood that long-winded expositions and speeches would grate against the smooth and sparse imagery on the screen. Rather, writers had to distill their stories and keep things tight and economical. If there was anything that Scott learned during this time, it was the importance of word choice: "Why use four words when one word will do?"

Scott continued his innovative story work at UPA contributing scripts for the groundbreaking shorts *Rooty Toot Toot* (1951) and *The Tell Tale Heart* (1953) before moving on to John Sutherland Productions, where he worked on commercials and industrial films. In 1956 Scott returned to UPA "by special invitation" to work on *The Boing Boing Show*, featuring the televised exploits of Gerald McBoing Boing. As he would later recount, the studio was so focused on getting the look and feel of the series just right that they forgot the humor that made people love the original story, so he was brought in to liven up the scripts where he could.

Throughout his career Scott was a strong proponent for artists' rights, his view perhaps skewed by the circumstances surrounding the Disney strike. He was very active in the Screen Cartoonists Guild (SCG) and in 1952 was named president (he would also later serve as business agent). While guild president, Scott helped the SCG remain a viable union alternative for the next several years. Unfortunately he would face his own series of problems when he would be forced out of UPA in 1952 during the crackdown of the House Un-American Activities Committee (HUAC) as it swept through Hollywood.

He spent his "free" time working as a freelance writer, where he began to carve out quite a niche for himself with television commercials because he could work "anonymously," outside of the prying eyes of HUAC. It looked as if that was going to be the next step in his career until he found himself in a meeting with Jay Ward.

Squirrel and Moose *or* Friendly Flier

In 1958 Jay Ward was one of the new pioneers in animation. A real estate salesman by trade, he had an innate understanding of animation and a belief in how it could most effectively be utilized in television. He backed up his ideas by producing *Crusader Rabbit,* the first animated program expressly made for television. Although it was popular, thanks to some questionable legal dealings, the show and Ward (against his wishes) were no longer together.[5] Ward eased the pain of losing his baby by turning his attentions to the creation of something new. After a few months of design and deliberation, Ward had created (with Alex Anderson) several characters for a program that never took off. While most were rather stock, there were a couple that he felt could be pretty special, especially in the right hands. Those hands turned out to belong to Bill Scott.

Ward needed someone who could take these initial character sketches and story ideas and tighten them into a show. When they met over lunch to discuss the work, Ward and Scott hit it off famously. Looking back, it's hard to imagine that they could not. Their personalities and philosophies fit as well as a married couple celebrating their 60th anniversary. They complemented each other's strengths and covered each other's weaknesses.

Scott and Ward agreed to work together to bring to life a happy-go-lucky moose named Bullwinkle and his gung-ho friend, a flying squirrel named Rocky. The goal that Ward and Scott set for themselves was to create first and foremost a program that would make *them* laugh, something that their friends would enjoy. If anyone else liked it, that would be gravy. They could have had no idea that from 1959 to 1964 they would run one of the most popular and influential shows in television history. The various series starring Bullwinkle and Rocky transcended animation; their appeal was universal, as was their influence.

Although there were many talented individuals collaborating on these programs, it can be argued that it was really Scott's show. Bill Scott is one of the very few mainstream animation artists to so fully impact a project. He wrote the scripts, which set the tone for the series; provided numerous voices; and was the show's producer, which allowed him to further set the style; plus he was a financial partner.

It's not just animation; over the history of television, there had been other strong personalities who have guided a program in one way or another, but there have been few who have so assuredly and with such talent worked from so many positions to create such a critically and commercially popular and influential series.

Vocal Star

As Scott and Ward were still working out the specifics of the show, Scott would write sample scripts to illustrate how things might play out. Because his scripts were so heavily verbal, Scott decided that the best way to present these to Ward was to act them out in character. Ward loved it so much that he asked Scott to read the parts in character during auditions for the cast. They finally reached a point where all of the major voices had been cast except for Bullwinkle. Scott asked Ward if he had anyone in mind for the part, to which Ward replied, "I thought you were going to do it." Scott went for it and was now not only writing the show, but also playing the lead. This was a writer's dream come true — being able to write what you want and not have to worry about an actor misinterpreting it and mangling the lines. Scott's vocal work is engaging, creative, interesting, professional and collaborative. Over the course of his time at Ward Productions, Scott provided the voice for Bullwinkle as well as Fearless Leader, Mr. Peabody, Dudley Do-Right, George of the Jungle, Jean La Foote, and other incidental characters.

When a program is as heavily verbal as shows from Ward Productions could be, it was imperative that there be strong vocal talents to help keep the action moving, which is why Ward and Scott assembled a bullpen of world-class voice artists including Paul Frees, Daws Butler, William Conrad, June Foray, Hans Conried and Edward Everett Horton. Scott more than held his own with this group.

Businessman

From the start, it was apparent that Scott would be a vital member of the team in regards to the creation of this new program. Ward was so certain of Scott's talents that he asked him to be a full partner in the company. Scott was excited by the opportunity but also worried about what people would say if they saw his name listed in the credits under writer, talent, producer *and* as one of the principals of the company. Not wanting to appear egotistical, he accepted the business offer but politely declined any outward credits, and so in 1958 he found himself a (somewhat silent) part of the newly formed Jay Ward Productions.

This could be seen as one of the few mistakes Scott made during his career. While he and Ward had an equal working partnership, the public never saw past the company's name and assumed that Ward was the driving force behind the shows. While Ward was instrumental in setting a tone and offering creative input, it was surely Scott who drove the tempo and style. And yet he did it all in a type of self-imposed anonymity.

Writer

As good as Scott was in the other areas of production, it was with his scripts that he really stood out. It wasn't just that he could create a strong, humorous story or pace it appropriately (an often-overlooked talent), Scott had an innate ability to tap into the collective subconscious of the popular culture and pull out the common memories. He also had a great ability to take the current situation of the world and expose it for the absurdity for which it really was. Everything that Scott wrote for these shows, though, was done so with tongue firmly in cheek. There was no malice in his work; an agenda or steady political slant could not be found. He chose to go after his targets with both the pointed tip of satire and the sloppiness of slapstick.

Certainly there were other programs at the time poking fun at the events, news and world of the day, but really none of them did it with such glee or "aw-shucks" goofy fun. That's part of the genius of Scott and company's work, that they make it seem so effortless, like it's all a big, grand old time, when in fact there are some rather serious undertones (capitalism, consumerism, war) to their stories. Part of the reason that his work went over so well was because it had a multitude of layers. In one scene you might find wild slapstick, a pun so bad it's good, and the mention of an obscure historical figure as a throwaway line.

All of this is what was poured into *Rocky and His Friends* (sponsored by General Mills) as it debuted on ABC November 29, 1959. It ran for two years, quickly becoming the number-one daytime program. Despite good ratings, in 1961 ABC dropped the show. It wasn't homeless for long, as NBC picked it up and gave it a primetime slot in that same year under the title of *The*

Bullwinkle Show. It stayed there until 1964 when it made way for other Ward Studio creations. Essentially both iterations of the show were the same: they each followed the same format and contained similar (if not the exact same) supporting segments within them.

Each program contained several different sketches that all fit neatly into one perfect whole. At the center of it all were the Rocky and Bullwinkle stories. These were fully realized adventures broken into three to three-and-one-half minute chapters. (The number of chapters for each adventure would vary, but a median might be 30.) Each program featured two chapters of the latest Rocky and Bullwinkle story—one would usually open the show and end in a cliffhanger. Then there would be some other short segments before we would return to the Rocky and Bullwinkle adventure in progress. This second chapter would again end in a cliffhanger, which would close out the show. These cliffhanger endings became quite popular, playing on the public's penchant for nostalgia and feeding their appetite for fun. Scott, an unabashed punster, saw that each cliffhanger ending was accompanied with two titles to promote the next adventure installment. These were usually plays off of famous entertainment works or popular sayings. One of the most famous examples came from an episode that ended with our heroes stuck in a leaky canoe. As the Narrator (William Conrad) lamented their situation, he implored viewers to return for the next exciting episode: "Canoe's Who or Look Before You Leak." It's a great joke, but it's safe to say that the network wasn't entirely thrilled.

The segments of the show that sat between the adventure chapters were:

Peabody's Improbable History—A dog and his pet boy go back in time to visit historical figures and help them along in times of crises.

Aesop and Son—A retelling of Aesop's stories.

Fractured Fairy Tales—They started out as the classic fairy tales but always ended not exactly as you remembered.

Dudley Do-Right—The 1890s melodrama of a brave and sure Canadian Mountie and his battles with the darkest of villains, Snidely Whiplash.

Even though Scott did not write all of the material on the shows, he certainly set the tone. He ensured that everything was focused on the characters and the situations they were in. When he wrote his scripts there was no extraneous business; every joke, every gag, every moment had a purpose. It was most likely a byproduct from his time at UPA. This writing style does a few things: it takes away the feeling of busy-ness that many cartoons have, and it helps the viewer keep a focus on the story, which keeps them engaged and invested. Scott's Bullwinkle scripts were plotted perfectly and with precision.

He knew that rather than write a script with 100 jokes hoping that at least 50 of them hit the mark, he would have 15 jokes that really killed.

There is a great example of the irreverence that Scott brought to the series from when *Rocky and His Friends* first started. In this initial run it opened and closed with a puppet show. During one episode, Scott (playing the Bullwinkle puppet) implored viewers to watch again next week. "To be sure you do," he instructed, "go ahead and take the knobs off your television set so you won't miss a thing." It was estimated that over 20,000 children followed the moose's orders. And of course this was at a time when people were lucky to have one TV, if they had one at all. Furious, the network demanded that the studio offer some sort of apology. So the very next week, the Bullwinkle puppet told everyone to put the knobs back on with glue, to make sure they stuck. (Needless to say, the puppet portion of the show didn't last much longer.)[6]

An example of the "Scott satire" sprinkled through the show can be seen in the story entitled *The Great Box Top Robbery*. This was a Rocky and Bullwinkle adventure in which it was discovered that the world's economy revolved around box tops. Things go awry when Bullwinkle is suspected of counterfeiting box tops (he has the world's largest collection). For this to really hit, remember that the show's sponsor was cereal giant General Mills.

On top of a penchant for comedy, a trait in Scott's characters is a knowing self-reference. They understand they are performers (there are often references from the characters or narrator wondering what the audience thinks or offering apologies for jokes gone bad) and play to that. It's played subtly and works as an invitation to the viewer, a declaration that they (the performers) know how ridiculous this all is and that we (the audience) should not search for the logic and just sit back and enjoy. So many animated shows either take themselves too seriously or refuse to embrace the conventions of their medium. Rocky and Bullwinkle not only acknowledged its medium but also reveled in it. Ward and Scott understood that television is not just an entertainment medium but also a communications device, and when considered in that light, it makes sense that they would utilize it as such. In 1998 the Museum of Television and Radio celebrated the Ward/Scott partnership with an exhibition entitled *The Adventures of Rocky and Bullwinkle and Friends*, which summed up the appeal of their work: "Ward and his associates combined topical satire with lighthearted flights of fancy."

An interesting angle of this exhibition was that it presented Ward and Scott's work not just from a cultural and artistic perspective, but from an academic one as well. For example the *Fractured Fairy Tale* segments were used as "a way to examine story structure and the elements common to all fairy tales."[7]

Would You Like to Buy ... or Cereal You Later

Among the many cultural "crazes" in the 1960s was the rise of the breakfast cereal. This was the golden age of morning meals, when new brands were being released almost weekly and each box had a bigger and better prize than the next. Competition among the cereal producers was fierce, but the rewards were great. So great that the Quaker Oats Company, a leader in the hot cereal market but virtually a non-existent player on the cold cereal shelves, decided things were too lucrative not to jump into the mix.

Because of the great overpopulation of the cereal shelves, in order for a new product to stand out it had to be carefully researched. The Quaker company used this research to create a cereal that contained all of the top elements that kids longed for in breakfast food. They ended up with what would be known as *Cap'n Crunch*. They took this cereal to Compton Advertising to give it a name and a story. Compton created a character and then took that to Jay Ward, who was no stranger to the world of breakfast, as the Bullwinkle programs were sponsored by General Mills, and asked them to make it interesting and fun. And that is exactly what they did.

Ward was not enthusiastic about getting mixed up with "advertising," but Scott saw an opportunity to have some fun with a steady stream of revenue. And so it was that the Jay Ward team sent Captain Horatio Crunch out on his maiden voyage in September 1963. Cap'n Crunch sailed the seas with a crew of children and a dog as first mate, and always were one step ahead of French pirate Jean LaFoote, who wanted nothing more than a handful of their delicious cargo. The spots all had that distinctive Ward/Scott feel, and they were an immediate smash hit. The spots drove people to the stores in such numbers that Quaker had to build a factory just to meet the demand.[8]

Hoping to capture lightning in a bottle twice, Quaker executives asked Ward in 1965 if they could create a new character for a cereal they were developing. Ward and Scott were having so much fun with the Cap'n that they jumped at the chance to be involved even earlier in the creative process. The results were Quisp (voiced by Scott), a flighty and fun alien, and Quake (given a voice by Ward stalwart William Conrad), a serious and strong miner from deep in the Earth's core. This meant that Quaker would have to create not one but two new cereals. Such was their trust in Ward and Scott that they agreed to do so without hesitation. These characters were great fun for the studio because not only did they have their own ads but they also often crossed over into each other's spaces.

The Ward Studio was now heavily involved in the breakfast wars. Besides their main cereal commercials, they also picked up production of spinoff brands (like Peanut Butter Crunch and Crunch Berries) and some new offerings (like King Vitaman). It was a fast-moving time. Artists didn't have the luxury of developing characters in a half-hour show, they had 30 seconds to capture and sell the audience. It was a constant challenge and one that Scott tore into. While he didn't write everything, he did a majority of the work, and as with the series work, anything that he didn't write inevitably fell under his watchful editorial eye.

This was what the studio did to supplement the series work, and before anyone realized it, this *was* the work. Scott, who had come so close to making advertising his professional line of work 20 odd years ago, found himself, in a way, fulfilling his destiny.

When they originally signed the contract, Scott and Ward had agreed that they would do the commercials as long as it was fun. By 1984 the battles with the advertising agency turks who were looking to put their own mark on the characters had drained the excitement, and so the two old friends decided they had had enough.

We Wanna Be Like You or *The Write Way*

> *"It affected people (Rocky and Bullwinkle), especially bright kids growing up. I'm fond of saying that we corrupted an entire generation."*— Bill Scott[9]

Rocky and Bullwinkle is a show that works on multiple levels and only grows richer the more time you spend with it. And the more time you spend with it the more you marvel at how perfectly it all works.

Matt Groening (creator of *The Simpsons*) was so influenced by the moose and squirrel that he sprinkled elements of it into *The Simpsons* (for example Homer and Bart each have the middle initial J., just as Rocky and Bullwinkle do, which was done as a tribute to Jay Ward).[10]

Craig McCracken, the creator of *The Powerpuff Girls*, among other shows, cites the influence this way: "It's just a matter of knowing where the best people are and learning from them, and all those influences are sprinkled throughout all our shows. There seems to be this focus on *Powerpuff* as just this tribute to anime, but they're missing the UPA tributes and the Jay Ward tributes."[11]

Of course it wasn't the animation industry that fell under Scott's influence. You can draw a line from *Rocky and His Friends* and *Bullwinkle* to shows like *M*A*S*H* and *Saturday Night Live*. There's not just a line of influence here, but an interconnectivity amongst these shows. Their attitudes, humor, controversy and general being are all tied together in a great cultural way. There are also people as diverse as Conan O'Brian (television host), Alan

Gilbey (British comedian and writer), the band Jack Off Jill, Jeff Smith (cartoonist), and Michael Vance (author) who have cited the impression that the world of Ward and Scott left on them.

On the Bullwinkle shows, Scott was the head writer on a veritable all-star team of comedy writers. There was George Atkins, Allan Burns, Jim Critchfield, Chris Hayward, Chris Jenkyns, John Marshall, Paul Mazursky, Jack Menelsohn, Larry Tucker and Lloyd Turner. These writers would go on to create such classic shows as *The Mary Tyler Moore Show, Rhoda, Taxi, Barney Miller, Maude,* and *Get Smart.* While each writer came ably equipped with their own style and comedy ideas, Scott impressed his personality and abilities on them through his guidance, direction and writing (while allowing each to retain their individuality). The result was a cohesive group that wrote from one comedy mind. As members of that group left to pursue other projects, they would always leave changed individuals for having worked with Bill Scott. They also would take a little bit of that Scott writing outlook and philosophy with them. As their success grew, so did the influence of Bill Scott.

And this is all just from the shows staring Bullwinkle and Rocky. There are throngs more who had the same epiphany when they saw a UPA short, huddled in front of the television to watch *Time for Beany*, or laughed themselves sick at a Warner Brothers cartoon. Such is the impact of Bill Scott's words. He was a man who set out to entertain and in doing so changed people's lives.

In the late 1990s there was a Ward Studios resurgence of sorts as all of the people who had grown up with the Ward shows were now old enough to make some business decisions, and starting in 1997 there were several live-action versions of Ward Studio cartoons released to the theaters: *George of the Jungle* (1997), *Dudley Do-Right* (1999), *The Adventures of Rocky and Bullwinkle* (2000). The films were mildly popular, and it was good to see the characters alive again, but in the transfer to live action something was lost. If there was any consolation for fans it was that *Dudley Do-Right* was preceded by an all new *Fractured Fairy Tale* entitled *The Phox, the Box and the Lox*. The even better news is that it was created from an original unused Bill Scott script. It may not have been premium Scott, but even his lesser work is head and shoulders above many of the other scripts floating around.

Bill Scott is one of the few figures in animation whose contributions transcended the industry. His work is one of those rare occurrences where pop culture transforms purely into culture.

To Scott writing was addictive; he couldn't help but write, he was the literary equivalent of a shark, and he had to keep his pen moving to stay alive. Toward the end of his career, as requests for his vocal abilities overtook those for his wordsmithing, Scott turned to the Tujunga, California, newspaper, for which he created a weekly column. His columns were general community pieces, but they were pure Scott — brilliant, funny, personable and relatable.

Talking It Out or *Write Word, Strong Way*

Such was the popularity of the Bullwinkle shows that for perhaps the first time in animation history, everyone took notice of, and wanted to learn more about, the writers. Scott seized this as an opportunity to build some good will for the show, for the industry and for the writing profession.

In 1961 he started lecturing at The University of Southern California. He believed strongly in education tracts for animators and lobbied many West Coast universities to establish degree-qualifying classes. These classes could have been considered master classes not just in writing but in animation as a communications medium. In them his passion for his work, his understanding of the audience, and his vast industry knowledge came through. Scott enjoyed giving these discussions/lectures/ presentations, so much so in fact that he often took them on the road. In November 1983 he spoke at an animation workshop at UCLA, where he presented his "C's" for creating good animation.

> Compression — Animation compresses action so greatly because it is the only film medium in which every square millimeter or every raster is under absolute and total control of the person making the film. As such it is a tremendously powerful, effective and forceful medium. It compresses time, it compresses action. You can get more done in animation in a short time than in any other way.
>
> Caricature — Animation is a medium of caricature. It is still an extension of, an intensification of life; of what you expect to see or what you think you are seeing. However subtle the metamorphosis may be, it is still caricature.
>
> Chimera — (Remember the chimera) is a mythological creature with the head of a lion, body of a goat, tail of a serpent. It (animation) is a chimerical medium. It is a medium which transcends life. It is a medium of make-believe. You must remember that, as a writer, you're constantly going to be called upon to invent things which do not exist: non-existent entities, characters, worlds, entire worlds.... Because of the chimerical nature, the fantasy nature, the fact that anything can happen in animation, it is much better at story telling than at reporting. It is much better at inventing than it is at simply giving you facts and figures.
>
> Confluence — "It has been my wonderful experience that I have never seen anything that I have written which I didn't think had been plussed as it went down the line. The director's timing of what I had written is a plus. The designer's idea about how it's supposed to look is a plus. The animator's bringing the things to life is a plus. The magnificent balance of color that occurs in some of the things was a plus. So the thing that happens on the screen, what started as the writer's idea, the writer's dream, is subject to the confluence of other skills and other arts down the assembly line.

He also had one other favorite C: the *Creative Process*. "(The) Creative process is the manipulation of memory. Nothing is ever *created*. Everything is simply remembered and put into new form. It is the manipulation of memory. So, if the creative process is the manipulation of memory ... have to have memory to manipulate. You have to have some things to call upon. You have to have some experience and some knowledge, some stuff up there in the attic. You go up and rummage through it when you need to create."[12]

Scott loved everything about the animation business and did all that he could to see it thrive and expand. From the early 1980s up until his death, he was the president of the U.S. chapter of AIFSA — the Association Internationale di Film D'Animation. He attended and often organized events, assisted with fundraising and acted as an overall industry ambassador. And being who he was, he also served as editor to the organization's magazine, *Graffiti*. For all of his efforts, Scott won the respect and admiration of his peers. In 1977 he was given the Inkpot award at Comic-Con and the Windsor McCay Award at the Annies.

While it would have been easy to focus all of his energies on "his" industry, Scott understood that animation was but one part of a larger arts community. With this holistic approach, Scott represented the industry as a member of the Board of Governors of the Motion Picture Academy, a member of the Television Academy and a member of the NAACP.

He remained busy until the end, when, on November 29, 1985, he passed away from complications of cancer, leaving behind happy moments for millions of people and, perhaps more importantly, raising the bar for writers everywhere.

HONORS

Winsor McCay Award, International Animated Film Association, 1977
Inkpot Award, Comic-Con International, 1977

SAMPLE FILM SELECTION

The Stupor Salesman (1941)
Gerald McBoing-Boing (1951)
The Bullwinkle Show (1961)
Cap'n Crunch commercials (1963–1983)

17. Michael Maltese: The Storyman

"The storyman says that there are no more zany seven-minute ideas and proceeds to write one anyway."
— Michael Maltese[1]

Much has been written about the "Shadow of Charlie Chaplin," how his influence over comedy, his position in film history, and of course his prominence as an international star lurks over entertainers to this day. Speaking strictly of the field of comedy, while Chaplin is certainly a leading light, through the years there have been a select number of others who have had some level of influence over the art form, people like Richard Pryor, Jerry Lewis, the original cast of *Saturday Night Live*, Jack Benny, Lenny Bruce, the Monty Python troupe. Always absent from the conversation, though, is a man who, for the last half of the twentieth century, made us laugh and in doing so shaped our sensibilities about *what* is funny. That man is Michael Maltese (2/6/08–2/22/81).

Throughout his long career, Maltese brought strength and clarity to several comedic storytelling conceits, weaving them into the language of animation. The narrated aside, having characters break the fourth wall and address the audience directly, the chase, the verbal sparring — these were not techniques discovered by Maltese, but he found a way to use them to strengthen his stories and heighten the humor in them. He was also able to keep a timelessness to his work. While there are some period-based gags in his writing, the overarching stories have held up well across the years.

His scripts also helped bring focus to many of the Warners characters who, up until he reached his creative full running speed in the mid–1940s, had been largely underdeveloped. Truth be told, there was no complete, fully rounded character in animation; even Mickey Mouse had holes in who he was. Maltese, though, working on a slightly more cerebral level, wrote scripts that found nuances in his "actors" that sharpened their personalities and, for some, like Porky Pig, gave them the definition and purpose they had, up to that point, never had. "The great achievement of Jones and Maltese (and composer Carl Stalling, versatile vocalist Mel Blanc and art director Maurice Noble) was their development of the Warners stock company. Porky Pig was now the harassed middle-management type; Elmer Fudd the chronic, choleric dupe; Sylvester J. Pussycat a feline of sputtering theatrical bombast. Bugs, originally a wild wabbit, wather than a wascally one, became the cartoon Cagney — urban, crafty, pugnacious — and then the unflappable underhare who wins every battle without ever mussing his aplomb; one raised eyebrow was enough to semaphore his superiority to the carnage around him."[2]

Conspicuously absent from this list of course is Daffy Duck, and that is because Daffy's character growth did not occur across a progression of shorts but congealed in one volcanic seven-minute stretch in 1953's *Duck Amuck*.

It can be surmised that without Maltese, we would have a very different collective sense of humor. Take any modern comedian or popular program, and when you begin to perform some ancestral research you find that one of their stated influences was the animation put out by Leon Schlesinger through Warner Brothers. Animation that was (more than likely) written by Michael Maltese. His situations, his language choices, his attitude have been absorbed by generations through repeated viewings of those Warner Brothers cartoons. They have instilled in us, regardless of class, age, race, or education, a joint comedic touchpoint. Phrases from his scripts are part of our language, and his comedic sensibilities have become part of our social DNA.

"We wrote cartoons for grown ups."— Michael Maltese[3]

Maltese started working in animation in the 1940s and continued behind a desk for 40 years. While his name may not be immediately recognizable, it is certain that he has made you laugh, that you've quoted his work, and that you subconsciously rewired your thoughts on what is funny based on what he made characters do.

Maltese started life on the opposite side of funny. He was a plumber. He did have the good fortune, though, of being a plumber in New York City in the early part of the twentieth century, which gave him a wonderful opportunity to perform "field research." All day he would work and listen to people fight and talk and share and, most importantly, laugh. He subconsciously studied people's penchant for humor — why they laughed, why they didn't, what some people thought was funny, what everyone did; it was a living focus group. He also consciously studied the silent film masters, particularly Charlie Chaplin, who Maltese remembers often imitating at home. When he wasn't watching a comedy he found himself drawn to films like *The Mark of Zorro* (1920), whose sense of adventure is apparent in the Maltese scripts for films like *Robin Hood Daffy* (1958) and *The Scarlet Pumpernickel* (1950).

Maltese finally decided that the path of a plumber was not for him, and he leaned on the other side of his brain and took a more artistic approach to work. In 1935 he had started working at the New York office of the Fleischer Studios as a cel painter. This gave him enough of a taste of the business to let him know that this was what he wanted, needed, to do. By 1936 he was headed west to carve out a career in Hollywood, when he made a stop at the Jam Handy Studios in Detroit. It was a short stay, and the following year he was on the Warner Brothers lot working as an inbetweener for the Leon Schlesinger animation unit. To pass the time, he wrote some essays for the studio newsletter. These were seen (and enjoyed) by the right eyes, and soon after publication, Maltese found himself a member of Schlesinger's Story Department.

At this time, the Story Department functioned as a "pool" system. Scheduling and availability dictated who worked with whom and on what. By the mid–1940s, though, this system was scrapped in place of a team or unit structure. He and Tedd Pierce were given the assignment to work with directors Friz Freleng and Chuck Jones.

While his work during this time was solid, it pales in comparison with his later output, when he would be paired exclusively with Jones. Still this was a fruitful and creative period that produced some good stories and one strong renowned character — Yosemite Sam, who made his first appearance in *Hare Trigger* (1945). Sam, the short, mustachioed, blustering fool, was often a cowboy, but his personality was so portable that he also appeared as a pirate, knight, cook, duke, soldier, and any number of other "stock in trade" antagonists. Sam is a great character because his traits are so universal that he is easily transported through scenarios, but his personality is so strong that he stands on his own in each short. The not-so-secret secret surrounding Sam is that he was modeled after Freleng, although Freleng would (or could) never acknowledge this. (In a double bit of irony, Freleng shepherded Sam through nearly every one of his on-screen shorts appearances.)

As Rachel Newstead pointed out in her review of the *Flintstones* episode "The Hot Piano," Maltese loved to play with language. From his "Duck Season, Rabbit Season, Duck Season" acrobatics in the 1940s to his clever turns for Fred Flintstone in the 1960s (helping him to move above a stock sitcom father to something more), Maltese infused his work with a certain "New York-ness" in his phrasing, his attitude, and the posturing of his characters. The characters in a Maltese scripted short were seen *as* New York. They were also very much seen as "characters," as regular actors and actresses playing a part. This decision, certainly one that had to be made consciously by the numerous members of the creative team, gave the writers, directors, and actors a wide range of freedom in what they could have each character attempt to do. It also opened the door to the outside world, the "real" world that these actors inhabited, which allowed for a particular mix of topicality and self awareness. This self reflexivity would later become the hallmark of the Warner Brothers studios: "Intertextuality was a trademark ... as they repeatedly referred to all aspects of the real world including themselves as cartoons."[4]

One of Maltese's stories for Freleng was *Notes to You* (1941). The plot is simple — Porky wants to sleep but can't because the cat outside his window won't stop singing. At least the plot *sounds* simple, but the story is layered with a tug of war between Porky and the Cat as each tries to get the upper hand. It's a rather rote cartoon concept, but under Maltese's sure hand, the script transcends the simple and takes on additional layers of meaning. And it does this without sacrificing any of the comedy. The film works because the audience can relate to Porky's plight, and yet the cat is such an innocent that you can't really root against it. Where other films might retread the same idea, Maltese's script tweaks each confrontation to keep it fresh, all the while escalating the action. We know where the story has to end, and yet we can't believe it will go there. When it does, it's both a shocking and funny conclusion because it defies our expectations.

Fellow writer Lloyd Turner remembers Maltese as being very "open" with his story ideas, which was a stark contrast to other writers on staff at the time. The writers at the studio were an eccentric bunch who generally guarded their scripts and ideas closely, although they were free to suggest ideas in their story "jam sessions," which were held to test the strength and ideas of a picture.

By many accounts, Maltese had a particular affection for the "sell." If he got an idea, he would go all out to sell the joke. He was a natural-born performer who was out of his seat during story sessions at the slightest suggestion (and sometimes not even then), acting out parts of a script or bringing a storyboard to life. Maltese would later elaborate on his process: "You're selling a mood, a pacing."[5] (This bent toward the performance side would make Maltese a fill-in actor. In 1943 he voiced the part of Hubie in *The Aristo-Cat*, and in 1940s he moved to the screen, playing a security guard opposite Porky Pig in *You Ought to Be in Pictures*. He also voiced a soldier, dog, mouse, "rabbit thug," a castaway — whenever an extra voice was needed, he jumped at the opportunity.)

This process of story discussion was particularly important for him because he leaned toward using sketches to "write" his scripts. In a typical cartoon there could be up to 150 of them. So these standup jam sessions allowed him to fill in the sequences and add the particular shading his story required. A master at his craft, he could also gauge the reaction he was getting and adjust the story path or change out a joke as he was going. Part of the reason that he could do this so quickly was because he loved the art of the joke, its construction and presentation, in all of its forms. According to his fellow animators, Maltese always had some little prop-joke he was working up or some gag for a story that he had to share (usually by re-telling the entire story he was working on, just to get the joke in context). In addition to providing a sounding board for his work, these sessions provided him with the opportunity to indulge his instincts for performance.

Maltese was also unsentimental about the work he did, as he had the confidence in his writing that there was always another joke coming. As he stated once to his collaborator Chuck Jones: "It works or it doesn't work, it's that simple."[6]

Late in his career, Maltese offered a telling thought about the working relationship of a team: "The beautiful part of animated cartoons is that, even though we may all hate each other, everyone is working for the same thing."[7] It's a sentiment offered in 1960 but fueled most likely by his relationship with the writers at Schlesinger's and Chuck Jones as the atmosphere at the studio was generally curt. There was somewhat of a "team" mentality, but the writers remained rather territorial.

The Partnership

By 1946 the studio writing system was "refined," and Maltese and Chuck Jones were paired exclusively together. This was the moment when he and Jones started what would become one of the most influential comedy teams of American entertainment. To understand how successful the duo was, you have to understand how disastrous the coupling *should* have been.

While Chuck Jones is now given a sort of super-status among the directors at the studio (and throughout animation, really), he had not always enjoyed such acclaim. His early work was pedestrian and in many cases overly saccharine. Consider his go-to character in the late 1930s and early 1940s — Sniffles the Mouse, an insufferable, overly cutesy bore who was pathologically sweet and whose one redeeming quality was that he was eventually retired. On the other side, Maltese had a tendency for aggressiveness, not so much in tone but in comic sensibility — everything was joke, joke, joke with no room for a breath let alone any form of character development. It was relentless, and while that style can work, it can also wear an audience down to a point of numbness. This approach is particularly on display in his work under director Friz Freleng including *The Wabbit Who Came to Supper* (1942); *The Hare-Brained Hypnotist* (1942); and *Double Chaser* (1942). Comparing Maltese's pre– and post–Jones work is important to discern his artistic growth, but it's also a little tricky because relatively few "scripts" from this period survive. Because of this, one must also look at the work of Maltese's collaborators and in turn make certain guided assumptions.

Soft-spoken sentiment vs. New York moxie. The pairing could have been calamitous, but in fact it was the perfect coupling, as the strengths and weaknesses of each man complemented the other in a way that brought a greater fullness to the finished piece. Jones, with his focus on character, slowed down Maltese's delivery, which allowed for things like character development to be woven across stronger story arcs, which in turn strengthened the script and enhanced the comedy within because it now had a certain relatability. In his book *Hollywood Cartoons*, Michael Barrier observes that in the relationship between the two men, "[Through Maltese] Jones learned how to use vigorous gags as vehicles for the caricature of emotion."[8]

Maltese could fall back into his old pattern, though, if not properly checked by an equally strong creative partner, which is what he would face after Jones. Toward the end of his career, Maltese was working at Hanna-Barbera, and William Hanna found him to have a "very smart-aleck approach to his humor. He had a way with words, especially clever rhyme phrases...."[9]

Jones also brought to the partnership a strong level of trust. A director less confident in his or her work would have pushed Maltese and tried to bend him to their artistic temperament. Jones, though, had confidence not only in his work, but also in the work of those around him and gave his collaborators the space they needed.

With a Maltese script Jones could play to their now-compatible strengths by "giving greater depth to the comedy that was already there by making it less a comedy of gags and more a comedy of character."[10]

Film critic Roger Ebert says that the Warners films of this time held "comic scenarios (that) were driven by eternal conflicts."[11] It's a nod toward the truth that what makes a Maltese story work so well is that it is grounded in human emotion (desire, love, fear, anger). There is a reality at play in his stories, and where Maltese's talent comes through is in his ability to move beyond a standard storytelling convention in getting to that reality.

If you have any memory of a cartoon distributed by Warner Brothers in the 1940s and 1950s, then you are most likely remembering a Maltese/Jones work. *Rabbit Fire. Duck Dodgers.* The Bugs Bunny operas. The frog who is an amazing song-and-dance man, but will only perform for an audience of one. *Duck Amuck* where Daffy Duck is at the mercy of his animator. The Coyote, the Road Runner, and the ACME Corporation.

While partnered with Jones, Maltese averaged one script roughly every five weeks, which helped the team put out over an hour of material each year (ten scripts at over an average of six minutes per finished short). To a person, everyone involved in creating great animation will state that they are working, first and foremost, to amuse themselves and their friends, and Maltese was no different. Take, for example, the creation of *Bully for Bugs* (1953). This very funny short finds Bugs Bunny taking one of his patented wrong turns at Albuquerque and ending up south of the border in the midst of a bullfight. For the next five minutes Bugs and the bull have a crescendoing back-and-forth battle (a highlight is Bugs' interpretation of the Mexican Hat Dance). It's a fully encapsulated comedy and one that only came about because an executive at the studio, Eddie Selzer, told Jones and Maltese that he never wanted to see anything about bullfighting because there was nothing funny about a bullfight. The two artists begged to differ and set about to successfully prove their point.

The Singing Frog

Jones and Maltese produced several comedy masterpieces, but together they also oversaw the creation of a set of cartoons that transcended the medium, becoming more than just animation bellwethers, but artistic (and even philosophic) touchpoints. One such picture was 1955's *One Froggy Evening,* a cartoon that film critic Jay Cocks said "comes as close as any cartoon ever has to perfection."[12] If you could see only one cartoon from the Maltese/Jones partnership, it should be *One Froggy Evening*. It's a wordless exploration of entertainment, fame, appreciation, and desire. And it's about as perfect as any animated short could be. The cartoon is set around the simplest of premises, but it is so expertly crafted across multiple levels that it transcends the one joke it is built around to become "a morality play in cameo."[13]

This dialogue-free short shares the story of a construction worker who, during the demolition of a building, finds a box that contains a singing and dancing frog. The construction worker sees dollar signs. The only hitch in his plan is that the frog will only sing when no one is watching, and so begins the furtive battle between the worker and the clock as he struggles to time things out so that the world will see his frog. At the end of the short the worker has lost everything, and, a broken man, he skulks back onto the construction site and reburies the live frog in the cornerstone. Jumping to 2056, the building is being demolished, a construction worker of the future uncovers the box, finds the frog, gets dollar signs, and the cycle begins again. "There are tragedies in conflict here: (a) a frog who is a song and dance star, who has been locked in the dark for decades but cannot perform in public, and (b) a worker who dreams of wealth and is considered a fool and a liar. The story of 'One Froggy Evening' involves an endless loop of frustration."[14]

Not only did Maltese write the story, but his is also the author of the frog's most famous number, the proto–1890s *The Michigan Rag*.

This film, like the Coyote/Road Runner series, has strong parallels of the eternal struggle of man vs. machine. It also plays to the idea of greed, exploitation, and art. "The construction worker might have simply enjoyed the frog's fine singing. He might have regarded it as a divine gift, for him alone or perhaps to be shared with a few friends. But, out of greed, he decides to exploit the frog."[15]

One Froggy Evening is a great standalone comedy, and it works fine as just that. What makes the film truly memorable, though, is that, upon repeated viewing, new layers of depth are uncovered. It's filled with ponderous thoughts, philosophical ideals, and social commentary. And it's a comedy. That's the key to this whole thing and what keeps everything pulled together. The genius of this film is that all of this disparate, deep thoughts are anchored in this one joke, a joke that is written so originally it carries the film while still feeling as fresh at the end as it did the first time we were shown it.

> "*The 1953 Chuck Jones short* Duck Amuck. *Watching this cartoon as a kid I realized the freedom of imagination and the creative possibilities that only animation can provide. Later watching it as a young adult I saw it as a 'meta' exploration of the animation process and the relationship between the animator and the worlds s/he creates. And on top of that, it's really, really, really funny.*"— Christopher Miller (director, *Cloudy with a Chance of Meatballs, Clone High*) on his favorite piece of animation[16]

One of the last films Maltese and Jones made before taking a forced break thanks to Warner Brothers (more on that later) was *Duck Amuck* (1953). It's a cartoon that, as critic Roger Ebert put it, "plays with the reality of the genre."[17] *Duck Amuck* is a completely original short starring Daffy Duck, with a complete understanding that he is a character acting out a story, who comes into a standard cartoon but is quickly sent spiraling as the action shifts and ebbs, changes and rechanges, vanishes then re-appears while tossing Daffy around, a helpless victim to the whims of an animator unseen. Daffy is squashed and shrunk, erased, redrawn and dropped into a number of locations, all the while berating the animator, who is unseen until the end, for every offense.

It's animation deconstruction, as the film offers the creators and the audience a chance to completely take apart the animated format while at the same time celebrating its uniqueness and flexibility. While it has its funny moments, the short is not an overall particularly hilarious one in and of itself. It works more on the execution of this mix of ideas of creator/creation, the filmmaking process, and the control (or lack of) that we all face. For some the short contains the trappings of existentialism, particularly when Bugs Bunny makes his appearance and we are forced to re-evaluate all that we have just seen.

This film also provides a tour-de-force performance by Daffy Duck, who in this span of a short seven minutes collects all of the traits he had ever carried and displays, spins, and refracts them and in doing so becomes perhaps the most multi-dimensional, fully realized character to grace an animated film at that point. Jones and animators Ken Harris, Ben Washam, and Lloyd Vaughan do an engaging job in the pacing of the action and in keeping an often-blank "stage" feeling alive and energetic.

Some believe the film is less a study on animation and more a showcase of character:

> 1953's *Duck Amuck*, a case study in both minimalism and clear delineation of character. Ostensibly, the short features two characters, Daffy and an off-screen God of Mischief. Make no mistake, however, this is Daffy's show and he rises up to give an Oscar-worthy performance. It is the perfect marriage of actor and material. In his book *Story*, renowned screenwriting guru Robert McKee said of character: "True character can only be expressed through choice in dilemma. How a person chooses to act under pressure is who he is — the greater the pressure, the truer and deeper the choice to character." This is the very essence of *Duck Amuck*. How Daffy reacts to the fact that his own medium has turned against him throws his character into sharp relief. His anger and desperation are paraded nakedly in front of us and — perhaps with amusement, perhaps with horror — we recognize them. We'd all like to think that, in Daffy's situation, we'd have the serenity to accept the things we cannot change, but, often, that is only a pipe dream. Most of us are more like Daffy than we'd like to admit.... *Duck Amuck* is ennobling. Each of us, in taking up arms against a sea of troubles, should endeavor to maintain our basic integrity as well as Daffy does.[18]

Maltese is interesting in that he obviously has an interest in the big ideas in life, and yet he rarely explores them in his scripts as individual elements. He more often combines common themes together, providing a broader viewpoint of his subjects.

Philosophic Comedy

The longest series that Maltese worked on while at Schlesinger was the Road Runner/Coyote battle, which started in 1949 with the *Fast and Furryous*.

The concept was inspired by an entry in the *Fox and the Crow* series from Columbia Studios entitled *The Fox and the Grapes* (1941) (made under the guidance of former Schlesinger director Frank Tashlin). It was the first in a series of films for the studio, and, in an interesting bit of serendipity, Jones and Maltese both contributed gags to the Academy Award–nominated *Robin Hoodlum*, a 1948 entry in the *Fox and the Crow* series produced by UPA. With the timing of the film, one has to wonder if they were using it as a sort of testing ground for some of their own ideas on the concept or just "having fun," and in the process discovering a new storytelling conceit.

Jones has credited Maltese with taking the initial idea and spinning it into the Coyote/Road Runner premise.[19] His intent was to make a parody of the straight-ahead chases that were so prevalently coming out of Hollywood at the time. What they ended up doing was creating the definitive comic chase series. This first entry is carefully structured yet with a very casual pace. While it feels as if the action is organic, Maltese and Jones were actually adhering to a very specific set of rules that include 1) there was the Coyote and the Road Runner and that was it in terms of characters, 2) each episode took place in the desert, 3) while the Coyote obviously wants to kill and eat the Road Runner, 4) the Road Runner never overtly harms the Coyote (that generally occurs thanks to his own ineptitude).[20]

This last "rule" provides the series with much of its charm and offers the viewer an emotional lynchpin — many a viewer has claimed to see in the Coyote some version of themselves — someone who wants something with all of their being yet is constantly thwarted by their own actions and by "the system" (in the case of the cartoon, the ACME Corporation).

Jones has said that they needed 11 gags for each Coyote and Road Runner film. That averages out to a gag every 38 seconds, which given the set-up, follow through and aftermath discovery keeps things at a pretty quick pace. This is why viewing multiple entries in the series back to back can be an exhausting feat. It can also be an interesting one, as in viewings separated by time, there is the tendency to remember only key moments, so that in separate films set-ups may appear the same, and you may experience a been there, done that sense. But you would be missing from a higher level one of the themes of the series and from a more base level a great sense and structure of comedy. This series has a number of comedic roots attached to it, one of which is the comedy of the unexpected. So set-ups are often repeated, sometimes within a single short, sometimes across shorts, but the payoff behind them is always different. This can be a completely new moment or simply a slight variation on the original, but the surprise for the viewer is still there. From a thematic sense, there is this large underlying theme of the Coyote and his battle against the world (a common theme for Maltese at this point in his career). In these scenarios we are experiencing "comedy as repetition-compulsion."[21] The Coyote sets up a trap; it fails. Later he attempts to set up the same trap but adjusts it slightly; he appears to have learned from his initial mishap and trusts that he can make the change needed to avoid repeating that mistake. But, Wham! It seems that no matter how he tries, the Coyote cannot escape his fate. The television show *Lost* dealt with this very issue when a character declared, "The universe has a way of course correcting itself."[22]

"*The coyote is the victim of a hostile universe.*"[23]

From a straight writing perspective, there is an impressive amount of inventiveness in the series, as it seeks new ways for the Coyote and Road Runner to engage in their struggle. Making the Coyote his (we can safely assume the character is male) own worst enemy has also provided the series a theological fan base, as there are those that see it as the start of a larger discussion on man's place in the universe (the Road Runner representing the constant "want," the Coyote standing in for Man, and the action standing in for Fate). Did Maltese intend to make the series an existential treatise? That each entry in the series has gone on to undergo such scrutiny, and on so many levels, only helps to illustrate the power and appeal of the story presented. In fact, some see this series as a companion to *One Froggy Evening*, with both offering parables on "the mechanics of self-destruction."[24]

Many of the Coyote/Road Runner cartoons are comedic rubrics that double back on themselves. The Coyote sets up a trap. It fails. We laugh. As the story progresses we return to the scene of this failed trap, and, at the most inopportune time for the Coyote, the trap detonates. We laugh harder. This format has elicited complaints from some that the Coyote/Road Runner films are too "repetitive," but they miss the point that this is a consistent effort by the filmmakers. Todd Taylor, in his essay *Coyotes and Visual Ethos*, puts it this way: "Prevalent visual cues can be assessing or establishing character or ethos."[25] At a more base level that repetition works; the endless cycle of chase/escape is not just a mechanism to spring the jokes — it *becomes* the joke. It's a comedy of "repetition-compulsion."[26]

The Genre-ist

There was no genre that Maltese could not turn into his own. True parodists need to completely understand their subjects in order to turn them inside out and subvert what would be considered their standard motifs. Maltese proved his mastery of this time and again as he skewered westerns, science fiction, horror, romance, action, and even high art. In 1950 he and Jones teamed on *The Rabbit of Seville*, which was really a marriage of the standard Bugs/Elmer hunting affair matched to Rossini's *The Barber of Seville*. It was an ambitious effort, jokey but reverent, but the duo would top themselves seven years later when they took on the topic of opera again with the retelling of Wagner's Ring cycle in essentially seven minutes in 1957's *What's Opera, Doc?* This film works so well because, unlike *The Rabbit of Seville*, the short plays very true to the source material, and the comedy comes from the juxtaposition of these characters in this setting, not, as in the earlier film, these characters using the setting for comedic effect.

As he had in earlier "musical" stories, Maltese wrote not only the script, but also the songs in the film, retrofitting Wagner's music to his lyrics of "Return My Love." Daniel Goldmark observes that Jones and Maltese were careful within *What's Opera, Doc?* to balance a respectful showing of the music with the comical actions of Bugs and Elmer. "They wanted to create a cartoon that was culturally accurate, satisfying the common notions of what Wagner's operas look and sound like."[27]

Music often played a key role in Maltese's work. In 1947 he worked with Freleng on *Rhapsody Rabbit*, a short starring Bugs Bunny as he attempts to play his way through Liszt's *Second Hungarian Rhapsody*. His piano-playing is fine; the hindrance comes along in the form of a mouse. While the concept is a good one, the film plays flat. This is most likely due to the choice of having Bugs Bunny star. While capable in nearly any role, his strength is in his words, and when those words are taken away (there is little dialogue in the picture) and his actions are confined to a piano bench, there is little to help him stand out. Were this short done with a new character, one that didn't carry Bugs's backstory or expectations, I think the result might have been much different. (In fact you can make your own argument for augmentation by watching MGM's release *The Cat Concerto* [1947], where Tom is the pianist and Jerry the meddlesome mouse. The film works better than the Freleng version because Tom is a better cipher, and the premise fits into their natural chemistry perfectly.)

Both films had their admirers. The 1946 Academy Award for Best Short Subject Cartoons went to *The Cat Concerto*, while no less than Pulitzer Prize–winning film critic James Agee, writing for *The Nation*, said, "The funniest thing I have seen since the decline of sociological dancing is *Rhapsody Rabbit*."[28]

When speaking about his time at Schlesinger's Maltese spoke about the writing process, particularly how the ideas formulate: "Everybody, right down the line, had somebody handing him some work that he had to do. But the writer went into the room and said 'Oh my God! What's funny?' And this was how you learned to live through the years; through death, illness, trouble in the family, and everything else. What I used to do was sit in a room and say 'Well what'll I do?' and I'd sit there. And the inspiration I got was the idea that if I didn't come up with anything, I wouldn't get paid. Economic pressure was the spur, known as a baby at home and the rent and all that; get funny. And I can't say exactly how it works, but ideas begin to come to you."[29]

In 1953, Warner Brothers shut the animation division down as a response to the exploding 3D boom. They were going to retool and only distribute

3D films, but no sooner had that decision been made then the boom went bust.

While that situation was being sorted out in the front offices, Maltese spent time at the Walter Lantz Studios (home of Woody Woodpecker and Chilly Willy). At this time, also working for Lantz was director Tex Avery. Avery was and remains a comedy legend, often called the "cartooniest" of all animation directors. Avery and Maltese had worked previously when both were at Warner Brothers including on Avery's final film there, *The Heckling Hare* (1941), but neither had fully hit his professional stride yet.

At this point in their careers, Avery working with a Maltese script would make even the most casual fan excited. Unfortunately they only had the opportunity to work on one release—1955's Academy Award–nominated Chilly Willy–starrer, *The Legend of Rock-a-Bye-Point*. The film is a loosely structured retread of an earlier Avery-directed Droopy Dog cartoon, MGM's *Deputy Droopy* (1955), which was itself a retelling of the story of an earlier Avery picture—1952's *Rock-a-Bye Bear*.

Maltese is able to freshen up the premise somewhat, but the re-pairing of the two masters is somewhat anticlimactic. This could be in part because they were saddled with Chilly Willy; it could also be quite simply that the working styles of the two just didn't mesh. Maltese hinted at such when he left Lantz and returned to the Warner Brothers lot when they re-opened their studio in 1954.

Some 45 years later the two would be posthumously reunited when the Academy of Motion Picture Arts and Sciences held a retrospective/tribute of their work, and again fans would be left to wonder, "What if."

One Last Creative Charge

Maltese left Lantz to return to Warner Brothers, but things were not the same, as television was coming of age and animation was slowly being phased out of theaters, not just from there, but across the industry. Maltese held out for a few years, but by 1958 the writing was clearly on the wall, and so he called upon Bill Hanna and Joseph Barbara (who had started their own studio after leaving MGM) and quickly found a home there. He remained with Hanna-Barbera until the early 1970s. Among the many shows he wrote for were *The Adventures of Penelope Pitstop*, *Quick Draw McGraw*, *Wacky Races*, *The Yogi Bear Show*, *The Huckleberry Hound Show*, and arguably Hanna-Barbera's flagship series, *The Flintstones*. In 1961 he wrote one of the most famous Flintstone episodes — *The Hot Piano*. Fred attempts to buy Wilma a piano for her birthday and ends up with one that was stolen. The whole thing ends up in a wild chase of police, thieves, Fred, Barney, and piano and culminates in a group serenade to Wilma (to the tune of "The William Tell Orchestra"), "Happy anniversary, happy anniversary, happy anniversary, haaappppyyy anniversary. For a cheerful toast and fill it happy anniversary, but be careful you don't spill it happy anniversary Oooooooo"(and continue on for two more choruses). It's fun, infectious, and the delivery is completely cartoony. Perfect Maltese.

To supplement his income Maltese turned, as many did, to the "ancillary" market — for example, he was already writing scripts for the *Quick Draw McGraw* show, so it was only natural that he write the daily comic strip as well. This also gave him the opportunity to dust off his drawing skills as he drew the strip, too. He had a similar arrangement earlier in his career when he wrote scripts for the Coyote and Road Runner cartoons "during the day" and wrote and illustrated the Coyote and Road Runner comics "at night."

During this period, Maltese re-teamed briefly with Jones from 1963 to 1967, when Jones had taken over the responsibilities to create more entries in another chase series — *Tom and Jerry*. These shorts suffer, though, from too strong of a deviation from the originals, and yet not a strong enough deviation to make the films seem new. Instead they play like odd copies, cobbled together by people who had seen a Tom and Jerry cartoon once and attempted to recreate it.

It is unfair to compare Maltese's work at Hanna-Barbera with what came before because the collaborators and finished products were so vastly different. He now had to worry about censors and sponsors and commercial breaks and in some cases stories that were four times longer than what he had been writing. In a *New York Herald-Tribune* article from 1960, Maltese explained the difference in the Hanna-Barbera process — he said that he was generally given character sketches and a general idea of character type but from that point was expected to name the characters, define them further, and then start knocking out scripts. For a free-ranging creative mind like Maltese's the opportunities presented in this type of environment were probably exciting to a point, but one has to wonder how much he missed the creative give-and-take that he had with Jones.

In the 1960s Warner Brothers made a deal to "sell" their animation catalogue to television stations across the country. This meant that the airways were now flooded with more Maltese. And the nation was better, and funnier, for it.

Today Maltese is finally beginning to receive the recognition he is due. After all, he has entertained millions around the world and had a definitive hand in structuring the comedic landscape of the twentieth century. Academy Award–winner Brad Bird calls Maltese "the king of the Warner Brothers shorts,"[30] and rightfully so.

HONORS

Winsor McCay Award, The International Animated Film Society, 1976
Named to the National Film Registry of the Library of Congress: *Duck Amuck* (1953),
    One Froggy Evening (1955) and *What's Opera, Doc?* (1957).

SELECTED CREDIT LIST

Horton Hatches the Egg (1942)
Baseball Bugs (1946)
Scent-imental Over You (1947)
Buccaneer Bunny (1948)
Fast and Furry-ous (1949)
Bear Feat (1949)
The Scarlet Pumpernickel (1950)
Feed the Kitty (1952)
Duck Amuck (1953)
Duck Dodgers in the 241/2th Century (1953)
Duck! Rabbit, Duck! (1953)
The Legend of Rock-a-Bye Point (1955)
One Froggy Evening (1955)
What's Opera, Doc? (1957)
The Flintstones: The Hot Piano (1961)

Epilogue

Sadly "Saturday Mornings," the type of pure Saturday mornings that I knew from my childhood, are no more. There are too many distractions, too many alternatives competing for time and attention, and to some this would be seen as a detriment to the youth of today. A lost cultural opportunity.

In place of a soggy cereal delirium, though, is something perhaps even better — opportunity. Children, everyone actually, find themselves with more opportunities to discover animation in all of its forms, to create their own animated stories, to harness their own creativity, and to fasten their own memories around this art form.

"Nothing demonstrates our collective conservatism as imaginative creatures quite so much as our response to animation. The medium has no practical limits on what it can do."[1]

Chapter Notes

Preface

1. Stephen Metcalf, "Beyond Bugs Bunny," Slate.com, June 2, 2006, http://www.slate.com/id/2142898/pagenum/all/.

2. John Hubley and Zachary Schwartz, "Animation Learns a New Language," in *Hollywood Quarterly: Film Culture in Postwar America, 1945–1957*, edited by Eric Smoodin and Ann Martin (Berkeley: University of California, 2002), http://www.escholarship.org/editions/view?docId=kt2f59q2dp&chunk.id=ss1.05&toc.id=ch02&toc.depth=1&brand=eschol&anchor.id=p076#X.

3. Alex Ben Block, "Anatomy of a Contender: 'Up,'" *The Hollywood Reporter*, November 17, 2009, http://www.hollywoodreporter.com/hr/content_display/film/news/e3i45e1bcc0b65a294fae37066c88506cfc.

Chapter 1

1. Art Babbitt, "The Art Babbitt Classical Animation Course," *Animator* 10, no. 4 (Autumn 1984), http://www.animatormag.com/archive/issue-10/issue-10-page-7/.

2. Art Babbitt, "Art Babbitt's Analysis of Goofy," *The Encyclopedia of Disney Animated Shorts*, http://www.disneyshorts.org/characters/goofy2.html.

3. *Ibid.*

4. "Art Babbitt — Disney Legend Bio," *The Walt Disney Company*, http://legends.disney.go.com/legends/detail?key=Art+Babbitt.

5. Noell Wolfgram Evans, "Popeye Pickets and Other Exploits in Animation Unions," *Written By* (Summer 2008): 59–65.

6. Tom Roth, Interview with author, March 21, 2010.

7. "Seventy Years On...," *Animation Guide*, November 5, 2009, http://www.animationguide.com/TB/?P=3089.

Chapter 2

1. Scott Bruce and Bill Crawford, *Cerealizing America: The Unsweetened Story of American Breakfast Cereal* (Boston: Faber & Faber, 1995).

2. John Hubley and Zachary Schwartz, "Animation Learns a New Language," in *Hollywood Quarterly: Film Culture in Postwar America, 1945–1957*, edited by Eric Smoodin and Ann Martin (Berkeley: University of California, 2002), http://www.escholarship.org/editions/view?docId=kt2f59q2dp&chunk.id=ss1.05&toc.id=ch02&toc.depth=1&brand=eschol&anchor.id=p076#X.

3. Sybil DelGaudio and Patty Wineapple, "Independent Spirits: The John and Faith Hubley Story," PBS, http://www.pbs.org/itvs/independentspirits/john.html.

4. Ramin Zahed, "The Toon That Changed My Life," *Animation Magazine*, February 5, 2010, http://animationmagazine.net/article/11097.

5. MOMA Press Release, "Gallery Exhibition Displays the Award Winning Work of the Hubley Studio," MoMA, December 19, 1997.

6. Amid Amidi, *Cartoon Modern* (San Francisco: Chronicle Books, 1996).

7. Jim Lochner, "Urbanissimo," *Film Score Click Track*, May 25, 2009, http://www.filmscoreclicktrack.com/2009/05/urbanissimo/.

8. *Ibid.*

9. Keith Scott, *The Moose That Roared: The Story of Jay Ward, Bill Scott, a Flying Squirrel and a Talking Moose* (New York: St. Martin's Griffin, 2002).

Chapter 3

1. Chris Gore, "Cel Out: The Plot to Kill Cartoons," *Wild Cartoon Kingdom* 1 (1993), http://wck-01.blogspot.com/.

2. "Learn from John Kricfalusi and Bill Plympton," *JacketFlap*, http://www.jacketflap.com/megablog/index.

3. John Martz, "Ottawa: John K and the Torch of Bob Clampett," *Drawn!: The Illustration and Cartooning Blog*, September 29, 2006, http://drawn.ca/tag/bob-clampett/.

4. Nathanial Stevens, "Question and Answer Session with Mighty Mouse: The New Adventures Co-creator John Kricfalusi," *Drawn!: The Illustration and Cartooning Blog*, http://digitalchumps.com/featured-electronics/132-features/4353-question-and-answer-session-with-mighty-mouse-the-new-adventures-co-creator-john-kricfalusi.html

5. John Martz, "Ottawa: John K and the Torch of Bob Clampett," *Drawn!: The Illustration and Cartooning Blog*, September 29, 2006, http://drawn.ca/tag/bob-clampett/.

Chapter 4

1. Bob McCabe, Graham Chapman, Terry Gilliam, Eric Idle, John Cleese, Michael Palin, and Terry Jones, *The Pythons Autobiography by the Pythons* (New York: Thomas Dunne Books, 2003).

2. Salman Rushdie, "Salmon Rushdie Talks with Terry Gilliam," *Believer Magazine* 1, no. 1 (March 2003), http://www.believermag.com/issues/200303/.

3. Mark Lewisoh, "The BBC.co.uk Guide to Comedy — Monty Python's Flying Circus," http://www.bbc.co.uk/comedy/guide/articles/m/montypythonsflyi_1299002137.shtml.

4. America Online Live Chat with Terry Gilliam, October 9, 1994, http://orangecow.org/pythonet/scripts/tgillive.html

5. Phil Stubbs, "Dreams: Gilliam's Childhood — An Interview," http://www.smart.co.uk/dreams/tgearly.htm.

6. Terry Gilliam, "The Ten Best Animated Films of All Time," *The Guardian Unlimited*, April 27, 2001, http://film.guardian.co.uk/features/featurepages/0,4120,479022,00.html.

7. Paul Wardle, "Terry Gilliam Interview," *The Comics Journal* 182 (1998).

8. Ella Christopherson, Interview with Terry Gilliam, *Index Magazine* 47 (February 2005), http://www.indexmagazine.com/interviews/terry_gilliam.shtml.

9. Mark Lewisoh, "The BBC.co.uk Guide to Comedy — Monty Python's Flying Circus," http://www.bbc.co.uk/comedy/guide/articles/m/montypythonsflyi_1299002137.shtml.

10. Stanley Reynolds, Television News, *The Times*, April 8, 1969.

11. "Terry Gilliam: Writer, Animator and Director," *BBC Guide to Life, the Universe and Everything*, http://www.bbc.co.uk/dna/h2g2/A716906/G12.

12. Jerry Beck, *Animation Art: From Pencil to Pixel, the World of Cartoon, Anime and CGI* (New York: Harper Design International, 2004).

13. America Online Live Chat with Terry Gilliam, October 9th, 1994, http://orangecow.org/pythonet/scripts/tgillive.html.

14. David Morgan, *Monty Python Speaks* (New York: Spike/Avon, 1999).

15. Glenn Whipp, "Arthur: A Long Time Ago in a Kingdom Far, Far Away," *Los Angeles Daily News*, July 6, 2004.

16. June 16, 1996, Press Release issued by *Monty Python's Daily Llama*.

17. Paul Fischer, "Cranky Critic Star Talk: Terry Gilliam," http://www.crankycritic.com/qa/terrygilliam.html.

Chapter 5

1. Stefan Kanfer, *Serious Business: The Art and Commerce of Animation in America from Betty Boop to Toy Story* (New York: Scribner, 1997).

2. Gordan Calma and Nenad Calma, "Fleischer Studios 'Popeye,'" Fleischer Popeye Tribute website, http://www.fleischerpopeye.com/history.php?section=fleischer_popeye&current=history.

3. Daniel Goldmark, *Tunes for Toons* (Berkeley: University of California Press, 2005).

Chapter 6

1. Jean-Luc Godard, *Godard on Godard* (New York: Da Capo Press, 1986).

2. Michael Barrier, *Hollywood Cartoons* (New York: Oxford University Press, 1999).

3. Jean-Luc Godard, *Godard on Godard* (New York: Da Capo Press, 1986).

4. Michael Barrier, "Frank Tashlin: An Interview," January 11, 2005, http://www.michaelbarrier.com.

5. Adrian Danks, "Bob Clampett," *Senses of Cinema*, http://archive.sensesofcinema.com/contents/directors/05/clampett.html.

6. Michael Barrier, "Frank Tashlin: An Interview," January 11, 2005, http://www.michaelbarrier.com.

7. Dave Keifer, "Unmanly Men Meet Womanly Women: Frank Tashlin's Satires Still Ring True," *New York Times*, August 20, 2006, http://www.filmforum.org/films/girlcant/girlcantnytimes.html.

8. Michael Barrier, "Frank Tashlin: An Interview," January 11, 2005, http://www.michaelbarrier.com.

9. Constantine Nasr, *Tish Tash: The Animated World of Frank Tashlin* (Los Angeles: New Wave Entertainment, 2005), video.

10. Noell Wolfgram Evans, "Popeye Pickets and Other Exploits in Animation Unions," *Written By.* (Summer 2008): 59–65.

11. Constantine Nasr, *Tish Tash: The Animated World of Frank Tashlin* (Los Angeles: New Wave Entertainment, 2005), video.

12. "Masters of Animation: The Prehistory of UPA," *Electronic Cerebrectomy*, February 12, 2008, http://samuraifrog.blogspot.com/2008/02/masters-of-animation-prehistory-of-upa.html.

13. Michael Barrier, "Frank Tashlin: An Interview," January 11, 2005, http://www.michaelbarrier.com.

14. "Animation: Hard to Find Films," http://animationhardtofind.blogspot.com/.

15. Adrian Danks, "Bob Clampett," *Senses of Cinema*, http://archive.sensesofcinema.com/contents/directors/05/clampett.html.

16. Dave Keifer, "Unmanly Men Meet Womanly Women: Frank Tashlin's Satires Still Ring True," *New York Times*, August 20, 2006, http://www.filmforum.org/films/girlcant/girlcantnytimes.html.

17. "The Way of Peace," *The Lutheran Standard* 105, no. 49 (December 6, 1947).

18. "Tashlin's Apocalypse," May 7, 2010, http://www.mardecortesbaja.com/blog/_archives/2007/5/7/2929815.html

19. Ray Davis, "The Road to Son of Paleface," *Pseudopodium*, http://www.pseudopodium.org/search.cgi?Jane+Russell.

20. John Cannemaker, *Tex Avery: The MGM Years, 1942–1955* (Atlanta: Turner Publishing, 1996).

21. Brandon Bentley, "Brandon's Movie Memory," http://www.deeperintomovies.net.

22. *Ibid.*

23. *Ibid.*

24. John Cannemaker, *Tex Avery: The MGM Years, 1942–1955* (Atlanta: Turner Publishing, 1996).

25. Dave Keifer. "Unmanly Men Meet Womanly Women: Frank Tashlin's Satires Still Ring True." *New York Times.* 8/20/2006 www.filmforum.org/films/girlcant/girlcantnytimes.html

26. Excerpts from Garcia, Roger, and Bernard Eisenschitz. *Frank Tashlin.* Locarno: Editions du Festival international du film de Locarno in collaboration with the British Film Institute, 1994. Posted on Brandon's Movie Memories, http://deeperintomovies.net/journal/archives/2051

Chapter 7

1. Richard Stayton, "Life in Hell & Heaven," *Written By* (Summer 2008): 53.

2. John Ortved, *The Simpsons: An Uncensored, Unauthorized History* (New York: Faber & Faber, 2009).

3. *Ibid.*

4. *Ibid.*

5. Eric Spiznagel, "George Meyer," *The Believer*, September 2004.

6. *Ibid.*

7. A. O. Scott, "Matt Groening," Slate.com, April 10, 1999, http://www.slate.com/toolbar.aspx?action=print&id=23430.

8. *Ibid.*

9. James Poniewozik, "The 100 Best TV Shows of All Time," *Time*, http://www.time.com/time/specials/packages/completelist/0,29569,1651341,00.html.

10. John Preston, "Overachiever, and Proud of It," *The Age*, January 10, 2010, http://www.theage.com.au/articles/2010/01/09/1262453696968.html.

11. Richard Stayton, "Life in Hell & Heaven," *Written By* (Summer 2008): 53.

12. Matt Groening, "Oh Boy, Charlie Brown," *The Guardian*, October 11, 2008, http://www.guardian.co.uk/books/2008/oct/

11/peanuts-matt-groening-jonathan-franzen/ print.

13. A. O. Scott, "Matt Groening," Slate. com, April 10, 1999, http://www.slate.com/ toolbar.aspx?action=print&id=23430.

14. *Ibid.*

Chapter 8

1. Ray Harryhausen and Tony Dalton, *A Century of Stop Motion Animation* (New York: Watson-Guptill Publications, 2008), 7.

2. Horatia Harrod, "Ray Harryhausen Interview," *The London Telegraph*, April 18, 2010.

3. Ray Harryhausen and Tony Dalton, *A Century of Stop Motion Animation* (New York: Watson-Guptill Publications, 2008), 113.

4. Don Hahn, *The Alchemy of Animation* (New York: Disney Editions, 2008), 100.

5. John Landis, Interview with Ray Harryhausen, *Jason and the Argonauts* DVD, 1998.

6. Henry Selick, Interview, August 16, 2008, Ultimate Disney website, http://www. ultimatedisney.com/henryselick-interview. html.

7. John Landis, Interview with Ray Harryhausen, *Jason and the Argonauts* DVD, 1998.

8. Ryan Brennan, "Harryhausen Dazzles Dallas," The Thunder Child website, http: //thethunderchild.com/Movies/MoviePeo ple/Harryhausen/HarryhausenDallas.html.

9. Henry Selick, Interview, August 16, 2008, Ultimate Disney website, http://www. ultimatedisney.com/henryselick-interview. html.

10. Horatia Harrod, "Nick Park's Tribute to Ray Harryhausen," Interview with Nick Park, *The London Telegraph*, April 19, 2010, http://www.telegraph.co.uk/culture/film/film -life/7593616/Nick-Parks-tribute-to-Ray- Harryhausen-Wallace-and-Gromit-stop-mo tion-animation.html.

11. Rusty White, "Ray Harryhausen: The Science Fiction Films," E-insiders website, http://www.einsiders.com/reviews/videor isks/harryhausen.php.

12. Tim Burton, *Burton on Burton*, ed. Mark Salisbury (London: Faber & Faber, 1995), 119.

Chapter 9

1. Michael Denning, *The Cultural Front* (London/New York: Verso, 1998).

2. Michael Riley, "Resume," http://www. earglasses.com/mriley/resume.htm.

3. Amid Amidi, "Ed Benedict," *Animation Blast* 8 (2002): 30.

4. Amid Amidi, *Cartoon Modern* (San Francisco: Chronicle Books, 1996).

5. John Rogers, "'Flintstones' Animator Dies at His Calif. Home," *Spartanburg Herald-Journal*, October 16, 2006, page B4, http: //news.google.com/newspapers?nid=1876&d at=20061014&id=6HUpAAAAIBAJ&sjid=n 9AEAAAAIBAJ&pg=3866,6488164.

6. Amid Amidi, "Ed Benedict," *Animation Blast* 8 (2002): 30.

7. John Kricfalusi, "Meet The Stars of the Flintstones," Flintstones Laserdisc, September 21, 2006, http://www.animationarchive.org/ labels/flintstones.html.

8. *Ibid.*

9. Amid Amidi, "Ed Benedict," *Animation Blast* 8 (2002): 30.

10. Steve Holland, "Ed Benedict — Obituary," *The Guardian*, http://www.guardian. co.uk.

11. John Kricfalusi, "Meet the Stars of the Flintstones," Flintstones Laserdisc, September 21, 2006, http://www.animationarchive.org/ labels/flintstones.html.

12. Amid Amidi, "Ed Benedict," *Animation Blast* 8 (2002): 30.

13. John Kricfaulsi, "Ed Benedict, 1912– 2006," John K. Stuff, August 31, 2006, http: //johnkstuff.blogspot.com/2006/08/ed-ben edict-1912-2006.html.

Chapter 10

1. Phillip Kemp, "Reiniger, Lotte (1899– 1981)," ScreenOnline, http://www.screenon line.org.uk/people/id/528134/index.html.

2. William Moritz, "Lotte Reiniger," *Mad Bad and Dangerous to Know*, http://by ronic.tumblr.com/post/230717912/lotte-rein iger-by-william-moritz.

3. Lotte Reiniger, *The Adventures of Prince Achmed*, Milestone Films Release Book, http://www.milestonefilms.com/movie.php/ achmed/.

4. Phillip Kemp, "Reiniger, Lotte (1899–

1981)," ScreenOnline, http://www.screenon-line.org.uk/people/id/528134/index.html.

5. http://www.lottereiniger.de/

6. Lotte Reiniger, *The Adventures of Prince Achmed*, Milestone Films Release Book, http://www.milestonefilms.com/movie.php/achmed/.

7. Chris Robe, "The Adventures of Prince Achmed: A Forgotten Tale," *Pop Matters*, December 3, 2002, http://www.popmatters.com/pm/review/adventures-of-prince-achmed/.

8. William Moritz, "Lotte Reiniger," *Mad Bad and Dangerous to Know*, http://byronic.tumblr.com/post/230717912/lotte-reiniger-by-william-moritz.

9. Lotte Reiniger, *The Adventures of Prince Achmed*, Milestone Films Release Book, http://www.milestonefilms.com/movie.php/achmed/.

Chapter 11

1. Ray Pointer, "Women Animators," Golden Age Cartoon Forums, November 3, 2007, http://forums.goldenagecartoons.com/showthread.php?t=10194&highlight=friedman&page=2.

2. Ashley Gerst, "Lillian Friedman — Rejected from Disney," *Gender and Race Critique in Animation*, May 16, 2008, http://theanimatedcritique.blogspot.com/.

3. Michael Mallory, "Move Over, Old Men," *L.A. Times*, Calendar Section, March 13, 2000, http://www.catalystagency.com/CLIENTS/CREDITS/MILLERcredits2.htm.

4. Elizabeth Bell, Lynda Haas, and Laura Sells, *From Mouse to Mermaid — the Politics of Film, Gender, and Culture*. (Bloomington: Indiana University Press, 1995).

Chapter 12

1. Bill Jones, "He Kept His Nightmare Alive," *The Phoenix Gazette*, October 22, 1993, http://www.timburtoncollective.com/articles/nmbc13.html.

2. Ray Harryhausen and Tony Dalton, *A Century of Stop Motion Animation* (New York: Watson-Guptill Publications, 2008).

3. Robert Ebert, "Tim Burton's *Nightmare Before Christmas*," Movie Review, *Chicago Sun Times*, October 22, 1993, http://rogerebert.suntimes.com/apps/pbcs.dll/article?AID=/19931022/REVIEWS/310220302/1023.

4. Bob Strauss, "Animation Goes Ape in Zany Monkeybone," *Los Angeles Daily News*, February 23, 2001.

5. Stephen Jones and Neil Gaiman, *Coraline: A Visual Companion* (New York: William Morrow, 2009), 115.

6. Sheila Johnston, "Coraline: Animation by Neil Gaiman," *The London Telegraph*, May 14, 2009, http://www.telegraph.co.uk/culture/film/filmreviews/5307595/Coraline-animation-by-Neil-Gaiman.html.

7. Henry Selick, Interview, August 16, 2008, Ultimate Disney website, http://www.ultimatedisney.com/henryselick-interview.html.

8. Tasha Robinson, "Henry Selick," The Onion A. V. Club, February 3, 2009, http://www.avclub.com/articles/henry-selick,23298/.

9. Stephen Jones, *Coraline: A Visual Companion* (New York: William Morrow, 2009), 55.

10. Bill Desowitz, "Selick Talks Coraline: The Electricity of Life," *AWN Magazine*, February 6, 2009, http://www.awn.com/articles/stop-motion/selick-talks-icoralinei-electricity-life/page/2%2C1.

Chapter 13

1. "Santa Ana Disney College Program," Santa Ana College, http://www.mickeysac.com/depthomeshellc.cfm?id=59613&rt=10&view=&sms=custom9&xsite=micke.

2. DVD Booklet, *Schoolhouse Rock 30th Anniversary* DVD (Burbank, CA: Buena Vista Home Video, 2002).

3. "Earth Promise: Earth Promise '21 in 21' Interview Series — George Newall — Creator of Schoolhouse Rock!," Earth Promises website, March 19, 2009, http://www.earthpromise.com/blog/2009/04/earth-promise-21-in-21-interview-series-george-newall-creator-of-schoolhouse-rock/.

4. George Newall, Interview with author, February 25, 2010.

5. *Ibid.*

6. DVD Booklet, *Schoolhouse Rock 30th Anniversary* DVD (Burbank, CA: Buena Vista Home Video, 2002).

7. George Newall, Interview with author, February 25, 2010.

8. DVD Booklet, *Schoolhouse Rock 30th Anniversary* DVD (Burbank, CA: Buena Vista Home Video, 2002).

9. George Newall, Interview with author, February 25, 2010.

10. DVD Booklet, *Schoolhouse Rock 30th Anniversary* DVD (Burbank, CA: Buena Vista Home Video, 2002).

11. George Newall, Interview with author, February 25, 2010.

12. Elaine Woo, "Thomas Yohe; Co-Created 'Schoolhouse Rock,'" *The Los Angeles Times*, December 26, 2000, http://articles.latimes.com/2000/dec/26/local/me-4734.

Chapter 14

1. "Real American Zero: The Adventures of Private SNAFU," *Looney Tunes Golden Collection Volume 5* (Burbank, CA: Warner Home Video, 2007).

2. Eric Smoodin and Ann Martin, eds., *Hollywood Quarterly: Film Culture in Postwar America, 1945–1957* (Berkeley: University of California, 2002), http://ark.cdlib.org/ark:/13030/kt2f59q2dp/.

3. Judith Morgan and Neil Morgan, *Dr. Seuss and Mr. Geisel* (New York: Random House, 1995).

4. *Ibid.*

5. Christopher Dow, "Private SNAFU's Hidden War," *Bright Lights Film Journal*, http://www.brightlightsfilm.com/42/snafu.php.

6. Eric Smoodin, *Animating Culture* (New Brunswick, NJ: Rutgers University Press, 1993).

7. "Real American Zero: The Adventures of Private SNAFU," *Looney Tunes Golden Collection Volume 5* (Burbank, CA : Warner Home Video, 2007).

8. Christopher Dow, "Private SNAFU's Hidden War," *Bright Lights Film Journal*, http://www.brightlightsfilm.com/42/snafu.php.

9. Eric Smoodin and Ann Martin, eds., *Hollywood Quarterly: Film Culture in Postwar America, 1945–1957* (Berkeley: University of California, 2002), http://ark.cdlib.org/ark:/13030/kt2f59q2dp/.

Chapter 15

1. John Cannemaker, *Before the Animation Begins* (New York: Hyperion, 1996).

2. John Cannemaker, *Paper Dreams* (New York: Hyperion, 1999).

3. Robin Allan, *Walt Disney and Europe* (Bloomington: Indiana University Press, 1999).

4. Charles Solomon, *The Disney That Never Was* (New York: Hyperion, 1995).

5. John Cannemaker, *Before the Animation Begins* (New York: Hyperion, 1996).

6. *Ibid.*

7. *Ibid.*

8. "Cinema: Mammal-of-the-Year," *Time*, December 29, 1941, http://www.time.com/time/magazine/article/0,9171,772928-1,00.html.

9. Charles Solomon, *The Disney That Never Was* (New York: Hyperion, 1995).

10. John Cannemaker, *Before the Animation Begins* (New York: Hyperion, 1996).

11. *Ibid.*

Chapter 16

1. Scott Bruce and Bill Crawford, *Cerealizing America: The Unsweetened Story of American Breakfast Cereal* (Boston: Faber & Faber, 1995).

2. John Cawley, "Frames of Time," http://www.cataroo.com/020204.html.

3. Keith Scott, *The Moose That Roared: The Story of Jay Ward, Bill Scott, a Flying Squirrel and a Talking Moose* (New York: St. Martin's Griffin, 2002).

4. Phil Denslow, ed., "The Animation Writer: Bill Scott at UCLA," *Graffiti Magazine*, March/April and May/June 1986, http://www.denslow.com/articles/bscott.html.

5. "Crusader Rabbit," Toon Tracker website, updated June 17, 2001, http://www.toontracker.com/crusader/crusader.htm.

6. "The Bullwinkle Show," Toon Tracker website, updated January 12, 2005, http://www.toontracker.com/bullwink/bullwink.htm.

7. Catalogue: Region Five ESC Electronic Field Trips, http://www.esc5.net/edtechweb/elecfieldtrips/museumoftvradio.html

8. Scott Bruce and Bill Crawford, *Cerealizing America: The Unsweetened Story of*

American Breakfast Cereal (Boston: Faber & Faber, 1995).

9. Stefan Kanfer, *Serious Business: The Art and Commerce of Animation in America from Betty Boop to Toy Story* (New York: Scribner, 1997).

10. "Hokey Smoke! Rocky and Bullwinkle," ToonZone website, 2005, http://bullwinkle.toonzone.net/secrets.htm.

11. Robert Lloyd, "Beyond Good and Evil," *LA Weekly*, November 24–30, 2000, http://www.laweekly.com/ink/01/01/features-lloyd.php.

12. Keith Scott, *The Moose That Roared: The Story of Jay Ward, Bill Scott, a Flying Squirrel and a Talking Moose* (New York: St. Martin's Griffin, 2002).

Chapter 17

1. Michael Barrier, *Hollywood Cartoons* (New York: Oxford University Press, 1999).

2. Richard Corliss, "That Old Feeling: Remembering Chuck Jones," *Time Magazine*, February 24, 2002, http://www.time.com/time/arts/article/0,8599,212624,00.html.

3. Steve Schneider, *That's All Folks—The Art of Warner Bros. Animation*, (New York: Henry Holt, 1988).

4. Daniel Goldmark, *Tunes for Toons* (Berkeley: University of California Press, 2005).

5. Michael Barrier, *Hollywood Cartoons* (New York: Oxford University Press, 1999).

6. William Hanna and Tom Ito, *A Cast of Friends* (Dallas: Taylor Publishing, 1996).

7. Jaime J. Weinman, "Mike Maltese Speaks in 1960," Something Old, Something New website, August 21, 2008, http://zvbxr-pl.blogspot.com/2008/08/mike-maltese-speaks-in-1960.html.

8. Michael Barrier, *Hollywood Cartoons* (New York: Oxford University Press, 1999).

9. William Hanna and Tom Ito, *A Cast of Friends* (Dallas: Taylor Publishing, 1996).

10. Michael Barrier, *Hollywood Cartoons* (New York: Oxford University Press, 1999).

11. Roger Ebert, "Chuck Jones: Three Cartoons (1953–1957)," RogerEbert.com, January 15, 2006,http://rogerebert.suntimes.com/apps/pbcs.dll/article?AID=/20060115/REVIEWS08/601150301/1023.

12. Steve Schneider, *That's All Folks—The*

Art of Warner Bros. Animation, (New York: Henry Holt, 1988).

13. *Ibid.*

14. Roger Ebert, "Chuck Jones: Three Cartoons (1953–1957)," RogerEbert.com, January 15, 2006, http://rogerebert.suntimes.com/apps/pbcs.dll/article?AID=/20060115/REVIEWS08/601150301/1023.

15. Mark Dilloff, "The Deeper Meaning of Michigan J. Frog," Deeper Questions website, March 1, 2010, http://blog.deeperquestions.com/blog/?p=143.

16. Ramin Zahed, "The Toon That Changed My Life!" Animation Magazine. 02/05/2010, http://animationmagazine.net/features/the-toon-that-changed-my-life.

17. Roger Ebert, "Chuck Jones: Three Cartoons (1953–1957)," RogerEbert.com, January 15, 2006, http://rogerebert.suntimes.com/apps/pbcs.dll/article?AID=/20060115/REVIEWS08/601150301/1023.

18. "The Great Cartoons: Duck Amuck," Paulietoons website, February 22, 2010, http://paulietoons.com/?p=656.

19. "Fun Facts About Wile E. Coyote and the Road Runner," Chuck Jones blog, April 29, 2009, http://blog.chuckjones.com/chuck_redux/2009/04/fun-facts-about-wile-e-coyote-and-the-road-runner.html.

20. *Ibid.*.

21. Robin Varnum and Christina T. Gibbons, *The Language of Comics: Word and Image* (Jackson: University Press of Mississippi, 2007).

22. "Flashes Before Your Eyes," *Lost*, season 3, episode 8, February 14, 2007 (Burbank, CA: Buena Vista Home Entertainment, 2007).

23. Michael Barrier, *Hollywood Cartoons* (New York: Oxford University Press, 1999).

24. Richard Corliss, "That Old Feeling: Remembering Chuck Jones," *Time Magazine*, February 24, 2002, http://www.time.com/time/arts/article/0,8599,212624,00.html.

25. Daniel Goldmark, *Tunes for Toons* (Berkeley: University of California Press, 2005).

26. Joe Adamson, *Bugs Bunny: Fifty Years and Only One Grey Hare* (New York: Henry Holt, 1990).

27. Daniel Goldmark, *Tunes for Toons* (Berkeley: University of California Press, 2005).

28. Joe Adamson, *Bugs Bunny: Fifty Years*

and Only One Grey Hare (New York: Henry Holt, 1990).

29. Michael Barrier, *Hollywood Cartoons* (New York: Oxford University Press, 1999).

30. Steven Gaydos, "Bird Wants Respect for Toon Scribes," *Variety*, December 28, 2007.

Epilogue

1. Mark Feeney, "Thinking Outside the Lines," *Boston Globe*, February 3, 2010, http://www.boston.com/ae/theater_arts/articles/2010/02/03/thinking_outside_the_lines_at_harvards_animation_exhibit/.

Bibliography

Adamson, Joe. *Bugs Bunny: Fifty Years and Only One Grey Hare*. New York: Henry Holt, 1990.

Allan, Robin. *Walt Disney and Europe*. Bloomington: Indiana University Press, 1999.

America Online Live Chat with Terry Gilliam, October 9, 1994, http://orangecow.org/python et/scripts/tgillive.html.

Amidi, Amid. *Cartoon Modern*. San Francisco: Chronicle Books, 1996.

_____. "Ed Benedict." *Animation Blast* 8 (2002): 30.

"Animation: Hard to Find Films." http://animationhardtofind.blogspot.com/.

"Art Babbitt — Disney Legend Bio." *The Walt Disney Company*. http://legends.disney.go.com/leg ends/detail?key=Art+Babbitt.

Babbitt, Art. "The Art Babbitt Classical Animation Course." *Animator* 10, no. 4 (Autumn 1984). http://www.animatormag.com/archive/issue-10/issue-10-page-7/.

_____. "Art Babbitt's Analysis of Goofy." *The Encyclopedia of Disney Animated Shorts*. http://www.disneyshorts.org/characters/goofy2.html.

Barrier, Michael. "Frank Tashlin: An Interview." January 11, 2005. http://www.michaelbarrier.com.

_____. *Hollywood Cartoons*. New York: Oxford University Press, 1999.

Beck, Jerry. *Animation Art: From Pencil to Pixel, the World of Cartoon, Anime and CGI*. New York: Harper Design International, 2004.

Bell, Elizabeth, Lynda Haas, and Laura Sells. *From Mouse to Mermaid—The Politics of Film, Gender, and Culture*. Bloomington: Indiana University Press, 1995.

Bentley, Brandon. "Brandon's Movie Memory." http://www.deeperintomovies.net.

Block, Alex Ben. "Anatomy of a Contender: 'Up.'" *The Hollywood Reporter*. November 17, 2009. http://www.hollywoodreporter.com/hr/content_display/film/news/e3i45e1bcc0b65a294fae 37066c88506cfc.

Brennan, Ryan. "Harryhausen Dazzles Dallas." The Thunder Child website. http://thethund erchild.com/Movies/MoviePeople/Harryhausen/HarryhausenDallas.html.

Bruce, Scott, and Bill Crawford. *Cerealizing America: The Unsweetened Story of American Break-fast Cereal*. Boston: Faber & Faber, 1995.

"The Bullwinkle Show." Toon Tracker website. Updated January 12, 2005. http://www.toon tracker.com/bullwink/bullwink.htm.

Burton, Tim. *Burton on Burton*. Edited by Mark Salisbury. London: Faber & Faber, 1995.

Calma, Gordan, and Nenad Calma. "Fleischer Studios 'Popeye.'" Fleischer Popeye Tribute web site. http://www.fleischerpopeye.com/history.php?section=fleischer_popeye&current=history.

Cannemaker, John. *Before the Animation Begins*. New York: Hyperion, 1996.

_____. *Paper Dreams*. New York: Hyperion, 1999.

_____. *Tex Avery: The MGM Years, 1942–1955*. Atlanta: Turner Publishing, 1996.

Catalogue: Region Five ESC Electronic Field Trips. http://www.esc5.net/edtechweb/elecfield trips/museumoftvradio.html.

Cawley, John. "Frames of Time." http://www.cataroo.com/020204.html.

Christopherson, Ella. Interview with Terry Gilliam. *Index Magazine* 47 (February 2005). http://www.indexmagazine.com/interviews/terry_gilliam.shtml.

"Cinema: Mammal-of-the-Year." *Time*. December 29, 1941. http://www.time.com/time/mag azine/article/0,9171,772928–1,00.html.

Corliss, Richard. "That Old Feeling: Remembering Chuck Jones." *Time Magazine*. February 24, 2002. http://www.time.com/time/arts/article/0,8599,212624,00.html.

"Crusader Rabbit." Toon Tracker website. Updated June 17, 2001. http://www.toontracker. com/crusader/crusader.htm.

Danks, Adrian. "Bob Clampett." *Senses of Cinema*. http://archive.sensesofcinema.com/contents/ directors/05/clampett.html.

Davis, Ray. "The Road to Son of Paleface." *Pseudopodium*. http://www.pseudopodium.org/ search.cgi?Jane+Russell.

DelGaudio, Sybil, and Patty Wineapple. "Independent Spirits: The John and Faith Hubley Story." PBS. http://www.pbs.org/itvs/independentspirits/john.html.

Denning, Michael. *The Cultural Front*. London/New York: Verso, 1998.

Denslow, Phil, ed. "The Animation Writer: Bill Scott at UCLA." *Graffiti Magazine*. March/April and May/June 1986. http://www.denslow.com/articles/bscott.html.

Desowitz, Bill. "Selick Talks Coraline: The Electricity of Life." *AWN Magazine*. February 6, 2009. http://www.awn.com/articles/stop-motion/selick-talks-icoralinei-electricity-life/ page/2%2C1.

Dilloff, Mark. "The Deeper Meaning of Michigan J. Frog." Deeper Questions website. March 1, 2010. http://blog.deeperquestions.com/blog/?p=143.

Dow, Christopher. "Private SNAFU's Hidden War." *Bright Lights Film Journal*. http://www. brightlightsfilm.com/42/snafu.php.

Drawn!: The Illustration and Cartooning Blog http://blog.drawn.ca/.

DVD Booklet. *Schoolhouse Rock 30th Anniversary* DVD. Burbank, CA: Buena Vista Home Video, 2002.

"Earth Promise: Earth Promise '21 in 21' Interview Series — George Newall — Creator of School- house Rock!" Earth Promises website. March 19, 2009. http://www.earthpromise.com/blog/ 2009/04/earth-promise-21-in-21-interview-series-george-newall-creator-of-schoolhouse- rock/.

Ebert, Roger. "Chuck Jones: Three Cartoons (1953–1957)." RogerEbert.com. January 15, 2006. http://rogerebert.suntimes.com/apps/pbcs.dll/article?AID=/20060115/REVIEWS08/601150 301/1023.

_____. "Tim Burton's *Nightmare Before Christmas*." Movie Review. *Chicago Sun Times*. October 22, 1993. http://rogerebert.suntimes.com/apps/pbcs.dll/article?AID=/19931022/REVIEWS /310220302/1023.

Feeney, Mark. "Thinking Outside the Lines." *Boston Globe*. February 3, 2010. http://www.bos ton.com/ae/theater_arts/articles/2010/02/03/thinking_outside_the_lines_at_harvards_ani mation_exhibit/.

Fischer, Paul. "Cranky Critic Star Talk: Terry Gilliam." http://www.crankycritic.com/qa/ter rygilliam.html.

"Flashes Before Your Eyes." *Lost*, season 3, episode 8. February 14, 2007. Burbank, CA: Buena Vista Home Entertainment, 2007.

"Fun Facts About Wile E. Coyote and the Road Runner." Chuck Jones blog. April 29, 2009. http://blog.chuckjones.com/chuck_redux/2009/04/fun–facts-about–wile-e-coyote-and– the-road-runner.html.

Gaydos, Steven. "Bird Wants Respect for Toon Scribes." *Variety*. December 28, 2007.

Gerst, Ashley. "Lillian Friedman — Rejected from Disney." *Gender and Race Critique in Ani- mation*. May 16, 2008. http://theanimatedcritique.blogspot.com/.

Gilliam, Terry. "The Ten Best Animated Films of All Time." *The Guardian Unlimited*. April 27, 2001. http://film.guardian.co.uk/features/featurepages/0,4120,479022,00.html.

Godard, Jean-Luc. *Godard on Godard*. New York: Da Capo Press, 1986.

Goldmark, Daniel. *Tunes for Toons*. Berkeley: University of California Press, 2005.

Gore, Chris. "Cel Out: The Plot to Kill Cartoons." *Wild Cartoon Kingdom* 1 (1993). http://wck- 01.blogspot.com/.

"The Great Cartoons: Duck Amuck." Paulietoons website. February 22, 2010. http://paulie toons.com/?p=656.

Groening, Matt. "Oh Boy, Charlie Brown," *The Guardian*, October 11, 2008, http://www. guardian.co.uk/books/2008/oct/11/peanuts-matt-groening-jonathan-franzen/print.

Hahn, Don. *The Alchemy of Animation*. New York: Disney Editions, 2008.

Hanna, William, and Tom Ito. *A Cast of Friends*. Dallas: Taylor Publishing, 1996.

Harrod, Horatia. "Nick Park's Tribute to Ray Harryhausen." Interview with Nick Park. *The London Telegraph*. April 19, 2010. http://www.telegraph.co.uk/culture/film/film-life/ 7593616/Nick-Parks-tribute-to-Ray-Harryhausen-Wallace-and-Gromit-stop-motion-ani mation.html.

_____. "Ray Harryhausen Interview." *The London Telegraph*. April 18, 2010.

Harryhausen, Ray, and Tony Dalton. *A Century of Stop Motion Animation*. New York: Watson-Guptill Publications, 2008.

"Hokey Smoke! Rocky and Bullwinkle." ToonZone website. 2005. http://bullwinkle.toonzone. net/secrets.htm.

Holland, Steve. "Ed Benedict — Obituary." *The Guardian*. http://www.guardian.co.uk.

Hubley, John, and Zachary Schwartz. "Animation Learns a New Language." In *Hollywood Quarterly: Film Culture in Postwar America, 1945–1957*, edited by Eric Smoodin and Ann Martin. Berkeley: University of California, 2002. http://www.escholarship.org/editions/view?doc Id=kt2f59q2dp&chunk.id=ss1.05&toc.id=ch02&toc.depth=1&brand=eschol&anchor.id= p076#X.

Johnston, Sheila. "Coraline: Animation by Neil Gaiman." *The London Telegraph*. May 14, 2009. http://www.telegraph.co.uk/culture/film/filmreviews/5307595/Coraline-animation-by-Neil-Gaiman.html.

Jones, Bill. "He Kept His Nightmare Alive." *The Phoenix Gazette*. October 22, 1993. http:// www.timburtoncollective.com/articles/nmbc13.html.

Jones, Stephen. *Coraline: A Visual Companion*. New York: William Morrow, 2009.

Kanfer, Stefan. *Serious Business: The Art and Commerce of Animation in America from Betty Boop to Toy Story*. New York: Scribner, 1997.

Keifer, Dave. "Unmanly Men Meet Womanly Women: Frank Tashlin's Satires Still Ring True." *New York Times*. August 20, 2006. http://www.filmforum.org/films/girlcant/girlcantny times.html.

Kemp, Phillip. "Reiniger, Lotte (1899–1981)." ScreenOnline. http://www.screenonline.org.uk/ people/id/528134/index.html.

Kricfalusi, John. "Ed Benedict, 1912–2006." John K. Stuff. August 31, 2006. http://johnkstuff. blogspot.com/2006/08/ed-benedict-1912-2006.html.

_____. "Meet the Stars of the Flintstones." Flintstones Laserdisc. September 21, 2006. http:// www.animationarchive.org/labels/flintstones.html.

Landis, John. Interview with Ray Harryhausen. *Jason and the Argonauts* DVD. 1998.

"Learn from John Kricfalusi and Bill Plympton." *JacketFlap*. http://www.jacketflap.com/ megablog/index.

Lewisohn, Mark. "The BBC.co.uk Guide to Comedy — Monty Python's Flying Circus." http:// www.bbc.co.uk/comedy/guide/articles/m/montypythonsflyi_1299002137.shtml.

Lloyd, Robert. "Beyond Good and Evil." *LA Weekly*. November 24–30, 2000. http://www.law eekly.com/ink/01/01/features-lloyd.php.

Lochner, Jim. "Urbanissimo." *Film Score Click Track*. May 25, 2009. http://www.filmscoreclick track.com/2009/05/urbanissimo/.

Mallory, Michael. "Move Over, Old Men." *L.A. Times*, Calendar Section. March 13, 2000. http://www.catalystagency.com/CLIENTS/CREDITS/MILLERcredits2.htm.

Martz, John. "Ottawa: John K and the Torch of Bob Clampett." *Drawn!: The Illustration and Cartooning Blog*. September 29, 2006. http://drawn.ca/tag/bob-clampett/.

"Masters of Animation: The Prehistory of UPA." *Electronic Cerebrectomy*. February 12, 2008. http://samuraifrog.blogspot.com/2008/02/masters-of-animation-prehistory-of-upa.html.

McCabe, Bob, Graham Chapman, Terry Gilliam, Eric Idle, John Cleese, Michael Palin, and

Terry Jones. *The Pythons Autobiography by The Pythons*. New York: Thomas Dunne Books, 2003.

Metcalf, Stephen. "Beyond Bugs Bunny." Slate.com. June 2, 2006. http://www.slate.com/id/2 142898/pagenum/all/.

Morgan, David. *Monty Python Speaks*. New York: Spike/Avon, 1999.

Morgan, Judith, and Neil Morgan. *Dr. Seuss and Mr. Geisel*. New York: Random House, 1995.

Moritz, William. "Lotte Reiniger." *Mad Bad and Dangerous to Know*. http://byronic.tumblr. com/post/230717912/lotte-reiniger-by-william-moritz.

Nasr, Constantine. *Tish Tash: The Animated World of Frank Tashlin*. Los Angeles: New Wave Entertainment, 2005. Video.

Newall, George. Interview with author. February 25, 2010.

Ortved, John. *The Simpsons: An Uncensored, Unauthorized History*. New York: Faber & Faber, 2009.

Pointer, Ray. "Women Animators." Golden Age Cartoon Forums. November 3, 2007. http://forums.goldenagecartoons.com/showthread.php?t=10194&highlight=friedman&page=2.

Poniewozik, James. "The 100 Best TV Shows of All Time." *Time*. http://www.time.com/time/specials/packages/completelist/0,29569,1651341,00.html.

Preston, John. "Overachiever, and Proud of It." *The Age*. January 10, 2010. http://www.theage.com.au/articles/2010/01/09/1262453696968.html.

"Real American Zero: The Adventures of Private SNAFU." *Looney Tunes Golden Collection Volume 5*. Burbank, CA: Warner Home Video, 2007.

Reiniger, Lotte. *The Adventures of Prince Achmed*. Milestone Films Release Book. http://www.milestonefilms.com/movie.php/achmed/.

Reynolds, Stanley. Television News. *The Times*. April 8, 1969.

Riley, Michael. "Resume." http://www.earglasses.com/mriley/resume.htm.

Robe, Chris. "The Adventures of Prince Achmed: A Forgotten Tale." *Pop Matters*. December 3, 2002. http://www.popmatters.com/pm/review/adventures-of-prince-achmed/.

Robinson, Tasha. "Henry Selick." The Onion A. V. Club. February 3, 2009. http://www.avclub.com/articles/henry-selick,23298/.

Rogers, John. "'Flintstones' Animator Dies at His Calif. Home." *Spartanburg Herald-Journal*. October 16, 2006, page B4. http://news.google.com/newspapers?nid=1876&dat=20061014&id=6HUpAAAAIBAJ&sjid=n9AEAAAAIBAJ&pg=3866,6488164.

Roth, Tom. Interview with author. March 21, 2010.

Rushdie, Salman. "Salmon Rushdie Talks with Terry Gilliam." *Believer Magazine* 1, no. 1 (March 2003). http://www.believermag.com/issues/200303/.

"Santa Ana Disney College Program." Santa Ana College. http://www.mickeysac.com/depthome shellc.cfm?id=59613&rt=10&view=&sms=custom9&xsite=micke.

Schneider, Steve. *That's All Folks—The Art of Warner Bros. Animation*. New York: Henry Holt, 1988.

Scott, A. O. "Matt Groening." Slate.com. April 10, 1999. http://www.slate.com/toolbar.aspx?action=print&id=23430.

Scott, Keith. *The Moose That Roared: The Story of Jay Ward, Bill Scott, a Flying Squirrel and a Talking Moose*. New York: St. Martin's Griffin, 2002.

Selick, Henry. Interview. August 16, 2008. Ultimate Disney website. http://www.ultimatedisney.com/henryselick-interview.html.

"Seventy Years On...." *Animation Guide*. November 5, 2009. http://www.animation-guide.com/TB/?P=3089.

Smoodin, Eric. *Animating Culture*. New Brunswick, NJ: Rutgers University Press, 1993.

_____, and Ann Martin, eds. *Hollywood Quarterly: Film Culture in Postwar America, 1945–1957*. Berkeley: University of California, 2002. http://ark.cdlib.org/ark:/13030/kt2f59q2dp/.

Solomon, Charles. *The Disney That Never Was*. New York: Hyperion, 1995.

Spiznagel, Eric. "George Meyer." *The Believer*. September 2004.

Stayton, Richard. "Life in Hell and Heaven." *Written By*. (Summer 2008): 53.

Stevens, Nathanial. "Question and Answer Session with Mighty Mouse: The New Adventures Co-creator John Kricfalusi." *Drawn!: The Illustration and Cartooning Blog.* http://digital chumps.com/featured-electronics/132-features/4353-question-and-answer-session-with-mighty-mouse-the-new-adventures-co-creator-john-kricfalusi.html.

Strauss, Bob. "Animation Goes Ape in Zany Monkeybone." *Los Angeles Daily News.* February 23, 2001.

Stubbs, Phil. "Dreams: Gilliam's Childhood — An Interview." http://www.smart.co.uk/dreams/tgearly.htm.

"Tashlin's Apocalypse." May 7, 2010. http://www.mardecortesbaja.com/blog/_archives/2007/5/7/2929815.html.

"Terry Gilliam: Writer, Animator and Director." *BBC Guide to Life, the Universe and Everything.* http://www.bbc.co.uk/dna/h2g2/A716906/G12.

Varnum, Robin, and Christina T. Gibbons. *The Language of Comics: Word and Image.* Jackson: University Press of Mississippi, 2007.

Wardle, Paul. "Terry Gilliam Interview." *The Comics Journal* 182 (1998).

"The Way of Peace." *The Lutheran Standard* 105, no. 49 (December 6, 1947).

Weinman, Jaime J. "Mike Maltese Speaks in 1960." Something Old, Something New website. August 21, 2008. http://zvbxrpl.blogspot.com/2008/08/mike-maltese-speaks-in-1960.html.

Whipp, Glenn. "Arthur: A Long Time Ago in a Kingdom Far, Far Away." *Los Angeles Daily News.* July 6, 2004.

White, Rusty. "Ray Harryhausen: The Science Fiction Films." E-insiders website. http://www.einsiders.com/reviews/videorisks/harryhausen.php.

Wolfgram Evans, Noell. "Popeye Pickets and Other Exploits in Animation Unions." *Written By.* (Summer 2008): 59–65.

Woo, Elaine. "Thomas Yohe; Co-Created 'Schoolhouse Rock.'" *The Los Angeles Times.* December 26, 2000. http://articles.latimes.com/2000/dec/26/local/me-4734.

Zahed, Ramin. "The Toon That Changed My Life." *Animation Magazine.* February 5, 2010. http://animationmagazine.net/article/11097.

Index